EXPLANATORY MODELS
IN LINGUISTICS

EXPLANATORY MODELS IN LINGUISTICS

A Behavioral Perspective

~ Pere Julià ~

PRINCETON UNIVERSITY PRESS
PRINCETON, NEW JERSEY

Copyright © 1983 by Princeton University Press

Published by Princeton University Press, 41 William Street,
Princeton, New Jersey
In the United Kingdom: Princeton University Press,
Guildford, Surrey

All Rights Reserved

Library of Congress Cataloging in Publication Data will be
found on the last printed page of this book

This book has been composed in Linotron Aldus

Clothbound editions of Princeton University Press books
are printed on acid-free paper, and binding materials are
chosen for strength and durability.
Paperbacks, while satisfactory for personal collections, are not usually
suitable for library rebinding.

Printed in the United States of America by Princeton
University Press, Princeton, New Jersey

To Maria del Tura

~ CONTENTS ~

	ACKNOWLEDGMENTS	ix
	INTRODUCTION	xi
1.	Psycholinguistic Context	3
2.	Structuralist Background	19
3.	The Transformational-Generative Proposal	42
4.	Explanatory Models	65
5.	Subsequent Refinements	93
6.	Performance and Competence	110
7.	Mentalism in Linguistics	126
	NOTES	143
	REFERENCES	204
	INDEX	219

~ ACKNOWLEDGMENTS ~

I am indebted to Antoni M. Badia-Margarit, Josep Roca-Pons, and Francesc Vilardell for unfailing help and encouragement. Henry and Danuta Hiż have read portions of the manuscript and have made many valuable comments about both content and presentation. The discussion of strictly linguistic matters is all the more precise for their help, even where they do not agree with my interpretation of the linguist's position. The influence of Stanley M. Sapon's work extends well beyond the explicit references cited below, as anyone familiar with the activities around the Verbal Behavior Laboratory of the University of Rochester in the sixties will detect immediately. My indebtedness to B. F. Skinner will be seen throughout, but it is a pleasure to acknowledge it at this point. My wife has helped me more than she knows.

I am grateful to the Fundación Juan March for a generous fellowship, which made possible the writing of this study and related work in preparation.

Pere Julià
Harvard University
August 1981

~ INTRODUCTION ~

Contemporary students of language have two courses open to them: they can approach the subject matter as a natural phenomenon or they can consider it a formal object. In the first case, the relevant techniques of analysis are those of behavioral science. Language is behavior. An effective treatment requires that the activity of speaker and listener be systematically related to the independent variables of which it is a function. If, on the other hand, they choose to study language as an object, they must be aware of certain self-imposed limitations. Basic among these is the fact that they are not studying behavior but its traces, written or spoken. In bringing to bear the general outlook of the formal sciences on natural languages, they are giving full expression to a long-standing tradition whereby a language is construed as a system of entities that can presumably be dealt with on its own terms.

The legacy of traditional philology is textual. Writing seems to have been responsible for the view, strengthened later by sound recording, that the physical effects of verbal behavior are the stuff of which languages are made. Numerous everyday expressions perpetuate the resulting view of language as a tool or instrument. But the modern analyst should be able to make the distinction.

For all its emphasis on spoken language, structural linguistics has followed in the same tradition. The development of ever more refined descriptive techniques has relied heavily on the preliminary transcription of recorded samples of speech. That leaves the analyst with data, say, the dependent variable, usually two steps removed from their original setting. Structuralists emphasize the notion of "system"; they necessarily capitalize on form. Form, not meaning, lends itself to systematic analysis (at least in principle). It has been said that linguistics can be scientific without being semantic. Meaning is reckoned with, at best, on the basis of posited formal relations. But meaning

~ INTRODUCTION ~

proves as inescapable as it proves elusive. The realm of meaning is the realm of the independent variables: to keep form and meaning apart is to retain, if not actually strengthen, traditional dualisms. It is a short step from there to some form of mentalism.

It was eventually felt that the elaboration of techniques for the manipulation of data (however restricted) was too ambitious a goal for descriptive linguistics. The alternative, as it turned out, was the construction of a general theory. As fully proposed, this general theory dictates the form of individual descriptions. In practice, actual data turn out to be of interest primarily when they exemplify abstract relations postulated by the a priori theory.

More important, a distinction is made between description and explanation: the theory must generate explanatory hypotheses about the "mechanism" of language and yield insight into the workings of speakers and listeners. Descriptive adequacy depends upon explanatory adequacy. But claims of explanatory power for an otherwise descriptive theory must necessarily appeal elsewhere: no measure of verbal argument is sufficient to justify a given descriptive strategy against another. More generally, there is no way to be sure of a system of organizing principles for the data except by going to the source of these data. This is what the structuralist does not do. To come up with explanatory hypotheses he is then forced to go beyond his "facts" and invoke a different dimensional system, typically the nervous system or the mind. The subject matter of modern linguistic theory is no longer what people do when they behave verbally (or even the traces of the speaker's activity) but an underlying competence presumably necessary for their verbal performance. The distinction between description and explanation arises due to an initial commitment to analyzing products of the behavior rather than the behavior itself.

The new trend in linguistics is largely the result of Noam Chomsky's speculations concerning the nature of language and language "users." A characterization of language as a recursively enumerable set represents the culmination of the tendency to look upon language as an object. Although a theoret-

~ INTRODUCTION ~

ically elegant abstraction, it loses contact with real speakers and listeners altogether. Chomsky is led to argue for the construction of models: the logical subject of the abstract theory is an idealized speaker-listener who, except for competence, shares none of the characteristics of the speakers and listeners whose "mechanism" is under analysis. The role of the environment being reduced to merely providing favorable conditions to set competence to work, the resulting "explanatory model" can amount only to a universal hypothesis about the form of language and the innate contribution of the organism to language learning and use. Beyond a given point, the entire argument has been directed primarily at a revival and justification of this special form of rationalism.

Chomsky argues that the study of human behavior is destined to irrelevance and triviality unless we have a preliminary formulation of relevant systems of knowledge and belief, since what a person does depends largely on what he knows, believes, and expects. In other words, we have to formulate hypotheses as to what is known and believed—in short, what is learned—before we can proceed to study "human learning and behavior" in a serious way. Language is deemed a good place to begin: not only is it a kind of knowledge acquired through "brief exposure" but it is largely predetermined. We seem to know beforehand. Its study ought to shed light on the characteristics of "human intellectual capacities" in ways that other systems of knowledge and belief cannot.

The proposal is predictably confused. Language is a good place to begin not because it is a "mirror of the mind" as suggested, but because a long-standing tradition provides a comfortable terminology to carry out the formalization of "what is learned." Under the circumstances, efforts to set up explanatory models are bound to reflect more the behavior of the analyst than the behavior under consideration. The two should not be confused.

Why not consider the possibility of beginning elsewhere? There are differences between verbal and nonverbal behavior (human or otherwise), but we are certain not to find out what they are by assuming a discontinuity somewhere along the line or postulating for the verbal case the status of a system of

~ INTRODUCTION ~

knowledge somehow independent of the behavior of speakers, listeners, and the variables which bring it about and keep it in strength. After all, what are knowledge and belief if not behavior?

The basic contention that exposure to a verbal environment is all that is needed to become a speaker-listener is an unsupported assumption, which psycholinguists seem to have taken at face value. By "verbal environment" is meant the "language" or system of forms characterized by the grammarian. But this, of course, will not do. It can easily be argued that if this were the case, a child surrounded by nothing but TV sets should be able to learn to speak and understand English by virtue of his innate competence. Nothing short of an analysis of the contingent relations between behavior and environmental events is likely to account for the processes whereby human organisms become members of verbal communities.

Chomsky's speculations have had an overwhelming impact in linguistics and, to a lesser extent, in philosophy, particularly the philosophy of language. Experts who claim to be interested only in establishing relations between sentences do not hesitate to make statements now about what people "do" with these sentences. The notion of explanatory value for descriptive statements has become pervasive, even among writers who would naturally reject competence as an explanatory fiction. The more serious consequences of Chomsky's writings are to be found, however, in psycholinguistics, a field of dubious status to begin with. The proposition that a formulation of linguistic competence based on an a priori theory of linguistic structure constitutes a prerequisite for the study of performance has been taken seriously. It may be that some analysts expected to find in the theory of generative-transformational grammar a measure of much needed direction for an essentially heterogeneous field. But it should be obvious by now that the study of language behavior cannot profit much from a priori formulations of language as an object. Linguistics faces serious epistemological problems of its own and the psychologist concerned with verbal behavior should be aware of them.

The present study centers primarily on Chomsky's work. His

~ INTRODUCTION ~

position is an extreme one; but extreme positions have a way of revealing overall methodological strengths and weaknesses. This study is decidedly critical but not entirely negative in character. The field of language is permeated with a multiplicity of pseudoproblems, to which recent speculations have contributed a substantial share. The need to keep them clearly in mind accounts for a certain amount of reiteration in the text. An effort has also been made to bring some of the more relevant issues into proper behavioral perspective. That should scarcely harm anyone, least of all the theoretically oriented. A section of notes has been included to complement the argument.

We may think that the model-building approach is misguided, that it is only made possible by an unrealistic appraisal of the subject matter—indeed, that the proposed "explanatory models" necessarily lead to fantastic conclusions. But it must also be recognized that Chomsky was originally addressing himself to the important question of the justification of grammars. In fact, one may venture the opinion that an understandable uneasiness in this respect was at least partly responsible for the immediate popularity of his proposal. In view of the acquired prestige of grammatical studies in contemporary research on verbal behavior, a detailed consideration of fundamental assumptions seems to be in order, for it may well be that, as usually formulated, they amount to little more than sophisticated *Scheinprobleme*.

EXPLANATORY MODELS
IN LINGUISTICS

~ CHAPTER 1 ~

Psycholinguistic Context

1.1 Scientific progress requires the realistic demarcation of fields of inquiry. Yet there is often a certain degree of arbitrariness associated with the delimitation of related topics, as the proliferation of "hyphenated" disciplines—say, biochemistry, astrophysics, neurophysiology, etc.—in recent decades clearly attests. Sciences with a long-standing tradition or a reasonably well-established set of procedures, techniques, and vocabulary, combine their independent knowledge in order to solve borderline problems more effectively. Sometimes a new and relatively autonomous field emerges out of this interdisciplinary contact.

There is a fundamental difference, however, between this sort of cooperation, where the contributing sciences have already proved capable of generating a reliable body of knowledge, and what amounts to a juxtaposition of fields lacking that minimum of methodological stability necessary for cumulative progress. In the latter case, the result may well be an even greater confusion about the status of the problems involved and the means available for coping with them; more generally, greater conceptual chaos is likely to ensue. Writing about physics and biology more than eighty years ago, Mach (1897) discussed the possible outcomes of the first type of cooperative enterprise in the following general terms:

> It often happens that the development of two different fields of science goes on side by side for long periods, without either of them exercising an influence on the other. On occasion, again, they may come into closer contact, when it is noticed that unexpected light is thrown on the doctrines

of the one by the doctrines of the other. In that case, a natural tendency may even be manifested to allow the first field to be completely absorbed in the second. But the period of buoyant hope, the period of overestimation of this relation which is supposed to explain everything, is quickly followed by a period of disillusionment, when the two fields in question are once more separated, and each pursues its own aims, putting its own special questions and applying its own methods. But on both of them the temporary contact leaves abiding traces behind. Apart from the positive addition to knowledge, which is not to be despised, the temporary relation between them brings about a transformation of our conceptions, clarifying them and permitting their application over a wider field than that for which they were originally formed.

It is probably too soon to tell the extent to which psycholinguistics will follow the pattern described by Mach. After roughly thirty years of virtually complete dissociation, psychology and linguistics were formally brought together in the fifties. Since then, linguistics has undoubtedly played the role of "absorbing science": modern linguistic metatheory includes explanatory power as an adequacy criterion for particular theories of languages or grammars; it also specifies the properties to be met by those grammars, with a previously unknown degree of specificity and formal rigor. This has lent syntactic analysis an unprecedented prestige and the a priori formulation of related "explanatory" hypotheses an unwarranted degree of credibility.

Although there are undeniable signs of growing skepticism, the period of buoyant hope and overestimation that has characterized the psycholinguistic community for the past two decades cannot be said to have given way to disillusionment yet. It is quite possible that both fields will again recoil into their own areas of expertise in their treatment of verbal phenomena. It may be worth asking then what the abiding traces of this temporary contact and the ensuing positive addition to knowledge are likely to be, and in what way it can bring about "a transformation of our conceptions, clarifying them, and permitting their application over a wider field than that for which they were originally formed." Perhaps what we must ask first, however, is whether psycholinguistics is a bona fide symbiosis of the kind alluded to by Mach or merely a complex case of juxtaposition. The best way to appraise the situation is to review, if in broad outline, the nature of this temporary contact and to weigh carefully the kinds of claims made by the engulfing field.

1.2 Osgood and Sebeok (1954) characterized psycholinguistics as the convergence of linguistics, information measurement, and learning theory. Not surprisingly, Saporta (1961) could still write: "it is clear that psycholinguistics is still an amorphous field, and the topics chosen as well as their arrangement represent only one arbitrary attempt at shaping a large body of available information about language." Adopting the above threefold demarcation two years later, Gough and Jenkins (1963) further pointed out the three aspects of "learning theory" relevant to psycholinguistics: (1) Osgood's theory of meaning, formulated in mediational terms; (2) Skinner's analysis of verbal behavior; (3) verbal associations, "a set of informal theoretical assumptions about verbal habits, elaborated and developed by individual psycholinguists into distinct theoretical conceptions." Presumably in an attempt to bring some order into this *mélange*, Osgood (1963) expressed the opinion that the important issues crystallize around the question of whether contemporary psychological theories can shed light on man's ability to create and understand new sentences. (Notice the uninhibited reference to the plurality of theories and the appeal to "sentences" as a priori analytical units. Osgood later became much concerned over the problem of "sentencehood.") A later characterization (Cofer, 1968) just about sums up the direction of subsequent trends: "information measurement is perhaps less influential than it once was; and of course, linguistics has recently become more influential, especially on the question of what knowing a language means for the psychology of the user of the language." This is a peculiar way of referring to psychology, one which in turn raises rather fundamental questions

~ CHAPTER 1 ~

about practically all of the adjacent terms. It becomes perhaps clearer in the light of the following statement: "there has been relatively little effort on the part of learning theorists to deal with language *as a system.*" Cofer then refers to various writers who, leaning heavily on linguistics, have concentrated on language acquisition and who "see their findings as making difficulties for current learning theory."

These developments can be attributed in large measure to the impact of Chomsky's speculations about the structure of language and the explanatory value claimed for his proposed model of transformational-generative grammar (TGG). Some underlying assumptions are important. Language is made up of an infinite set of sentences and its "use" is a matter of linguistic rule. The job of a grammar is to specify the structural features of this infinite set by finite means: a generative system of rules will meet the case. The evaluation of competing grammars is made in accordance with an overall metatheory that says what any natural language must be like; this general theory is identified with a model of the innate abilities responsible for language learning. The metatheory thus becomes an explanatory model. Moreover, speakers of natural languages constantly produce and understand sentences they have never heard before, and this unlimited use of language on the basis of finite experience suggests a relation between the finitary descriptive means proposed and mental processes of some sort. (The details, not always equally explicit, of Chomsky's proposal will be taken up below.)

These are strong claims, elegantly expressed as a general rule. To account for the "use" (that is, production and understanding alike) of novel utterances has become something like the raison d'être of psycholinguistics, with developmental studies conforming to specification as well. This is not to say that all psychologists concerned with language have embraced Chomsky's proposal uncritically or to the same degree. But it is fair to say that research on verbal behavior has been weakened (sometimes seriously) by this latter-day linguistics-dominated outlook: it is not unusual to see its findings contrasted with, if not discussed as a function of, the latter's demands and expectations as a matter of course (see, for example, Glanzer, 1967; Clifton, 1967; and more generally, Dixon and Horton, 1968). Mainstream psycholinguistics has found itself progressively committed to the "justification" of the formal outlook on language (see, for example, Miller, 1962, 1965; and, despite Fodor and Garrett, 1966, Blumenthal, 1970; Fillenbaum, 1971; Johnson-Laird, 1974; Danks and Glucksberg, 1980). The new psycholinguists, as they were soon called, reversed the prevailing empirical outlook in rather drastic ways: the well-rooted tendency to keep close to the data and thus to concentrate on the emerging functional relations (for what they might have been worth) gave way to a frank priority to theoretical speculation; all too often, experimental work has become ancillary. Indeed, many linguists and a number of philosophers have automatically become experts on the psychology of language and, emboldened by their immediate impact, on psychology at large.[1] Some aspects of psychology have necessarily been emphasized at the expense of others.

Whatever its intrinsic interest, the forcefulness with which the new standpoint has been put forth is probably not sufficient in itself to explain its overwhelming impact.[2] Traditional psychological study of language was vulnerable; it was based on poorly understood behavioral processes and half-hearted formulations. Gough's and Jenkins' characterization of the study of verbal associations above must be reckoned as accurate. Similar remarks apply to the venerable field of verbal learning. The two traditions share a commitment to conditioning principles (within a narrow Stimulus-Response conception) and a moderate indulgence in theoretical speculation. Whatever measures of theoretical analysis are available have merely a local interest; even so, the gap between data and theory seems to be growing wider. These "miniature" theories are usually anchored in largely inconclusive results, and they are generally disconnected from one another. Moreover, it does not seem reasonable to expect any significant degree of integration in the future. The major outcome of a large-scale conference convened with this purpose in mind was a more direct scrutiny and ultimate rejection of the S-R frame of reference as well as a general consensus as to the need for "greater theoretical complexity." It should perhaps be added that this position was strongly reinforced by the presence of mainstream psycholinguists, who argued in the same sense on grounds of formal principle. Some participants rather unnecessarily appealed to perceptual variance, ethology, and computer simulation of cognitive functions to add strength to what should have been nothing more than a reasonable and straightforward recognition of empirical insufficiency.

Cofer (1968) points out "that students of verbal learning have concentrated their efforts on retention and transfer, that the psychological psycholinguists have emphasized meaning and associative processes (and, from information theory, sequential aspects of language), and that the overall system, which a language is, has not been given much consideration. It may also be said that human learning and retention, in some overall or broadly gauged perspective, has not been given attention either." The basic problem is less likely to be a neglect of language as an "overall system" (whatever this may ultimately prove to mean) than the obvious lack of procedural unity and theoretical direction in the study of learning among students of verbal learning and the psychological psycholinguists. (These are by no means the only areas of psychology similarly affected.)

It is partly understandable that against this background of experimental and theoretical chaos, the linguist's formally impressive, all-encompassing descriptions of "what is learned" should appear particularly enticing and (at least to some) his corresponding broader claims persuasive. Anyone looking at the proceedings of the aforementioned conference (Dixon and Horton, 1968) is bound to conclude that psychology at large, and the behavioral study of language in particular, are in serious trouble. A more informed point of view, however, puts the S-R paradigm and the broad variety of traditional "problem areas" there represented in proper historical perspective and clears the way to a more realistic view of "language" as an object of behavioral science.[3]

1.3 A generally recognized feature of the expository style of the new psycholinguists is the ease with which rival proposals have been habitually dismissed as "uninteresting" and "trivial," almost since the very inception of the TGG movement (see Verhave, 1972, for an exposition). Information theory, for example, was originally introduced as a framework for the regularization and possible quantification of language and other complex behaviors; as Glanzer (1967) also points out, it eventually played an important part in bringing into focus the formulation of theories of linguistic structure incorporating the assumptions listed above. Chomsky appropriately discussed the inadequacies of related finite-state models in his early work, and similarly, those of any form of assignment of grammatical categories to consecutive phrases roughly on the phrase-structure pattern (see chapter 3). Reference to these shortcomings became part and parcel of any argument in favor of the TGG model for years; typically, these references tended to become indiscriminate (and sometimes equivocal) as the movement gathered momentum.

Outside of linguistics, the (psychological) study of meaning should not count as an alternative position in itself; but it is rendered so by the extreme formalist's insistence that syntactic analysis must be performed first. The following early statement illustrates the subsidiary role accorded semantics in general and (to go back to Gough's and Jenkins' appraisal) to Osgood's work in particular: "To introduce the process of comprehension, however, raises many difficult issues. Recently there have been interesting proposals for studying abstractly certain denotative (Wallace, 1961) and connotative (Osgood, Suci, and Tannenbaum, 1957) aspects of natural lexicons. Important as this subject is for any general theory of psycholinguistics, we shall have little to say about it in these pages. Nevertheless, our hope is that by clearing away some syntactic problems we shall have helped to clarify the semantic issue if only by indicating some of the things that meaning is not" (Chomsky and Miller, 1963). Meaning is unquestionably a difficult subject. Any clarification of what it is not would be an important contribution in itself. But this is not what the reader is presented with, probably because the implied dependence of semantics on syntactic analysis cannot be upheld. Neither is prior to the other. Indeed,

~ CHAPTER 1 ~

where natural languages are concerned, the entire notion of "abstract study" of lexicons may well prove meaningless altogether.

Criticisms have been particularly hostile with respect to behavioral science in general and what Chomsky understands to be Skinner's position in particular. They originate principally with Chomsky's widely reprinted review (1959) of Skinner's *Verbal Behavior* (1957), which went largely unchallenged for over ten years. MacCorquodale (1970) provided a comprehensive reply, in which he accurately characterized the review as "an amalgam of some rather outdated behavioristic lore including reinforcement by drive reduction, the extinction criterion for response strength, a pseudo-incompatibility of genetic and reinforcement processes, and other notions which have nothing to do with Skinner's account."

Chomsky missed the point of Skinner's experimental framework in rather fundamental ways; having misunderstood the "premises," against which his review is mainly directed, his conclusions concerning a strictly empirical extrapolation of laboratory findings to the verbal field could hardly be expected to be correct. For all its superficial brilliance, Chomsky's review gave a thoroughly distorted, if not specious, picture of Skinner's analysis. (MacCorquodale fittingly calls its tone "ungenerous to a fault, condescending, unforgiving, obtuse, and ill-humored.") It also provided a series of statements that have become, over the years, standard (rather repetitive and unimaginative) invectives against any unqualified view of language as behavior. Postal (1964a) offers a typical early example: "it is clear that enough is already known about the nature of language to show that views of language learning which restrict attention to the gross phonetic properties of utterances, either by adherence to psychological theories which do not countenance concepts more abstract and specific than 'stimulus,' 'chaining,' 'response,' etc., or linguistic structure representable by final derived phrase markers, cannot teach us very much about the fantastic feat by which a child with almost no direct instruction learns that enormously extensive and complicated system which is a natural language." The operant formulation of behavior, verbal and nonverbal, is still usually referred to as an example of S-R psychology.[4] Here too psychologists are partly to blame.

In fairness to Chomsky, it must be pointed out that he does acknowledge the existence of "certain nontrivial applications of *operant conditioning* to the control of human behavior":

> A wide variety of experiments have shown that the number of plural nouns (for example) produced by a subject will increase if the experimenter says "right" or "good" when one is produced (similarly, positive attitudes on a certain issue, stories with particular content, etc.). . . . It is of some interest that the subject is usually unaware of the process. Just what light this gives into normal verbal behavior is not obvious. Nevertheless, it is an example of positive and not totally expected results using the Skinnerian paradigm. (1959, fn. 7; his one reference is Krasner, 1958)

In the nature of things, verbal authority is of no avail in the face of tangible achievements. Much operant conditioning of verbal and nonverbal behavior alike has since taken place in the laboratory,[5] not to speak of large-scale application in such fields as education (special and otherwise) and psychotherapy. Yet remarks about a strictly behavioral approach to language have not kept abreast of these developments. In a retrospective self-appreciation, Chomsky (1967c, p. 142) himself has said more recently: "Rereading this review after eight years, I find little of substance that I would change if I were to write it today. I am not aware of any theoretical or experimental work that challenges its conclusions." Five years later he still writes:

> there is no hope in the study of the "control" of human behavior by stimulus conditions, schedules of reinforcement, establishment of habit structures, patterns of behavior, and so on. Of course, one can design a restricted environment in which such control and such patterns can be demonstrated, but there is no reason to suppose that any more is learned about the range of human potentialities by such methods than would be learned by observing hu-

~ CHAPTER 1 ~

mans in a prison or an army—or in many a classroom. (1972)

Statements of this sort reveal a profound misunderstanding of the function of the laboratory in the natural sciences and of the interplay between basic research and engineering applications. Over four decades of cumulative research in the experimental analysis of behavior, with its characteristic emphasis on the behavior of the single organism, have yielded a highly sophisticated body of knowledge on the subject matter, in terms of both laboratory techniques and the conceptual framework developed—often approximating a degree of rigor comparable to that in some areas of biology and the physical sciences. The surprising lawfulness and generality of the results with a large variety of species, man included, constitute the main force behind the growing literature. Such results would appear to demand closer consideration than mainstream psycholinguists seem willing to give them. Instead, a sharp dichotomy has been drawn between basic laboratory research and ethology: the former is typically dismissed as restrictive and irrelevant, presumably on account of its emphasis on decomposition of complex processes and the systematic isolation of variables; explanatory linguistics has turned instead to ethology for support of a clearly nativistic position.[6] As Skinner (1947) has pointed out, however:

> To simplify the material of a science is one of the purposes of a laboratory, and simplification is worthwhile whenever it does not actually falsify. But the experimental psychologist has no corner on simplification. The psychoanalytic couch is a simplified world, and so is any test situation.

Experimentation generated by prior models of the type proposed reduces to some form of testing. To be consistent, it should also be discarded as restrictive and irrelevant. That would leave the overall theory, for all its formal complexity and sophistication, as a grand unverifiable hypothesis. Chomsky seems to be aware of this, in part at least—hence the priority given to overall theory, intuition, and formal adequacy over actual experimental work (see especially chapter 4). His approach is too radically aprioristic to allow for a different kind of theory, one based on data and serving only to organize their treatment into more general statements.

A fundamental difference in outlook accounts for the great disagreement under discussion. A linguist and logician, Chomsky is almost necessarily committed to a traditional view of language as well as the correspondingly narrow scope of its description—one with which Skinner's analysis is at great variance.[7] A causal account centers on the behavior of the individual speaker and listener; it places the burden of explanation outside the organism, in the controlling relations responsible for the rise and maintenance of verbal behavior. A minimal acquaintance with it suffices to show one that any such description has very little room to accommodate formal devices worked out with an abstract view of language in mind. An analysis of behavior as a function of environmental variables is novel enough where nonverbal repertoires are concerned; when it comes to verbal behavior, it becomes much more difficult to grasp in view of the explicit training that, to a greater or lesser extent, we have all gone through in the course of a formal education. As it happens, the linguist is bound to exhibit an even more elaborate and uncritical repertoire about the repertoire he is trying to describe.[8]

1.4 Obviously many additional details could be added to the psycholinguistic story as portrayed above, but their discussion would be inimical to the present argument. A fairly up-dated view of the state of the art can be found in Reber (1973). The author classifies current trends into three different "paradigms." The "associationist paradigm" indiscriminately encompasses all efforts to extend a behavioristic frame of reference to the verbal case, including such "neobehavioristic" proposals as Staats' (1968), and attempts to compromise with the demands of mainstream psycholinguistics—notably Osgood (1968, 1971; see also Osgood, 1967, p. 104). The "process paradigm" assumes that the explanation of language behavior (learning and use) requires the postulation of an initial set of general cognitive mechanisms. This position has gathered strength from the rad-

~ CHAPTER 1 ~

ical (and surprising) shift of orientation of such investigators as Premack (see, for example, Premack, 1971). The "content paradigm" is the more linguistically determined; it postulates a different though not entirely unrelated kind of nativism whereby an innate *faculté de langage* sets language apart from the rest of behavioral repertoires and the role of learning is minimized to the point of neglect. Clearly, there is no room in such a classification for an operant approach to verbal behavior (which is not even mentioned).

These three paradigms are then systematically examined in terms of how they handle certain issues extant in the contemporary literature, namely, the biological foundations of language, its presumed uniqueness within human behavior, the acquisition "problem," the competence/performance distinction; some interesting paragraphs are also devoted to the relations between behaviorism and mentalism, and reductionism. Many generally confused issues are brought sharply into focus. Not surprisingly, the process and content paradigms (a distinction first suggested by Slobin, 1966) converge: their similarities far outweigh their differences; in particular, they share a strong reliance on a prior description of "that enormously extensive and complicated system which is a natural language" (to use Postal's phrasing). The so-called learning theory approaches are ruled out of account.

It may be interesting to note that the general conclusion of Reber's paper is that the process paradigm, intermediate between the more polarized associationist and content ones, is in fact the more radical of the three in that "it (1) treats language as generative in nature and (2) views language as fundamentally equivalent to other cognitively based behaviors." The author deems it the most likely to provide psycholinguistics with much-needed pragmatic direction, even though refinements will have to be made in general cognitive theory as currently formulated. Adherents to this point of view, probably the author himself included, would no doubt argue that cognitive theory stands to gain much from a close association with the content orientation in psycholinguistics.

Two observations are pertinent at this point. First, the one important weakness of this otherwise lucid and influential study is its treatment of "associationism." Some typical (and a few atypical) errors of appreciation are echoed without further thought. Reber's argument loses force precisely on this account. And second, the author does not expatiate on the shortcomings of general cognitive theory. Instead, the article ends on this vague note of promise: "Such an approach would call for a new learning theory, hardly a conservative or reformist proposal." This is unfortunate in that the reader is thereby deprived of a hopeful glimpse of the future (see, however, Salzinger, 1973a, for a discussion of the inherent difficulties of the approach in this context; see also Skinner, 1969, 1974).

Mainstream psycholinguistics can indeed be said to have come under the sway of "explanatory linguistics," as clearly shown by the choice of basic issues (as Reber calls them) in terms of which the various paradigms are evaluated. Nor have things changed subsequently in any fundamental way (see, for example, Danks and Glucksberg, 1980). Perhaps the most important departure from the standard position is the emphasis on "larger psychological context" in lieu of the earlier commitment to an "idealized, literal, context-free sentence" and the need to recognize the shared interests of such disciplines as anthropology, sociology, and philosophy. These interests are seen, however, merely as "complementary contributions to the study of human mental life." Research is still conceptualized in terms of word and sentence representations, processing mechanisms, and the like (with special attention to the listener). These and other writers see nothing wrong with the liberal incorporation of procedures developed in the field of artificial intelligence. The cognitive outlook, forced by a view of language as an object, appears to be more entrenched than ever. Yet the basic question remains the same: Why does verbal behavior occur when it does and why does it have the form it has on every particular occasion?

1.5   To go back to the beginning, the psychological study of language has suffered a radical change of orientation in recent decades, which can easily be traced to the formal recognition of

~ CHAPTER 1 ~

the new and necessarily hybrid field of psycho-linguistics. What the "abiding traces" of this temporary contact between linguistics and psychology will prove to be remains to be seen. Nevertheless, it is fair to say that the immediate effect has been so far unilateral, owing largely to the advent of the TG school of grammarians. Various reasons have been suggested above for the reasonable ease with which psychologists of various persuasions have submitted to the linguist's redefinition of their subject matter and, more surprisingly, to his dictates concerning the nature of its investigation.

The formulation of explanatory models in linguistics involves a number of conceptual and methodological assumptions that explicitly (and sometimes implicitly) violate well-established principles of empirical research. Some standard preconceptions about the object of study have gone unchallenged in the course of this formulation, and as a result, the formal aspects of language have predictably been given undue prominence. The generative grammarian's claims regarding the psychological implications of his essentially descriptive proposal inevitably reflect these initial limitations; yet the proposal's overwhelming impact must probably be attributed in large measure to these explanatory claims rather than to the model's intrinsic formal merits alone. These claims are also responsible for the present estrangement between psycholinguistic theory and behavioral science—hence this general reference to the genesis and development of psycholinguistics, meant primarily as an immediate background for the direct examination of the proposed model itself.

Reference has already been made to the role of the metatheory in the evaluation of alternative sets of rules. The underlying motivation is the justification of grammars—the notion that over and above considerations of strict descriptive convenience, grammatical analysis should yield, in theory at least, some insight into the conditions of speakers and listeners. It is here, if anywhere, that "a positive addition to knowledge" (to come full circle to Mach's statement above) must be sought. There probably is more to this proposal than initially meets the eye. It does not follow, however, that the most suitable procedure is the construction of formally motivated models and the postulation of broad explanatory hypotheses. The new emphasis on theory has led a vast majority of experts to overlook the fact that where behavior is concerned strictly formal constructions are likely to prove more elegant than instructive.

The analyst with a less speculative turn of mind is bound to question not only the linguist's right to stipulate the range and nature of legitimate questions and his arbitration over the adequacy of the methods brought to bear on them, but ultimately also the validity of the assumptions underlying his formulation of presumably explanatory models. This will constitute the object of the present study.

SUMMARY

Two decades of collaboration between linguistics and psychology have little to show for themselves. Linguistics has played the role of "absorbing" science; the contribution of psychology has been reduced, in the best of cases, to providing the technical know-how for testing the linguist's hypotheses about "what is learned." Psychologists have also unquestioningly accepted the linguist's criticisms of behavioral science, based though they are on outdated views and a profound misunderstanding of the function of the laboratory in the study of natural phenomena. The avowed goal of psycholinguistics is to account for the fact that people produce and understand sentences they have never heard before. But the standard reference to speaking and understanding as the "use of language" reveals all the fundamental biases of the formalistic outlook. The contemporary distinction between competence and performance is forced by this basic outlook and the explanatory claims of mainstream linguistic theory. Formalism entails dualism. At issue is of course the so-called psychological reality of linguistic constructs. After what was thought to be encouraging initial evidence, some experts renounced the expected isomorphism between linguistic descriptions and psychological activity. Dissatisfaction has been mounting over the years and a future psycholinguistics without linguistics is now envisaged in some quarters. This is, however,

CHAPTER 1

an unrealistic program so long as language is thought of as a system of forms and the starting point for research. Such an outlook affords at best a trivial kind of predictive power—a form of prediction of behavior from behavior alone. What is more, language is a priori declared a different kind of behavior. Explanation is then necessarily sought inside the organism, in cognitive structures postulated on the basis of formal hypotheses and invoked in order to lend some sort of substance to even more elusive mental processes. The naturalistic alternative is to abandon the cognitive metaphor and face verbal activity in all its functional complexity.

~ CHAPTER 2 ~

Structuralist Background

2.1 The development of modern structural linguistics can be mainly characterized, in its early stages, not only by such theoretical distinctions as de Saussure's *langue* versus *parole*, diachrony versus synchrony, and so on, but also (especially in the United States) as an attempt to work out descriptive techniques devoid of commitments to a priori philosophies of language or the classical grammatical paradigms. The fact that many early exponents of the new trend in America were also anthropologists greatly contributed to the initial thrust of the movement: the application of the grammatical systems of Greek and Latin to unwritten, unknown, and often unrelated languages proved conspicuously awkward. Franz Boas is usually mentioned in this connection (Bloomfield called him "the teacher in one or another sense of us all"), even though his thinking is not always consistently evaluated.

According to the new outlook every language had its own "logic," and it was the analyst's task to discover the relevant facts. To put the matter bluntly, one was to speak about specific languages, not Language. The emphasis was upon field techniques and the catchword was 'objectivity.' This attitude, undoubtedly salutary at first, had also a number of built-in biases—notably, a highly restrictive view of the data under description. Its implications became increasingly acute when linguists eventually began to make inductive statements again in the course of developing a general descriptive methodology. Subsequent increases in formal sophistication only strengthened these biases; indeed, they are still with us, probably more entrenched than ever, in current discussions of linguistic theory.

~ CHAPTER 2 ~

Joos (1957, p. v) summarized the subsequent developments as follows:

> What actually happened consisted principally of the advent of Sapir and Bloomfield.
>
> Both trained in traditional historical linguistics and specifically in Germanics, and always sympathetically attentive to such studies here and abroad; Sapir by instinct what is popularly called "a psychologist" and possessing unsurpassable empathy and quickness of wit, while Bloomfield was distinguished in disinterested wisdom and love of solid structure, their impacts upon American Linguistics were quite different in essence while both serving similarly to advance linguistic thought beyond the Boas pattern. . . .
>
> They valued de Saussure's contribution in equal measure, but used it in ways as different as their personalities. Sapir gained insights, and stimulation to think out patterns of what very likely goes on inside the skull of *homo loquens*, taking him one at a time. Bloomfield took what he found either solid or well shaped, and shaped the first and made the second firm, for use in constructing his model for what plainly goes on between person and person in speech communication. For him there was enough that demanded unambiguous statement in what we all see and hear; why borrow trouble by explaining the invisible?

In a general way, this excerpt contains many of the issues that are bound to recur in one form or another in the following discussion. Some general comments are in order.

Both Sapir and Bloomfield were neogrammarians. Their adherence to the principle of "regularity of sound change" and their continued sympathetic outlook on historical studies were bound to leave a conceptual mark upon their work, even when their efforts centered on synchronic matters. That both Sapir and Bloomfield equally valued de Saussure's contribution is not only historically relevant but symptomatic: drawing a basic distinction between *signifiant* and *signifié*, de Saussure considered language "un système où tout se tient et qui ne connaît que son ordre propre," which amounts to the narrowest possible demarcation of this aspect of human behavior.[1]

The differences in Sapir's and Bloomfield's personalities and the attendant effects upon the field have often been pointed out. Sapir's closer association with anthropology is well-known. Interestingly enough, however, it is mostly for his intuitive psychological leanings that he is now frequently "rehabilitated" by linguists who at the same time repudiate Bloomfield's linguistics for being merely "descriptive." Contemporary theory demands "explanation" as well. Ultimately, the distinction between the two approaches is philosophical: it involves questions about the nature and scope of the subject matter, the aims of its scientific analysis, and the techniques best suited to this end. Joos' quotation captured twenty years ago what now some interpret as a fundamental difference between the two men. The inside of the skull of *homo loquens* notwithstanding, Joos' somewhat cryptic "taking him one at a time" deserves closer scrutiny than it has received. Joos applied the term 'model' to Bloomfield's endeavors either in a loose, undefined sense or else because the term was very much in vogue among post-Bloomfieldians at the time.

Influential though Sapir has been throughout, Bloomfield's methodology has prevailed. Hymes (1972) offers a sober historical appraisal:

> Before World War II, to be sure, there was not the sense of opposition between a Sapir and a Bloomfield tradition that was to be fostered in the 1940's, after Sapir's death in 1939, in terms of Sapir as "vague" and "intuitive" vs. Bloomfield as "hard-headed" and precise (a view that conveniently neglected to note that Sapir's grammars represented the high point of precision in actual description at that time) . . . and what the climate of American linguistics might have been, had Sapir lived, is worth conjecture. As it was, Whorf also died before World War II (in 1941), and the continuity of the perspective became ravelled and peripheral. The methodological climate came to be dominated

~ CHAPTER 2 ~

by men who took a certain conception of Bloomfield as its symbol.

"A certain conception of Bloomfield as its symbol" is an apt expression. Fries (1961) goes as far as to say that in general Bloomfield "rather tended away from practice and explicit formulation and codification of doctrine" and that he "very rarely dealt with specific procedures and techniques." More important:

> If, then, there is anything of a Bloomfield "school" it must arise out of the fact that a considerable number of workers in the field of linguistics have adopted and use the fundamental principles which guided Bloomfield's own work. For him it was these basic principles that were important—not specific techniques and procedures of operation in themselves.

It has been said that Bloomfield's concept of "scientific statement" turned American Linguistics into "a way of stating" rather "a set of statements." Indeed, this would explain, in part at least, the diversity of neo-Bloomfieldian approaches that were to come out of his (and sometimes Sapir's) stimulation and influence during the forties and fifties. Fries codifies Bloomfield's principles as follows:

A. The "Regularity" of Sound Change
B. The "Exclusion" of Psychology
C. Scientific Descriptive Statements
D. The Use of Meaning
E. The Field of Linguistic Science

Obviously, principles A, C, and E are closely interrelated. Actually, E comprises both C and A. As Fries puts it,

> His progressive succession of emphases in certain fundamental principles was from the implication of "strict regularity" in the mechanistic operation of sound change, through the uncompromising demands of rigorous "scientific" demonstration and statement in physical terms, to the complete transfer of linguistic significance from items to patterns in an over-all unifying "structuralism."

Bloomfield's attitude toward the "regularity" principle, which he considered a fundamental working assumption, is both representative and illuminating. He valued it because it was scientifically productive in that it yielded verifiable results; it also permitted a proper treatment of exceptions.

Principles B and D have been the source of much independent, though by no means unrelated, misunderstanding. Much has been made in recent years, for example, of Bloomfield's "commitment to behaviorism." Thus Bloomfield's empirical outlook, which amounts to no more than a form of positivism prevalent during the first decades of the century, is often attributed to a presumed alliance with behavioral psychology.[2] This would be in direct contradiction to principle B. Bloomfield's views on meaning (generally held to be the most affected area) and its use in linguistic analysis, principle D, have been similarly misconstrued. While it is true that he often appeals to terms like 'stimulus,' 'situation,' 'response,' and so on, the case has been overstated. His numerous references to meaning are frequently at variance with one another and may have proved ultimately not very constructive, but Bloomfield was consistent about the need to take meaning into account in any serious study of language. Some of his followers (for example, Bloch, 1948; and Harris, 1951b) later advocated its exclusion, at least in theory. Their respective views have sometimes been confused. The ensuing inability of the post-Bloomfieldians to develop a semantic theory has also been blamed in recent years on Bloomfield's pernicious association with behaviorism.

The interested reader is referred to Fries' exegetical paper for exact references in Bloomfield's own writings. The following excerpts are, however, relevant in an overall way to the present discussion and show Bloomfield's robust disposition to set up an autonomous science of language, free from unnecessary mentalistic verbiage and what he called on various occasions "randon theorizing," "teleological explanations," and "premature psychologizing." (Most of these topics have, of course, been widely discussed in the literature. Where accuracy is concerned, however, there is no substitute for direct sources; hence the present density of quotations.)

~ CHAPTER 2 ~

In the 1870's when technical terms were less precise than today, the assumption of uniform sound-change received the obscure and metaphorical wording, "Phonetic laws have no exceptions." It is evident that the term 'law' has here no precise meaning, for a sound-change is not in any case a law, but only a historical occurrence. The phrase "have no exceptions" is a very inexact way of saying that non-phonetic factors, such as frequency or meaning of particular linguistic forms, do not interfere with the change of phonemes.   (1933, p. 354)

the postulational method saves discussion, because it limits our statements to a defined terminology; in particular, it cuts us off from psychological dispute. . . . The existence and interaction of social groups held together by language is granted by psychology and anthropology.

Psychology, in particular, gives us the series: to certain stimuli (A) a person reacts by speaking: his speech (B) in turn stimulates his hearers to certain reactions (C). By a social habit which every person acquires in infancy from his elders, A-B-C are closely correlated. Within this correlation, the stimuli (A) which cause an act of speech and the reactions (C) which result from it, are very closely linked, because every person acts indifferently as speaker or as hearer. We are free, therefore, without further discussion, to speak of *vocal features* or sounds (B) and of *stimulus-reaction features* (A-C) of speech. (1926, probably as close as Bloomfield ever came to a conceptual and methodological systematization.)

Whatever one may think of this description of the A-C mechanism, it can hardly be called a compromise with, let alone a commitment to, behaviorism. Of course, some confusion may have arisen from his appeal to the formula S—r—s—R, where "r—s denotes the act of language" and complements for man "the normal biological series S—R" (1939, p. 15). Moreover, calling verbal behavior "substitute responses" elsewhere could not do much justice to the case. The formula was meant to symbolize only the function of language in society: "language enables one person to make a reaction (R) where another has the stimulus (S)." Bloomfield's concern was with speech itself (B). Thus he writes:

> De Saussure's system is . . . : (1) actual object, (2) concept, (3) acoustic image, (4) speech utterance; the series to be reversed for the hearer. . . . The totality of this is *le langage*, the socially uniform language pattern. De Saussure's careful statement lays clear the point at issue: What he calls "mental" is exactly what he and all other linguists call "social"; there is no need for the popular finalistic terms. We shall do better to drop (2) and (3) and speak instead of a socially determined correspondence between certain features of (1) and (4). (1927a)

Albeit in a different vein, the importance of concept/acoustic image over actual object/speech utterance as the true object of linguistic theory has been brought to the fore in recent years again in the form of "explanatory mentalism" versus mere "descriptivism."

With regard to meaning, Bloomfield fluctuated between insightful statements that should not prove too difficult to paraphrase into *modern* behavioral terms and hopelessly vague or downright discouraging, though probably realistic, views:

> We have defined the *meaning* of a linguistic form as the situation in which the speaker utters it and the response which it calls forth in the hearer. (1933, p. 139)

> The term 'meaning' which is used by all linguists, is necessarily inclusive, since it must embrace all aspects of semiosis that may be distinguished by a philosophical or logical analysis: relation, on various levels, of speech-forms to other speech-forms, relation of speech-forms to non-verbal situations (objects, events, etc.), and relations, again on various levels, to the persons who are participating in the act of communication. (1939, p. 18)

> The situations which prompt people to utter speech, include every object and happening of the universe. In order to

give a scientifically accurate definition of meaning for every form of a language, we should have to have a scientifically accurate knowledge of everything in the speaker's world. The actual extent of human knowledge is very small, compared to this. (1933, p. 139)

Most of this was naturally intuitive and outside the scope of a narrow S-R psychology. Bloomfield was not referring, of course, to relations in the *functional* sense disclosed by an experimental analysis of the behavior of single organisms. His concern was with *langue*. In practice, descriptive efforts probably demanded no more than criteria of "sameness" or "difference," as has been repeatedly observed. It was only consistent that Bloomfield should cling to a formalistic solution: "The first task of the linguistic investigator is the analysis of a language into distinctive sounds, their variations, and the like. When he has completed this, he turns to the analysis of the semantic structure,—to what we call the morphology and syntax of the language, its grammatical system" (1914). As Hockett (1968, p. 19) has pointed out, "Here we have the very opposite of a proposal that grammar and semantics are separable. A language has forms (words, morphemes, sentences); forms have meanings; the correspondence between forms and meanings *are* the 'semantic structure' which *is* the 'grammatical system.' This view of Bloomfield's never really changed." It was also fraught with difficulties, as subsequent workers found. For one thing, it suggests a restriction of "meaning" to the traditional notion of "reference." (Bloomfield, 1943, seems to be aware of this but again insists that "in all study of language we must start from forms and not from meanings.") Subordination of meaning to form, if feasible, makes the former liable to all of the procedural vagaries of analyzing the latter. It imposes structure, which may do violence to our data: our units of analysis may thereby reflect more the behavior of the analyst than the behavior of the speakers whose language we are trying to account for.

Most of these views, as well as the domain to be covered, are conveniently brought together in Bloomfield's review (1927b) of Jespersen's *Philosophy of Grammar* (1924):

> For Jespersen language is a mode of expression: its forms express the thoughts and feelings of speakers, and communicate them to hearers, and this process goes on as an immediate part of human life and is, to a great extent, subject to the requirements and vicissitudes of human life. For me, as for de Saussure . . . and, in a sense, for Sapir . . . , all this, de Saussure's *la parole*, lies beyond the power of our science. We cannot predict whether a certain person will speak at a given time, or what he will say, or in what words or other linguistic forms he will say it. Our science can deal only with those features of language, de Saussure's *la langue*, which are common to all speakers of a community,—the phonemes, grammatical categories, lexicon, and so on. These are abstractions, for they are only (recurrent) partial features of speech utterances. . . . They form a rigid system,—so rigid that without adequate physiologic information and psychology in a state of chaos, we are nevertheless able to subject it to scientific treatment. A grammatical or lexical statement is at bottom an abstraction.
>
> It may be urged that change in language is due ultimately to the deviations of individuals from the rigid system. But it appears that even here individual variations are ineffective; whole groups of speakers must, for some reason unknown to us, coincide in a deviation, if it is to result in a linguistic change. Change in language does not reflect individual variability, but seems to be a massive, uniform, and gradual alteration, at every moment of which the system is just as rigid as at every other moment. . . .
>
> In the study of linguistic forms, therefore, I should not appeal, as Jespersen sometimes does, to meaning as if it were separable from form, or to the actual necessities and conveniences of communication. On the other hand, we flatter ourselves when we think that we (as linguists, at

CHAPTER 2

any rate) can estimate these; . . . they do not affect the somewhat meagre abstraction which we can and do study. In setting up the grammatical categories, such as the parts-of-speech system, I should not appeal beyond the actual forms of the language under consideration. Under forms we must of course include substitutive and syntactic features.

Whatever the ultimate status of thoughts, feelings, and so on in a scientific analysis, it is not clear what the difference is between these "actual necessities and conveniences of communication," which are to be neglected, and meaning, which is not to be treated "as if it were separable from form."

Bloomfield's admission of ignorance as to the *reasons for change* in language as a "massive, uniform, and gradual alteration" is characteristically honest. That "at every moment . . . the system is just as rigid as at every other moment" should be rather a matter for perplexity. His (like de Saussure's and Sapir's) historical-comparative interests and training, the attendant orthographic biases, and the acceptance of the "regularity of sound change" principle as a necessary working assumption constitute the immediate background for the delimitation of *langue*.[3]

2.2   Bloomfield never really reconciled the empirical fact that our data differ at different times and places with the need to consider language a "rigid system." Nor could he have been satisfied with a solution in terms of "coalescence of phonemes," as suggested by Sapir (1921) and proposed by Swadesh (1935), for this was but an explication in terms of the system itself. The problem may well lie in the definition of the subject matter as a "system": "language" has become a convenient construct for the study of forms ("those features of language . . . which are common to all the speakers of a community,—the phonemes, grammatical categories, lexicon, and so on. These are abstractions, for they are only [recurrent] partial features of speech utterances.") In 1933 Bloomfield seems to be aware of this:

~ STRUCTURALIST BACKGROUND ~

> The language of any speech-community appears to an observer as a complicated signalling-system. . . . A language presents itself to us, at any one time, as a stable structure of lexical and grammatical habits.
>
> This, however, is an illusion. Every language is undergoing, at all times, a slow but unceasing process of *linguistic change*. . . . The ninth-century English of King Alfred the Great, of which we have contemporary manuscript records, seems to us like a foreign language; if we could meet English-speakers of that time, we should not understand their speech, or they ours. (1933, p. 281)

The term 'habit' should not be taken too literally. Also, 'stable' is less strong than the previous 'rigid,' but 'structure' makes up for the difference in an attempt to characterize the "system."[4] The question arises whether we are entitled to call two unintelligible "versions" of English the same language. Indeed, what becomes of "a language" apart from the corresponding speech-community, that is, when it ceases to be "signalling"?

At any rate, we have "lexicon" (= forms) and "grammar" (= patterns of arrangement of smaller forms in larger ones). Meaning, elusive though it may be, must also be taken into account. Thus, phonemes (minimum meaningless elements) combine into morphemes (minimum meaningful elements). These are the "forms." Likewise, taxemes (minimum meaningless features of arrangement) produce certain combinations or tagmemes (minimum meaningful features of arrangement). Included are not only "patterns" of order but also of selection, modulation, and phonetic modification (1933, ch. 16). As Hockett points out, this is one of Bloomfield's obscurest views.

The post-Bloomfieldians continued to zero in on language (the "meagre abstraction which we can and do study") in yet more radical ways. They were dissatisfied with at least two aspects of Bloomfield's approach, however. A discussion of subsequent developments can best profit from Hockett's (1968, ch. 1) revealing exposition. In the first place, appeal to meaning, however intuitive, became suspect: philosophical apriorism might thereby be introduced, and much in the Boas spirit, this had the risk of imposing semantic categories from one language to the next. Although semantics would probably have to be included in any complete description of a language, it should play no part in the grammatical analysis proper. In the process, the concept of "grammar" (or grammar-and-lexicon) underwent a considerable change, too. Meaning was thus to be excluded as a criterion for studying "the patterns by which meaningful forms (not mere phonemes) combine or arrange themselves into larger forms." That this was more a matter of principle than of actual practice is shown by the quick provision made to the effect that occasional resort to meaning was acceptable as a "practical shortcut" (compare Harris, 1951b; Hockett, 1952). Aside from the explicit separation of grammar and semantics, the main outcome was a further reification of language as an *autonomous* set of formal patterns. (This priority of the formal statement and its independence from semantics were later an integral part of Chomsky's 1957 "generative manifesto" as well.)

A second, not entirely unrelated, point of disagreement had to do with the relation between phonology and the rest of grammar. Tacit in Bloomfield's thinking was a dichotomy between morphology and syntax via word boundaries—a surprising criterion in view of the recalcitrant nature of the concept. This view (which he shared with Sapir) Bloomfield considered more important than the lexicon-grammar distinction. It is no doubt fundamental—indeed, it is only part of the broader question, "How relevant are these formally defined entities and dichotomies to the treatment of effective speech units?" Words themselves are often fragmented or merge into larger units, boundaries are generally blurred in actual speech, and suprasegmental features may be all but overriding (to mention only relatively formal criteria). Hockett goes as far as to say: "The problem in phonemic analysis was, as Bloomfield saw it, first and foremost to be certain of the articulatory-acoustic features that serve to keep *words* apart. . . . One might almost say that Bloomfield split phonology into morphological phonology (phonemics) and syntactical phonology, though he used no such pair of terms."

Several workers, particularly Trager, Bloch, and Hockett, thought the dichotomy between morphology and syntax less important than that between phonology and grammar-and-lexicon. Phonemic analysis should aid in the delimitation of *utterances*, not just "words," and this implied taking into consideration "any relevant differences of speech melody, contrasts of stress, and whatever phonemic stigmata might turn out when he had examined the grammatical structure of sentences." On close inspection, the *when* clause in this quotation is methodologically revealing. So is the fact that certain inherent features of utterances are called "suprasegmental."[5] In any case, Hockett says, "we regarded words as grammatical units, not as phonological or overriding ones, and thus we considered the morphology-syntax dichotomy to be a subdivision within grammar, not necessarily paralleled by any comparable break-up of the phonological system." (It is interesting to note that Hockett adds: "I am inclined to say that, today, the phonological views of the transformationalists are the rather direct descendants of those of Bloomfield, Sapir, and the Prague school.") The broader question is not thereby answered, of course, and words as units continued to play a prominent role in subsequent work on morphology and syntax (later, of course, syntax and morphology).

For some time questions centered on methodological precision exclusively, with periodic stock-taking efforts (compare Joos, 1957, interspersed commentary). Rigor meant exclusion of meaning (as far as possible) and inclusion of lexicon (but not phonology) in the study of grammar. Phonology provided, however, a good model for morphology: what phonemes were to allophones, morphemes could be to allomorphs, or Harris' original "morpheme alternants." Just as allophonic differences became nugatory in the study of phonemic patterning or structure ("phonotactics"), so the actual shape of morphemes was unimportant when their way of clustering into larger units was under study. Hockett appropriately called the latter "tactics" and sees it, in retrospect, as "obviously hierarchical."

Eventually a view of the design of grammar emerged, mainly under the leadership of Harris, in which procedures and terminology of the "grammatical process" (or "taxeme") type had no part. The result was an "item-and-arrangement" model. But as Hockett—one of the principal protagonists—tells us, "we had

~ CHAPTER 2 ~

no sooner achieved a pure item-and-arrangement model (not yet called that) than we began to wonder whether it was really what we wanted." Written in 1950, Hockett's paper appeared in 1954. Such doubts were only too reasonable.

In re "grammatical process," Joos (1957, p. 115) has this to say:

> besides the "morphemes," there was still something of an essential different kind called "process," without which the morphemes would not be glued together into utterances but would be left loose in the analyst's hands. Sapir's vitalistic way of thinking welcomed this duality as an essential dualism in human nature. But these were other times, and Sapir's disciple Harris drove out the spirit and showed that the structure of the utterance was still there.
>
> Later this building-block style of description was extended systematically, especially in terms of immediate-constituency theory, into the higher levels of grammar, where we find it well elaborated by 1947.

Joos is referring, of course, to Harris' 1942 statement about morpheme alternants and to Wells' 1947 influential formulation of immediate constituent (IC) analysis, in which the well-rooted notion of "hierarchical organization" found explicit expression. Surprisingly, Bloomfield seems to have introduced taxemes and tagmemes in order to capture that "something of an essential different kind." But the spirit was driven out to be replaced later by similarly mystical "rules." (One need not be a dualist, of course, to realize that when the emphasis is on *structure* procedural refinements—no matter how effective formally—are insufficient to tell why the analyzed utterances are put together the way they are.)

Eventually questions of broader methodological import were brought up (for example, simplicity of description, predictive power over inventory-type analysis, and so on) and the concept of "model" brought in. There was also some preliminary talk about the relation between linguistic descriptions and the condition of speakers of natural languages.

The first linguist to make use of the term 'model,' if loosely, was Harris (1944, 1951a; it reappears, perhaps more purposefully, in the title of a brief paper in 1959), but it was Hockett (1954) who made full and explicit use of the concept:

> By a "model of grammatical description" is meant a frame of reference within which an analyst approaches the grammatical phase of a language and states the results of his investigations. In one sense, there are as many models as there are different descriptions. . . . But in another, and very important sense, most grammatical descriptions seem to cluster about a relatively small number of distinct models; it is with these archetypal frames of reference that we are concerned here.

These archetypal frames of reference were the traditional word-and-paradigm (WP), which he discussed but briefly, and item-and-arrangement (IA) and item-and-process (IP), which he described in detail. The latter were clearly the product of more recent efforts. The various kinds of morphophonemic problems involved were understandably the primary object of attention. Hockett concludes that neither IA nor IP is completely satisfactory, but such problems as choice of construction over homophonous sequences and criteria of hierarchical structure (not unrelated to the grouping of IC's in such classical examples as "old men and women" or, more generally, "A N and N") make the IP model inviting.[6] The notion of "process," however, is open to dangerous extradescriptive interpretation.

A disturbing feature of Hockett's discussion, it should be noted, is his conspicuous tenacity to evaluate the relative merits of these two models within what could be called "WP coordinates." In IA, where only the classified occurrence of recurrent partials is stated ("without moving parts," as Hockett put it), biases probably do not transcend the imposition of terminological schemes. (Compare, for example, the five solutions reported by Hockett, following Bloch, to account for the relation between /tuk/ and /teyk/.) In IP, however, certain forms are explicitly posited as "basic" and others as "derived," and the problem becomes, or should become, more apparent. It is not quite clear, for instance, why the present tense or the homophonous infinitive should be so insistently taken as the base from which to derive /tuk/ in purportedly synchronic studies. Hockett's five "solutions" are framed within the terms of IA analysis; but /tuk/ occupies the right-hand term of a rewrite rule whose left term is *take + past* in Chomsky (1957, p. 32). At play, of course, are general criteria of descriptive economy having to do with broader correlations among structural features throughout the "system." But the fundamental nature of the argument remains the same: there exists a permanent risk of inadvertently applying new techniques to old ways of thinking. Considerations of this sort become especially relevant when explanatory demands are also made of purely descriptive devices, as we shall see. In any case, Hockett (1968) comments:

> it is not quite correct to characterize our predominant theoretical leanings in the late 1940's as "phrase structure grammar" (Postal, 1964b), since that term occupies an exact position in a frame of reference much more highly formalized than any we were using. But it is true that the only obvious formalization (within that particular frame of reference) of the item-and-arrangement model is a phrase-structure grammar; transformations require item-and-process.

Questions of simplicity (sometimes 'clarity' was used as a synonym) ranged between strictly descriptive convenience (Hockett, 1947) and a concern with practical uses of the final statement (Lounsbury, 1953). There are sensible echoes of the latter position in Hockett's 1954 paper: "Whether a grammatical description of a language is satisfactory or not depends in part on the use we want to make of it." Even so, the chasm between a patient empirical treatment of data (which, as it was, forced an almost endless terminological proliferation) and "theory," some felt, had grown too wide—hence, Hockett's desiderata and full-fledged recourse to the notion of model:

(1) A model must be *general*: it must be applicable to any language, not just languages of certain types.
(2) A model must be *specific*: when applied to a given language, the results must be determined wholly by

the nature of the model and the nature of the language, not at all by the whim of the analyst. It is not lack of specificity if the model requires us to subsume certain facts more than once, from different angles. It would be a lack of specificity if the model *allowed* us to take our choice in such cases, instead of *forcing* one choice or other or their joint option.
(3) A model must be *inclusive*: when applied to a given language, the results must cover all the observed data and, by implication, at least a very high percentage of all the not-yet-observed data. This is the analog of the "guidebook" criterion (not Metacriterion) mentioned earlier.
(4) A model must be *productive*: when applied to a given language, the results must make possible the creation of an infinite number of valid new utterances. This is the analog of the "prescriptive" criterion for descriptions.
(5) A model must be *efficient*: its application to any given language should achieve the necesary results with a minimum of machinery.

This was a far cry from Bloomfield's well-known statements, "The only useful generalizations about language are inductive generalizations" and, in a more Boasian spirit, "Features that we think ought to be universal may be absent from the next language that becomes accessible." Hockett goes well beyond codification of current practices.

The generality of (1) is only strengthened by the specificity of (2). The analyst should check his whims, of course, but placing the nature of the model before the nature of the language suggests an excessive commitment to preestablished schemes (compare the opposition between "allowing" and "forcing"). Although both (3) and (4) have to do with predictive power, (4) makes a stronger case of it by virtue of its greater scope—the "very high percentage" of (3) becomes "an infinite number" in (4)—and the addition of "creation" and "validity." Another passage in the same paper helps interpret these terms: "by following the statements one must be able to generate any number of utterances in the language above and beyond those observed in advance by the analyst—new utterances most, if not all, of which will pass the test of casual acceptance by a native speaker." This was not "generative" in the later formalized sense of "recursively enumerating," but in the more pedestrian sense of "production," and thus appropriately labeled by Hockett. In the hands of such analysts as Harris and Hockett, concerns over rigor and simplicity had begun to give linguistics only an elementary algebraic look. Simplicity, or Hockett's "efficiency" desideratum (5), is of course important, so long as one does not make a fetish of it.

Questions of creativity as well as validity (later grammaticalness or well-formedness) were to pass a stronger test than mere "casual acceptance" when models became more specific shortly thereafter. So was generality. Linguistics was becoming theoretical.

Productivity had been in the air for some time. One article is especially relevant to the present discussion. Hockett (1948) based a distinction between structural linguistics as a "game" and as a "science" on the predictive value of descriptive statements. In the former case, the one rule is that all the data in the corpus be covered, whatever the procedures involved. In the latter, descriptions account for utterances outside the corpus as well: "as a result of his examination he [the linguist] must be able to predict what *other* utterances the speakers of the language might produce, and, ideally, the circumstances under which those other utterances might be produced."

To a larger extent than is usually recognized, this brief paper may have set the stage for later developments. By dint of a special twist, that is, by considering the learning child's coinage of novel utterances a kind of prediction, Hockett could draw a parallel with the analyst's task of devising predictive techniques ("The child in time comes to *behave* the language; the linguist must come to *state* it") and thus presumably lend a more tangible justification to descriptive efforts. Despite the desirability of also predicting the circumstances under which utterances are produced, these circumstances held no intrinsic interest from this point of view. In a footnote we read: "Attempts to include

~ STRUCTURALIST BACKGROUND ~

prediction of the circumstances (except in terms of preceding utterances) constitute semantic analysis. Structural analysis can be scientific without being semantic." 'Circumstances' is undoubtedly too broad a term to suggest precise investigative strategy. Appeal was made to the nervous system instead:

> The structure of a language may be regarded as the end product of a game: in this sense structure is created by the person who plays the game. But every speaker of a language plays just such a game, the end product being a state of affairs in his nervous system rather than a set of statements. The linguistic scientist must regard the structure of the language as consisting precisely of this state of affairs. His purpose in analyzing a language is not to create structure, but to determine the structure actually created by the speakers of the language.

Similar and more extravagant claims have been made during the following decades in order to give linguistics, an empirical set of descriptive techniques so far, a more "scientific" status. Controversy over "description" versus "explanation" has loomed large in linguistic circles. The structuralist must necessarily turn to other dimensional systems (physical or nonphysical) when he is not satisfied with his descriptive work and demands an explanation of his data into the bargain. It is interesting to note that in his 1968 book, a severe criticism of Chomsky's "explanatory linguistics," Hockett eschews his own influential 1948 paper. We must probably take this as a disavowal of this earlier proposal, which is not included (at least explicitly) in his 1954 methodological constraints on models, either. Yet both publications were probably instrumental to a large extent in bringing about many of the subsequent theoretical trends. (Chomsky, 1961, acknowledged this, at least in part.) Hockett's game-science distinction is not, moreover, entirely unrelated to later arguments over "God's truth" versus "hocus-pocus" linguistics, neither of which holds the answer to an understandable dissatisfaction with mere structural statements, no matter how sophisticated.

Hockett's comments on transformational analysis, with which, appropriately, he ends his discussion of the post-Bloomfieldian period, are directly relevant here. (Stratificational grammar and tagmemics can be comfortably shunned in the present context—except perhaps for noting the former's claims also to reflect something about the speakers of natural languages, and Pike's efforts to make his linguistic analysis relevant to other aspects of human behavior.) As he sees them, transformations are "largely a corrective to certain temporary extremisms of the 1940's, a reintroduction, with improvements and under a new name, of certain useful features of the Bloomfieldian and Sapirian view of language." Indeed, his praise of transformations is couched in two statements by Bloomfield:

> Syntactic transformations, in either the Harris or the Chomsky version . . . yield a special sort of item-and-process model of grammatical design that is not only more powerful but also, in my opinion, much more realistic than any item-and-arrangement model can be. . . . Recall Bloomfield's remarks of 1945: "Systematic description . . . tries to assemble all forms that have any common feature and to unite them under a single statement." Transformations are a great help in this, in that limitations of cooccurrence can be stated once for a whole group of transformationally related phrase-types, instead of separately for each (Harris, 1957; Chomsky, 1957). Again from Bloomfield: "The reader [of an overly "rigorous description"] finds difficulty in interpreting, applying, and combining separate statements." The effective ordering of rules does much to combat this difficulty. Transformations are heuristically valuable: if nothing else told us so, transformational tests would quickly reveal that the predicates of *I found the village* and *I walked a mile* are not parallel (Chomsky, 1957). Outside of syntax, ordered rules are a wonderfully clarifying device in morphophonemics.

A characterization of transformations as "heuristically valuable" is surely correct; elsewhere we read that "transformations are not a theory, but only a possible ingredient of a theory."

~ STRUCTURALIST BACKGROUND ~

For obvious reasons, it is around the emphasis on theory that the present preliminary discussion will be brought to a close.

Although this last quotation captures the essence of the transformational device as originally conceived, both formulations have of course undergone substantial changes since (see especially, Harris, 1965; Chomsky, 1965). Except for Chomsky's recognition that meaning deserves an explicit role in grammatical studies, his and Harris' formulations have grown consistently apart with respect to both technical detail and philosophical outlook.

Transformations are generally recognized as Harris' most important contribution to linguistics, yet Hockett seems to bring Harris in primarily as background for discussing Chomsky. In fact, he takes Harris to task for his reluctance to go beyond the data: "It is fair to say, I believe, that Harris has been a superb *methodologist*, but never at any time a *theorist* of language." Theoretical concerns have to do with the relation between language and its users and with the role of language in human affairs. Thus, the fact that Harris drew no "broader or deeper inferences" from his 1957 classic paper (or after),[7] whereas Chomsky immediately went on to theorize in the above sense, counts as a point for Chomsky. Indeed, Chomsky's unremitting insistence against heuristics vis-à-vis theory is traced to an overreaction to Harris' "theoretical nihilism." Hockett's implicit sympathies, though critical, are probably the result of his own lingering proclivities.

This is not the place to discuss the differences between the two approaches, but it may be well to point out that Harris' emphasis on data manipulation is clearly in keeping with the original thrust of the movement. Transformations can be studied for their own sake, as relations between sentences or between sets of sentences and a sentence. This is the essence of Harris' method. In contrast, Chomsky's formulation incorporates a phrase-structure component and transformations are construed as relations among trees. It is true that the absence of anything like a "semantic component" may indeed help to lend Harrisian-style grammar the aspect of an unmotivated game. As Hiż (1976) points out, however, Harris' syntax has always been

~ CHAPTER 2 ~

semantically motivated. 'Motivated' may be a strong term, but how could it have been otherwise without talking nonsense at every stage?

Whatever the deficiencies of the approach, in what respects can a formulation developed in terms of a priori models prove more like a science? Chomsky's overall theory is couched in a metatheoretical framework (much more sophisticated but not entirely unlike Hockett's cruder proposal of 1954) which *claims* explanatory power. Whether this makes his approach more like science than like a game, however, is seriously open to question. The daring discussion of the implications of a generative-transformational view for a characterization of linguistic knowledge may come closer to drawing "broader and deeper inferences," but a data-tied formulation is more likely to reveal relevant relations among the data, at least in principle.

One can only sympathize with the urge to go beyond structure (whatever the means used for its specification) and get back to the actual behavior of speakers and listeners. But it is doubtful whether this can best be accomplished through the construction of models and the subsequent imputation of their formal conveniences to speakers of natural languages, all the more so when the basic descriptive apparatus has been developed in terms of abstract syntactic representations then mapped onto actual sentence structures. Nor are certain self-imposed initial limitations irrelevant here: for example, Chomsky's sentence atomism is not only unwarranted but also bound to force a host of further unfruitful formal elaborations and, in turn, unduly emphasize certain aspects of semantics at the expense of others. What is more, such built-in biases are likely to raise misleading rather than pertinent questions as far as the *behavior* of speakers and listeners is concerned.

SUMMARY

Structural analysis studies language as an abstraction. The outcome is a conception of the subject matter as a self-contained, independent system of forms that can presumably be described without explicit appeal to speakers, listeners, and their common environments. This view underlies all efforts to establish an autonomous science of language. As originally conceived, this was to be a descriptive science, free from random theorizing, teleological explanation, and premature psychologizing. It was to avoid the imposition of a single mould on the great variety of "self-contained systems" called languages: experts were to speak of specific languages, not Language. The primary concern was methodological precision: the emphasis was on method rather than theory; on form rather than meaning (which was, however, to be taken into account). Large quantities of data were gathered, but these were narrowly determined by the eliciting setting itself. The approach was fraught with difficulties, as linguists found out when they began to make inductive statements in the course of developing a general methodology. Eventually there emerged a concern with general criteria, such as generality, efficiency, and productivity; the notion of model was brought in. Descriptions should account for data outside the corpus at hand; the need for rules came to the fore. Some reference to speakers, without whom there would be after all no "abstract system" to analyze, was perhaps inevitable. When the emphasis is on structure, procedural refinements are insufficient to tell why the utterances under analysis have the form they have. There exists a permanent risk of merely applying new techniques to old ways of thinking. At the root lies the perennial confusion between products of behavior and the behavior itself. A long tradition and the consequent wealth of conceptual systems stand in the way of any attempt to look at verbal behavior simply as behavior which is verbal.

~ CHAPTER 3 ~

The Transformational-Generative Proposal

3.1   Chomsky's more permanent (for some, irreversible) contribution to linguistics, by many accounts, lies in the mathematical rigor of his strictly formal work on the properties of grammars. It is probably equally safe to say that the overall impact of the transformational-generative proposal stems from claims regarding the relevance of its descriptive framework for a general theory of language. But although the precision afforded by the application of techniques from finite automata theory and recursive function theory was no doubt useful to Chomsky's original work, it has ultimately proved less than beneficial as the persuasive cogency of the resulting theory has lent an otherwise unwarranted credibility to ever stronger explanatory claims.

The formal details and scope of the descriptive apparatus of Chomsky's theory have undergone considerable change over the years. These technical changes are not the object of the present study. General acquaintance with the formal descriptive means will be assumed. Enough will be presented below, however, to bring forth what constitutes our primary concern, namely, the fundamental assumptions underlying Chomsky's work. These have varied little during the past two decades (see, for example, Chomsky, 1956 and 1976); they are intimately related to his explicitly formulated goals for linguistic theory. Indeed, they have permitted, if not actually motivated, the gradual shift of emphasis concerning explanatory value.

3.2   Certain initial assumptions are already explicit in Chomsky's "Three models for the description of language," published in 1956, two years after Hockett's "Two models of grammatical

~ TRANSFORMATIONAL-GENERATIVE PROPOSAL ~

description." Some of these initial assumptions have to do with a view of science and the overall nature of linguistic theory. In this early statement, Chomsky defined the two central problems of descriptive linguistics as (1) the discovery of simple and "revealing" grammars for natural languages, and (2) the formulation of a general theory of linguistic structure based on an examination of the underlying conceptions of these grammars, if successful. At play are such concepts as model, structure, rules, grammar, and a conception of language. The first two are, of course, taken for granted. Rules, grammar, and language, however, though closely interrelated with structure and among themselves, demand closer scrutiny.

Scientists aim to establish general laws on the basis of a necessarily finite set of observations. These general laws are formulated, in Chomsky's view, in terms of certain hypothetical constructs. Scientific theories permit the prediction of an unlimited number of unobserved events; mathematical theories have "the additional property that predictions follow rigorously from the body of theory." The linguist attempts to describe a language on the strength of a finite set of data; this places linguistics on a par with empirical science at large. Chomsky makes the proposal that the resulting grammar be considered a theory of the structure of the language under analysis: as such, it "projects" the stated interrelations discovered among the items in the corpus to the rest of the language. It does so via rules "framed in terms of such hypothetical constructs as the particular phonemes, words, phrases, and so on." These grammatical rules are the "laws" of the language. An adequate grammar should determine the set of grammatical sentences unambiguously.

The relation between rules and grammar is clear. Less so is the relation between rules of grammar and (empirical) laws, which probably holds only for a given conception of language. The following excerpt provides just this conception and further clarification of its relation to grammar:

> By a language, then, we shall mean a set (finite or infinite) of sentences, each of finite length, all constructed from a

finite alphabet of symbols. If A is an alphabet, we shall say that anything formed by concatenating the symbols of A is a string in A. By a *grammar* of the language L we mean a device of some sort that produces all of the strings that are sentences of L and only those.

This definition is clearly at odds with the interest in natural languages set forth in (1) and (2) above. Gone also is what feeble suggestion of inductive principle might be contained in that proposal. Abstraction and reification, alluded to before, seem now complete to anyone bent on looking at language as a natural phenomenon. 'Rule' and 'law' may be synonymous within some abstract analytical context such as this, which is perfectly in keeping with Chomsky's obvious predilection for mathematical treatment. But though this view may momentarily forestall possible quibbles about the essential role assigned to hypothetical constructs in the formulation of general laws, it does little to allay one's possible concern over the empirical status of words, phrases, and the like, in terms of which linguistic rules are framed. Indeed, such doubts are bound to carry over into the rules themselves, which play a predominant role in TGG. This switch from particular languages to Language (L) for purposes of theorizing (and back again for convenient examples) is at the basis of Chomsky's entire effort to set up an overall framework for linguistic theory.

In fact, general linguistic theory is not reached through a consideration of successful grammars of natural languages. Instead, it becomes a metatheory in terms of which we establish what a successful grammar must be like. Alternative proposals are investigated, again in abstract terms. A grammar should make explicit the relation between an available corpus and the language of which it is a subset. Obviously, structure should be assigned through finite means. By drawing a parallel with the native speaker's (limited) experience, and assuming an intuitive knowledge of sentencehood on his part, it is then postulated that an adequate linguistic theory should ultimately be able to account for the ability to produce and understand an infinite number of novel sentences.

~ TRANSFORMATIONAL-GENERATIVE PROPOSAL ~

The notion of "grammaticalness" is at the core of Chomsky's formulation, and operational criteria of sorts are suggested for characterizing the concept of "grammatical sentence." The weight of the argument rests, however, on rather more theoretical grounds. The determination of clear-cut cases of grammatical sentences in an isolated language provides a weak test of adequacy for a given grammar and, therefore, for the theoretical conception underlying it. But it provides a strong test if we insist that such cases "be handled in a fixed and predetermined manner" for every language.

The central issue is the relation between the set of observed sentences and the set of grammatical sentences, about which, Chomsky admits, a great deal must be learned. The bulk of the paper under discussion is devoted to studying the formal properties (structures) of the set of grammatical sentences (the language). Thus, a given conception of linguistic structure must be rejected if some "interesting language" lies outside its descriptive scope. One such language is English. If this conception is retained, we go on to ask also whether it can account for all possible interesting languages in reasonably simple ways. Grammars must also be "revealing," that is, significant semantic properties must follow from the syntactic analysis thus performed. What is more, the corresponding conception of linguistic structure must shed light into nothing less than the "mechanism of language," not specific languages or subsets thereof.

Chomsky assumes that natural languages are made up of an infinite set of grammatical sentences. The emphasis being on syntax, the sentence is taken as the initial category; presumably, we should expect to remain within its boundaries. Fixed structural assignments are taken for granted, as well as their immediate relevance to both speaking and understanding, that is, the "use of language." A unique model for all languages is implied throughout.

3.3 Three "nontrivial" models of grammatical description are carefully considered in Chomsky's 1956 paper, namely, finite-state, phrase-structure, and transformational grammars (FSG,

~ CHAPTER 3 ~

PSG, and TG, respectively). We need not go into the formal details of the argument here, beyond stating briefly the reasons why Chomsky rejects the first two as inadequate, in favor of the third or, rather, a combination of PSG and TG.

Finite-state Markov processes provide the formal machinery for discussing the simplest grammatically interesting device that will generate an infinite number of sentences. It is based on "a familiar conception of language as a particularly simple type of information source," a conception with which Chomsky is rightly displeased. Its inadequacy stems from the fact that English is not a finite-state language and therefore outside the descriptive range of left-to-right devices with a finite set of dependency states. The assignment of an arbitrary finite upper limit of sentence length in English is no solution either: the resulting grammar will be extremely complex, though simplifiable through the inclusion of recursive means (closed loops in the present case). But then either many nonsentences will be generated, or else perfectly grammatical sentences will be left out. A sequence of such devices, likewise, will not do:

> Suppose, for example, that for fixed n we construct a finite-state grammar in the following manner: one state of the grammar is associated with each sequence of English words of length n and the probability that the word X will be produced when the system is in state S_i is equal to the conditional probability of X, given the sequence of n words which defines S_i. The output of such grammar is customarily called the $n+1^{st}$ order of approximation to English.

As n increases, the generated sequences are also more likely to resemble ordinary English, where the probabilities were determined to begin with. There are properties of sentence formation in English which such devices, whatever their interest in other contexts, are simply not equipped to handle, however.

Chomsky states categorically that "there is no general relation between the frequency of a string (or its component parts) and its grammaticalness." Models based on statistical order of approximation (with which such devices are usually associated) fail to distinguish between such pairs as the now classic examples

~ TRANSFORMATIONAL-GENERATIVE PROPOSAL ~

(1) "Colorless green ideas sleep furiously" and (2) "Furiously sleep ideas green colorless," even though (1) is grammatical whereas (2) is not.

A question may be raised about the grounds on which (1) is declared a grammatical sentence. Chomsky's notion of an operational criterion (the only one actually suggested) involves the fact that whereas a native speaker of English will read (2) with falling intonation on each word, he will read (1) with normal intonation; also, (1) will be learned and remembered much more easily than (2). The latter statement probably needs qualification, particularly as strings illustrating nonsense become longer. It is not entirely unrelated to the observation that "as n increases, an nth order approximation to English will exclude (as more and more improbable) an ever-increasing number of grammatical sentences, while it still contains vast numbers of completely ungrammatical strings." 'Improbability' is the key, and reliance on *words* may be the problem. Utterances, whether they are sentences or not, do not occur unmotivated—a fact that theoretical linguists are often too wont to ignore. In fact, as far as regular speakers and listeners are concerned, (1) is not a "sentence" at all, carefully constructed though it was to conform to well-known patterns of English while containing no two or more words that "make sense." Chomsky was really putting forth a particular point of view about well-formedness and meaningfulness. But one may question the view that well-formedness alone suffices to turn a string of words into an English sentence: (1) and (2) constitute excellent examples of a deep-rooted tendency in this type of study to bring to bear on natural languages exceedingly artificial examples conveniently worked out for purposes of theoretical speculation. The representativeness of these examples justifies the otherwise uncalled-for space devoted to the FSG proposal.

Chomsky devoted considerable space to a discussion of the formal relations between FSG and PSG, the older immediate-constituent analysis, which he relabeled "phrase-structure grammar." A rigorous formalization of PSG shows that this model is much more powerful and simpler than a word-by-word model. Even so, it is insufficient on several counts, forcing the

~ CHAPTER 3 ~

introduction of transformational rules. (Not everyone agrees that PSG and IC analysis are necessarily the same. See, for example Harman, 1963.) Chomsky writes: "A phrase-structure grammar is defined by a finite vocabulary (alphabet) V_p, a finite set Σ of initial stings in V_p, and a finite set F of rules of the form: $X \rightarrow Y$, where X and Y are strings in V_p. Each such rule is interpreted as the instruction: rewrite X as Y."

As elsewhere in Chomsky's work, abstract formulations such as this are then mapped onto actual sentences. Chomsky offers a general characterization of his proposal in the following terms:

> we picture a language as having a small, possibly finite kernel of basic sentences with phrase structure . . . along with a set of transformations which can be applied to kernel sentences or to earlier transforms to produce new and more complicated sentences from elementary components. We have seen certain indications that this approach may enable us to reduce the immense complexity of actual language to manageable proportions and, in addition, that it may provide considerable insight into the actual use and understanding of language.

(1) The kernel of basic sentences is obtained by application of obligatory transformations to the terminal strings of the phrase-structure grammar; Chomsky points out that "the grammar can be greatly simplified if we limit the kernel to a very small set of simple, active, declarative sentences." (2) All other sentences—that is, questions, passives, sentences with compound noun phrases, with conjunctions, and so on—are derived by applying optional transformations to the strings underlying the kernels. (3) Each type of transformation can be finitely characterized; a finite restricting class indicates the information needed to apply a transformation to a given string. (4) Transformations carry grammatical sentences into grammatical sentences, effecting a structural change. The constituent structure of given sentences can be investigated in terms of their behavior with respect to sets of transformations. (5) In addition, there is a sequence of morphophonemic rules that convert a string of morphemes into a string of phonemes: for example,

have past → had, be en → been, take past → took, and so on. (6) Phrase-structure and morphophonemic rules apply directly: we only need to know the shape of the recipient string. Not so transformational rules, which require some knowledge of the derivational history of the strings to which they apply. (7) Grammars thus have a tripartite structure.

The actual *modus operandi* is summarized as follows:

> To generate a sentence from such a grammar we construct an extended derivation beginning with an initial string of the phrase structure grammar, e.g., # Sentence #. . . . We then run through the rules of phrase structure, producing a terminal string. We then apply certain transformations, giving a string of morphemes in the correct order, perhaps quite a different string from the original string. Application of the morphophonemic rules converts this into a string of phonemes. We might run through the phrase structure grammar several times and then apply a generalized transformation to the resulting set of terminal strings.

Simplicity in the overall description, a formal criterion, played a prominent role. Revealing syntactic analysis should also point up meaningful semantic properties, as we have seen. Reference to semantics is only implicit throughout; indeed, interaction between syntax and semantics is limited to such marginal comments as "transformations are, by and large, meaning preserving." Discussion of their general relation is shunned. A final, brief section is devoted to explanatory power in linguistic theory, however.

Throughout this final section, systematic appeal is made to "understanding" alone. This is consistent with the emphasis laid on structural ambiguity before. An ambiguous sentence is one liable to be understood in more than one way. PSG will account comfortably for the constructional ambiguity of such examples as "they are flying planes," analyzable as "they-are-flying planes" or as "they-are flying-planes." PSG alone, however, cannot handle cases like "the shooting of the hunters," where "hunters" can be subject or object: "shoot" and "hunters" are differently related in the two underlying kernels ("hunters shoot" and "they shoot hunters"). These are examples of constructional homonymity on the transformational level: two different transformational origins explain the structural and semantic ambiguity of "the shooting of the hunters," which, Chomsky points out, must be struck out of the kernel and reintroduced through different transformations. He further writes: "transformational analysis enables us to reduce partially the problem of explaining how we understand a sentence to that of explaining how we understand a kernel sentence." A proposed grammar that does not provide correspondingly different analyses casts doubt on the metatheory in accordance with which it has been constructed. The addition of a T-component to PSG makes the resulting TGG model more powerful than PSG alone and, of course, more powerful than FSG.

The ultimate relevance of these examples and analyses is not altogether clear. There seems to be an implicit assumption that the ambiguity of cases like the ones reported, taken in isolation for the sake of formal analysis, reflects an inevitable ambiguity where actual speech situations are concerned. This is on a par with previous observations about the artificial character of examples brought to bear on grammaticalness. There is also a strong assumption made in "grouping" various sentence types around one and the same underlying kernel; moreover, taking simple declarative active sentences as kernels is probably only a matter of formal convenience, supported by traditional practices.

A terminological note may not be out of place at this point. Chomsky often uses the term 'use' interchangeably with 'production,' rather than with 'understanding.' In a truly empirical context, involving the behavior of real speakers and listeners, it would seem advisable to place 'production' and 'understanding' on a similar footing, and leave 'use' (with all due reservation) to refer to both taken together. (As we shall see, Chomsky later came to interchange 'use' with 'understanding' more frequently. The same observation applies there.)

3.4 These same arguments, along with their explicit and implicit assumptions, were expanded in less technical terms a year later (Chomsky, 1957). Sometimes the phrasing is the same and many of the same examples are included, especially for FSG and PSG. Discussion of grammaticalness, despite the emphasis placed here on the notion of degrees, remains the highly theoretical issue that, as formulated, it is safe to say it can only be. Transformations are discussed more extensively, however, and their relation to Harris' work is put in proper perspective (if casually). A whole chapter is devoted to transformations in English. Special reference to *Syntactic Structures* is justified here, aside from its impact and popularity, by the fact that in it Chomsky made fully explicit the goals of linguistic theory and the relation between syntax, semantics, and explanatory power.

The proposition, occasionally put forth, that by 1957 Chomsky was still much of a Bloomfieldian must rest, presumably, on his stand on the relation between syntax and semantics, at least in theory. As we have seen, the more sophisticated sector of post-Bloomfieldian linguistics had become uneasy about the development of descriptive techniques by essentially *ad hoc* procedures; greater attention was being paid to syntax, and a preoccupation with "going beyond the corpus" was clearly in the air: Harris had included it implicitly (1951, see especially ch. 16, to which Chomsky has repeatedly referred in this connection); Hockett (1954) was more explicit about it, and his desiderata came close to a rudimentary metatheoretical proposal as well. During this period, as we saw in chapter 2, it was generally assumed that what was needed was a formal analysis, from which meaning had better be excluded. Chomsky may be said to have carried these aspirations to the end. So much so, that his proposal hardly looked Bloomfieldian, or rather post-Bloomfieldian, at the time. This was due, to a considerable extent, to his exclusive emphasis on syntax, his drastic reformulation of the concept of "linguistic level," and his introduction of recursive devices and abstract characterizations. The notion of model acquired concreteness. Above all, he was addressing himself to the important question of the justification of grammars, intimately related to his proposed goals for linguistic theory and ultimately explanatory power. As Hockett puts it,

~ CHAPTER 3 ~

"By moving away from the rest of us at a wide angle, Chomsky has achieved a different perspective. We cannot reject his opinions merely because we fail to see, from our angle of view, what he thinks he can discern from his" (Hockett, 1968, p. 36).

3.5 It may be well to review, in synthesis, what Chomsky's actual position was in 1957, before going on to discuss his subsequent stronger claims. According to Chomsky a grammar is a device that generates all and only the grammatical sentences of a language. Everything hinges on infinity. Reference has already been made to the relation between the set of observed sentences and the set of grammatical sentences, as well as to what constitutes a strong test of adequacy as far as grammaticalness is concerned. The formulation of a general theory centers on L, whatever that may be, not on specific languages. Chomsky writes: "To use Quines's formulation, a linguistic theory will give a general explanation of what 'could' be in language on the basis of 'what *is* plus *simplicity* of the laws whereby we describe and extrapolate what is' " (p. 14, fn.).[1] (Like Chomsky's, Quine's [1953] argument is strictly formal. Indeed, "what 'could' be in language" smacks of reification. At any rate, it is class K, infinity, of his classic four-level characterization of domain. Like the lower levels, J, I, and H, the finite corpus, K is made up exclusively of grammatical sequences. Notice also the appeal to simplicity and laws.)

Although there is a suggestion made that steps can be taken to establish a behavioral criterion of "grammaticalness," intuitive knowledge is assumed for the purpose of discussing the sorts of grammar that will meet a strong test of adequacy; the formulation is based on clear-cut cases, letting the grammar, once constructed, determine the intermediate cases. We face "a familiar task of explication of some intuitive concept—in this case, the concept 'grammatical in English,' and more generally, the concept 'grammatical' " (p. 13).[2] This is achieved through the establishment of metatheoretical constraints rather than on strictly empirical grounds, that is, through the systematic elaboration of a data-tied set of techniques. An abstract system ensues. Thus, for example, a "condition of generality" is imposed whereby particular grammars, as theories of particular languages, are constructed in terms of concepts defined without reference to specific languages. As it turns out, this is more a matter of principle than of practice: while true for rules, "level," and the like, a great many of the concepts employed are those discovered by structural linguistics. What is more, Chomsky takes traditional categories for granted.

This is not to say that heuristic devices have no place, but the overall thrust is to get rid of them as much as possible. A linguistic theory is not a manual for the discovery of grammars. This would be an unreasonable demand. It would also be too strong a requirement to expect the theory to decide whether a proposed grammar is the correct one. In Chomsky's view, careful inspection of earlier proposals purporting to provide discovery procedures shows that they are in reality evaluation procedures. This is the most that the linguist can expect from a general theory.

> Our ultimate aim is to provide an objective, non-intuitive way to evaluate a grammar once presented, and to compare it with other proposed grammars. We are thus interested in describing the form of grammars (equivalently, the nature of linguistic structure) and investigating the empirical consequences of adopting a certain model for linguistic structure, rather than in showing how, in principle, one might have arrived at the grammar of a language. (p. 56)

It seems therefore desirable that the goals of linguistic theory should be made both explicit and rigorous. Chomsky offers a view of such a theory as a machine with inputs and outputs. For discovery procedures (largely the kind of structural analysis referred to in 2.2), the input is a corpus and the output is the grammar; for decision procedures, the input is a corpus and a grammar, and the output a "yes"-or-"no" choice ("yes" entails that the proposed grammar is the best); for evaluation procedures, the input is a corpus and two grammars, and the output the *better* of the two proposed grammars. There is room for improvement of both general formulation and particular grammars, whether "from the discovery of new facts about particular languages or from purely theoretical insights about organization of linguistic data" (p. 50). The crucial question has to do with the relation between the general theory and specific grammars.

There are formal conditions to be met. Again, special emphasis is laid on simplicity: to be significant, this simplicity must be systematic (affecting the overall description), not local. Much of the discussion revolves around the separability of descriptive levels (associated with discovery procedures) versus interdependence of abstract levels of representation: "when we lower our aims to the development of an evaluation procedure, there remains little motivation for any objection to mixing levels, and there is no difficulty in avoiding circularity in the definition of interdependent levels" (p. 57). A transformational-generative model, with mixed levels, is favored by the theory. If adopted, a number of well-known problems that had long baffled descriptive linguistics vanish and the bulk of the description is reduced. A discussion of these problems would lead us into marginal issues in the present context, however. More important here, there are certain "external conditions of adequacy" to be met as well. These have to do with what Chomsky calls the "empirical consequences of adopting a certain model of linguistic structure." We have already touched on some of them (see also chapter 5).

3.6 Chapter 8 of *Syntactic Structures* is entirely devoted to the explanatory power of linguistic theory. Chomsky writes: "There are many facts about language and linguistic behavior that require explanation beyond the fact that such and such a string (which no one may ever have produced) is or is not a sentence" (p. 85). The distinction between "language" and "linguistic behavior" is of course consistent with a view of the former as an abstraction.

As in "Three models for the description of language," Chomsky falls back on structural ambiguity and understanding as the central issues. A criterion of adequacy for a linguistic theory and the set of grammars associated with it lies in their power to assign different structural descriptions to cases of constructional homonymity or ambiguously represented phoneme sequences: each case of constructional homonymity should correspond to a real case of ambiguity and to each proper kind of ambiguity should correspond a real case of constructional homonymity, whether on the morphological, phrase-structure, or transformational level. Several kinds of structural ambiguity besides those pointed out above are discussed. The importance of adding a transformational component is of course emphasized. Words like "have," "be," "seem," and so on, superficially irregular, prove to be cases of higher-level regularity. In particular, it is shown that appropriate transformational representation permits an "intuitively" correct classification of sentence types, which, though having different lower-level representations, are understood in similar ways. This is the case, for example, of certain types of questions.

The redefined notion of "level" plays a fundamental role. The matter is fairly summed up in the following excerpt:

> What we are suggesting is that the notion of "understanding a sentence" be explained in part in terms of the notion of "linguistic level." *To understand a sentence, then, it is first necessary to reconstruct its analysis on each linguistic level*; and we can test the adequacy of a given set of abstract linguistic levels by asking whether or not grammars formulated in terms of these levels enable us to provide a satisfactory analysis of the notion of "understanding." (p. 87; italics added)

The heavy appeal to "understanding" suggests a special reliance on (the behavior of) the listener, yet discussion of explanatory power is generally phrased in terms of the *speaker*'s intuition (less vaguely, sometimes his actual behavior):

> Any grammar of a language will *project* the finite and somewhat accidental corpus of observed utterances to a set (presumably infinite) of grammatical utterances. In this respect, a grammar mirrors the behavior of the speaker who, on the basis of a finite and accidental experience with language, can produce and understand an indefinite number of new sentences. Indeed, any explication of the notion

~ CHAPTER 3 ~

"grammatical in L" (i.e., any characterization of "grammatical in L" in terms of "observed utterance in L") can be thought of as offering an explanation for this fundamental aspect of linguistic behavior. (p. 15)

Grammatical processes are assumed to be the same for both speaker and listener. Elsewhere, the terms 'synthesis' and 'analysis' are brought in as synonyms for 'production' and 'understanding': "In fact, these two tasks, which the speaker and hearer must perform are essentially the same" (p. 48). This is clearly reminiscent of Bloomfield's outlook (see section 2.1 above). Of course, speakers speak and listeners respond to them, but it is doubtful whether processes of synthesis and analysis thus formulated can account for the actual processes through which they come to emit the particular behaviors so labeled, whether these are the same, or whether any tasks of synthesis and analysis must indeed be performed at all in order to speak and understand. In any case, this is probably as far as Chomsky went in 1957 regarding the psychological implications of linguistic theory. Notice also the cautionary "in part" in the next-to-last quotation.

Given the relevance attributed to ambiguity, it may be appropriate to point out also that there are powerful reasons, on formal grounds alone, to believe that circumscribing the analysis to sentence boundaries is an unnecessary, indeed a complicating and artificial, restriction (see note 2, next chapter). In fact, it is not quite clear what is meant by "a proper kind of ambiguity."[3]

Chomsky argues that "there is independent evidence in favor of our method of selecting grammars" (p. 55) and, it follows, in favor also of the globally simpler TG model he proposes. The native speaker's intuition, which remains an undefined form of external evidence, became later part of the data (as it were) when a sharper distinction between linguistic "competence" and "performance" was drawn in the course of formulating even stronger explanatory claims. However convenient from a formal point of view, a conceptualization of linguistic metatheory as a machine with inputs and outputs is not entirely aseptic, as these last paragraphs suggest and subsequent developments prove.

~ TRANSFORMATIONAL-GENERATIVE PROPOSAL ~

3.7 A final comment about Chomsky's views on the relation between syntax and semantics is probably in order at this point, for at least two reasons. First, nowhere else in the book are Chomsky's dualistic assumptions clearer. His arguments for the independence of grammar from semantic criteria lead him to a radical separation of "language" from its "use"; reification of L, hinted at before, finds full expression here: "In §§3-7, then, we were studying language as an instrument or a tool, attempting to describe its structure with no explicit reference to the way in which this instrument is put to use" (p. 103). Semantic considerations have to do with "use" and are therefore related to explanatory power. The basic contention is that syntax can help semantics, but not vice versa. Two distinct and separate fields are implied. Second, as indicated above, it is here that the more sophisticated post-Bloomfieldians could probably sense an affinity with Chomsky's overall proposal, in spirit if not in actual detailed practice. Chomsky takes them to task on this score; his more detailed criticisms were aimed, however, at those grammarians who still contemplated the appeal to semantic clues seriously.

Chomsky attributes this confidence to the assumption that semantic criteria are misjudged as simple and immediately given, and argues to the contrary. Thus, he devotes special attention to the consequences of approaching phonemic distinctness in terms of differential meaning. He correctly points out that sometimes phonemically distinct utterance tokens are synonymous, while homonymous forms may have different meanings. The prospect of accounting systematically for such facts would be a forbiddingly laborious task, in part because of the bulk of the corpus needed, but also because of the difficulty of drawing the line between sameness and difference of meaning in many cases. Of course, where phonemic distinctness is concerned, field workers have a much easier task of it through the use of such "nonsemantic" devices as the pair test, which amounts to a (rudimentary) operational test of behavior. But the development of a semantic equivalent seems also a hopeless task, for very much the same reasons. In Chomsky's view, an appeal to meaning through such criteria as the way in which utterance

~ CHAPTER 3 ~

tokens can be used (class of situations, type of response they evoke, and so on) is not a solution either, without a prior notion of utterance types. But these are presumably part of what the grammarian is after.

A second (and related) source of confidence stems from a confusion between "meaning" and "informant's response." Consider Lounsbury's statement: "In linguistic analysis we define contrast among forms operationally in terms of difference in meaning responses" (quoted on p. 99). Chomsky suggests that dropping the word 'meaning' turns this statement into an acceptable form of the pair test; but then, in his view, the pair test is nonsemantic (though it involves an informant's response). He concludes that a view of meaning as "response to language," as such approaches suggest, is inadequate. He finds it so broad as to be devoid of significance. (The fact is that it is too narrow.) Yet he himself inevitably falls back on such devices in his own work.

Chomsky's discussion of syntax and semantics begins with a reiteration of the preceding argument about the role of the redefined notion of linguistic level in understanding. He now adds:

> In particular, in order to understand a sentence it is necessary to know the kernel sentences from which it originates (more precisely, the terminal strings underlying these kernel sentences) and the phrase structure of each of these elementary components, as well as the transformational history of development of the given sentence from these kernel sentences . . . these being considered the basic "content elements" from which the usual, more complex sentences of real life are formed by transformational development. (p. 92)

This is followed by: "In proposing that syntactic structure can provide a certain insight into the problems of meaning and understanding we have entered onto dangerous ground." Indeed. Chomsky argues that much effort has gone into answering the question, "How can you write a grammar with no appeal to meaning?" (where the implication is that it *can* be done), instead of the real question, "How are the syntactic devices available in a given language put to work in the actual use of language?" (which implies a view of grammar and of language), or better yet, "How can you write a grammar?"—which easily leads to the construction of a metatheory.

He quickly points out that remarks about possible semantic implication in discussions of explanatory power should not be misinterpreted. The theory has been developed on strictly formal grounds, and such remarks only indicate "some ways in which the actual use of available syntactic devices can be studied" (p. 93). This is doubtful at best. The theory has been *worked out* on formal grounds, but as soon as actual examples from a natural language are brought in, "responses to language" are forced upon the analyst. One does not detect ambiguity in an unknown language, nor does one fully appreciate its available syntactic devices or come by, say, transformationally related forms—no matter how good a theory one may have. Responses to language (necessary but not sufficient for the listener, of which linguists are a very special subspecies) are implicit in statements like the following: "We can describe circumstances in which a 'quantificational' sentence such as 'Everyone in the room knows at least two languages' may be true, while the corresponding passive 'at least two languages are known by everyone in the room' is false under the normal interpretation of these sentences" (pp. 100-101). Presumably 'circumstances' and 'interpretation' cover such things as "class of situations," "responses they evoke," and so forth, dismissed before. Judgments of truth and falsehood imply them. The theory may have been elaborated formally, but the validity of the formulation or its relevance to "interesting" *natural* languages (which have been kept in mind all along) and relevant judgments inevitably appeal to meaning, colorless green ideas notwithstanding.

Chomsky argues that belief in the relevance of meaning to grammatical studies stems from "an unfortunate tendency to confuse 'intuition about linguistic form' with 'intuition about meaning,' two terms which have in common only their vagueness and their undesirability in linguistic theory" (p. 94). Replacing these concepts by a rigorous and objective formulation

~ CHAPTER 3 ~

is a major goal of linguistic theory, even though "intuition about form" is undeniably helpful to the grammarian, whereas "intuition about meaning" is not. One could just as well argue that where real verbal data are involved, "intuition about meaning" is less arbitrary than "intuition about form," which entails tacit decisions about verbal units and categories and their interrelations (grammarians often do not agree about these, hence the arguments over the treatment of data). These decisions cannot be made on strictly formal grounds alone, particularly where explanatory power is sought. Nor is reliance on orthographically defined segments warranted.

Biases of this sort are clear when such "counterexamples" as the morphemes "to" in "I want to go" and "did" in "did he come" (p. 100) are contrasted with *gl-* in "gleam," "glimmer," "glow." While it is hard to assign an independent meaning to the former, it is reasonable to assign "meaning of some sort to such non-morphemes" as the latter, whereby the notion that morphemes are minimal meaningful elements is discredited. Yet, meaning of some sort can be assigned to "to" and "did" if we stop considering them free-standing units. Indeed, how else is "did," for example, given a role as a "dummy-carrier" for certain past tense forms and thus becomes "an available syntactic device"? Like *gl-*, "to" and "did" do not occur alone in speech; unlike *gl-* they recur alone, in writing.

Chomsky is right in showing the untenability of proposals assigning "structural meanings" to grammatical categories and constructions on a par with the assignment of "lexical meanings" to words and morphemes. Thus, for example, actor-action cannot be assigned to the grammatical relation subject-verb in "the fighting stopped" and action-goal cannot be assigned to verb-object in "I will disregard his incompetence." Significantly enough, however, he adds, "if meaning is taken seriously as a concept independent of grammars" (p. 100). The active-passive pair mentioned a while ago was brought in to show that "not even the weakest semantic relation (factual equivalence) holds in general between active and passive" (p. 101).

The correspondences that hold between the structures discovered in a formal analysis and given semantic functions indicate that the syntactic devices are used fairly systematically. But these correspondences are sufficiently inexact to suggest that grammatical analysis must proceed on strictly formal grounds alone: "To put it differently, given the instrument language and its formal devices, we can and should investigate their semantic function . . . but we cannot, apparently, find semantic absolutes, known in advance of grammar, that can be used to determine the objects of grammar in any way" (p. 101, fn.).

These correspondences cannot be ignored, however; they should be studied with a view to an eventual "general theory of language that will include a theory of linguistic form and a theory of the use of language as subparts" (p. 102). The emphasis is clearly on theory construction rather than on direct techniques to handle the data; syntax and semantics are to remain distinct fields. Again, syntax can help semantics, but not vice versa. "In other words, we should like the syntactic framework of the language that is isolated and exhibited by the grammar to be able to support semantic description, and we shall naturally rate more highly a theory of formal structure that leads to grammars that meet this requirement more fully" (p. 102).

In fact, the process is not as unidirectional as these lines suggest. Interconnections immediately come up, as we have seen, as soon as explanatory power is discussed, yet Chomsky insists that the formal nature of his proposal is not thereby altered: "Such semantic notions as reference, significance, and synonymy played no role in the discussion" (p. 103). Of course, this implies a preconceived view of each field and justifies the allusion to an underlying dualism at the beginning of this section. This view was modified later, though not in fundamental ways. We also read: "To understand a sentence we must know much more than the analysis of this sentence on each linguistic level. We must also know the reference and meaning of the morphemes or words of which it is composed; naturally, grammar cannot be expected to be of much help here" (pp. 103-104). This observation is realistic but falls short of the mark by restricting "reference" and "meaning" to words and morphemes; moreover, it is at odds with the correspondences just referred to. Aside from obvious preconceptions about units, let alone

CHAPTER 3

about the range of "semantic functions," it suggests a process of analysis whereby longer utterances are "taken apart" in understanding, presumably after they have been "put together" in a process of synthesis before.

At any rate, the emphasis on understanding may be consistent with the close relation between this way of formulating the syntax-semantics "dichotomy," explanatory power as a metatheoretical constraint, and the goals of linguistic theory; but it is somehow inconsistent with the view that "a grammar mirrors the behavior of the speaker." A surprising remark toward the end tilts the balance completely: "What we have pointed out . . . is that this formal study of the structure of language as an instrument may be expected to provide insight into the actual use of language, i.e., into the process of understanding sentences" (p. 103). The speaker is literally slighted here, unless we are ready to assume with Chomsky that being a listener implies being a speaker and vice versa—a very doubtful behavioral proposition. The implication that the final descriptive statement applies to both is of course fallacious; such a view favors the reification of language purely as a set of forms. The identification of "use of language" with understanding clearly reflects the linguist's condition with respect to the subject matter, narrowly defined.[4]

Meaning is a suspiciously elusive concept, for very good empirical reasons. It may also be that attention is being focused on the wrong cues (for example, paraphrase may prove a more expedient device than appeals to reference); or it may be that a general sifting of concepts in both fields is necessary—we may want to ask, for example, what is the meaning of "knowing the analysis of a sentence" and of "knowing the reference and meaning" of a morpheme or word. The problem lies not in meaning itself, whatever its ultimate treatment may be, but in looking for absolutes, semantic or grammatical. This is only part of a broader underlying tendency to take traditional schemes and categories for granted; in particular, separation of syntax and semantics apears to lead to an inescapable circularity, where natural languages are concerned.

~ TRANSFORMATIONAL-GENERATIVE PROPOSAL ~

SUMMARY

Underlying the formulation of TGG are certain fundamental assumptions concerning science in general and linguistic theory in particular. Scientific laws are unreservedly conceived as general statements formulated in terms of hypothetical constructs; grammatical rules are equated to laws in the well-established sciences. Mathematical treatment is favored without further question. The general theory of linguistic form becomes a metatheory that determines the form of individual grammars. In turn, a grammar becomes a device that generates all and only the grammatical sentences of a language. The emphasis is on *abstract study rather than on the development of data-tied techniques*. Isolated textual examples constructed for purposes of theoretical argumentation are brought to bear on largely ersatz issues, such as infinity, grammaticalness, and ambiguity. The goal of linguistic theory is to provide an evaluation procedure, conceptualized as a machine with inputs and outputs: in go, say, a corpus and two grammars, and out comes selected the better of the two grammars. More important, there are also "external" conditions of adequacy—referred to as the empirical consequences of adopting a certain model of linguistic structure. These have to do with the "explanatory power" of linguistic theory and, despite all efforts to relegate meaning to a subordinate position, with the relation between syntax and semantics. The redefined notion of linguistic level plays a central role: thus, to understand a sentence it is necessary to reconstruct its analysis on each level. A special reliance on the listener is clear throughout; this is consistent with the importance attached to disambiguation in the evaluation of alternative theories. Yet the presumed priority of the study of form over the study of meaning falls flat: one does not detect ambiguity in or appreciate the available syntactic devices of a language one does not know. Where natural languages are concerned, strict formalism is a self-delusion. Meaning—obliquely equated here with the "use of language"—is to be found among the independent variables which bring verbal activity about. At stake is the justification of grammars: for significance, grammars should yield insight

~ CHAPTER 3 ~

into speaking and understanding. In view of the inherent arbitrariness of structural analysis, this is no mean proposal. Questions cannot but arise, however, about the status of linguistic constructs and the rules themselves. It is doubtful whether much progress can be expected so long as language and language behavior are kept as two different domains.

~ CHAPTER 4 ~

Explanatory Models

4.1   The full extent of the explanatory power proposal became clear later (Chomsky, 1962a). The same arguments, more technically explicit, can be found in Chomsky and Miller (1963), Chomsky (1963), and Miller and Chomsky (1963), included in a handbook of mathematical psychology "to make psychologists more realistically aware of what it is a person has accomplished when he has learned to speak and understand a natural language" (Luce et al. 1963, pp. 271-272). (Where no reference is given, quotations in this chapter can be understood to come from this 1962 statement;[1] otherwise, pages cited are those in the 1963 handbook. Section 4.6 is an exception.)

By 1962 Chomsky's thinking had undergone what was probably an inevitable change. As part of a further conceptual and methodological shift away from empiricism, vaguely conceived, the previous "language" (the infinite set of grammatical sentences) and "corpus" (the finite sample with which a linguist must necessarily work) became a matter of "competence" and "performance," respectively. Grammaticalness continued to play a fundamental role. Two assumptions were at the basis of this development: (1) the job of a grammar is to separate grammatical and ungrammatical sentences of L; (2) the task of linguistic theory is to construct a device that will allow particular grammars constructed in accordance with it to do just that, assigning structure in illuminating ways.

Linguistic corpora, made up of samples of "performance," cannot be taken at face value, for they are likely to contain sentences that are ungrammatical for linguistically irrelevant reasons. The data of linguistic theory must therefore be idealized. (We have seen something of the same strategy above, but

~ CHAPTER 4 ~

here it plays a vastly more fundamental role and leads to radically different consequences.) Chomsky contends that there is nothing contrived about this proposal: it only reflects the native speaker's ability to tell grammatical from ungrammatical sentences. What is more, he does so by virtue of his linguistic competence; linguistic theory is concerned with the native speaker's "knowledge of L." It is only logical that linguistic intuition, which had played a secondary role so far (appealed to for judgments of grammaticalness and ambiguity), should now come to the fore as the object of study proper.

A conception of linguistic theory as a machine with inputs and outputs was a preliminary step in this direction. As pointed out above, this conception is not as aseptic as it might seem. Where explanatory power provides the justification of grammars, this switch to competence as linguistic knowledge and intuition (still undefined, it is what the theory is trying to characterize) is proof enough of it. The next step, a formulation of language learning on a par with this abstract proposal, and the subsequent postulation of innate linguistic abilities were probably inevitable too. Chomsky's rationalistic leanings, explicit enough at this point, were to become more marked later.

Obviously, a host of ultimately psychological questions immediately come up. Some of these will be discussed at appropriate points below; others are taken up in the notes. One might want to ask, for example, on what grounds are reasons for ungrammaticalness declared "linguistically irrelevant"; or one might challenge the assumption that people talk in sentences, grammatical or otherwise; indeed, the behavioral relevance of grammaticalness, as formulated, becomes suspect. Answers to these and similar questions prove hardly satisfactory unless all traces of effective empirical training are left behind and one settles for the self-contained view offered by Chomsky—wherein lies, one is led to conclude, the originality of his proposal.

Actually, the overall conception can be found in de Saussure (1916), referred to in Section 2.1. The linguistic system (*langue*) could be acquired on the basis of "fragmentary" linguistic behavior (*parole*) by virtue of an innate *faculté de langage*, seated in the brain. Chomsky makes de Saussure's general outlook explicit (pp. 327-328) and points out that his approach, though fundamentally the same, is different in two respects: (1) semantics is shunned here (this was mended later); (2) de Saussure looked upon *langue* as "a storehouse of signs," which forced him to attribute the creation of sentences to *parole* rather than to systematic rule. The availability of appropriate mathematical techniques permits now a formulation of language in terms of a finite recursive generative process, thus avoiding the "bizarre consequence" of de Saussure's standpoint. (It also brought about a further reification of "language," an acknowledged abstraction.) Chomsky has discussed these historical and philosophical antecedents in broader terms many times since (see, for example, Chomsky, 1964 and particularly 1966).

4.2   Chomsky and Miller (p. 271) write:

The fundamental fact that must be faced in any investigation of language and linguistic behavior is the following: a native speaker of a language has the ability to comprehend an immense number of sentences that he has never previously heard and to produce, on the appropriate occasion, novel utterances that are similarly understandable to other native speakers. The basic questions that must be asked are the following:

1. What is the precise nature of this ability?
2. How is it put to use?
3. How does it arise in the individual?

The overall methodological outlook is well synthesized in the authors' preliminary remarks concerning possible answers. Thus, (1) has to do with competence and must be answered by making explicit "the underlying structure inherent in all natural languages." Grammar becomes the critical concept. Question (2) has to do with performance and "calls for an attempt to give a formal characterization of, or model for, the users of natural languages." About (3), "far less progress has been made in formulating it in such a way as to support any abstract inves-

CHAPTER 4

tigation. What goes on as a child begins to talk is still beyond the scope of our mathematical methods."

About each of these questions respectively we learn (a) that "associating vocal responses with visual stimuli—a feature that has attracted considerable psychological attention—is but one small aspect of the total language learning process"; (b) that "psychologists, who might have been expected to attack this question as part of their general study of behavior, have as yet provided only the most programmatic (and often inplausible) kinds of answers"; (c) that "we can only mention the genetic issue and regret its relative neglect in the following pages." Clearly, the phrasing of question (3), "how does it *arise in the individual*" (italics added) suggests more than a manner of speaking, which (c), in turn, makes all too explicit.

> By presenting (1) and (2) as two distinct questions we explicitly reject the common opinion that a language is nothing but a set of verbal responses. To say that a particular rule of grammar applies in some natural language is not to say that the people who use that language are able to follow the rule consistently. To specify the language is one task. To characterize its users is another. The two problems are obviously related but are not identical. (p. 272)

No serious behavioral formulation would entertain the notion that language is *nothing but* a set of verbal responses—a view that would appear to be more in keeping with Chomsky's own definition of L as an infinite set of sentences. Such a statement shows a profound misunderstanding of the most elementary concepts of contemporary behavior theory and points up the difficulty of reconciling the linguist's conception of language with the inescapable fact that people simply do not produce sentences *in vacuo*. The phrase "on appropriate occasion" in the excerpt at the beginning of this section is revealing enough. But stimuli are not the only independent variable to be taken into account; and the restriction to their visual variety is absurd. Appeal to "association" as the (presumably central) mechanism is equally misleading. References to psychological proposals are

~ EXPLANATORY MODELS ~

generally eclectic and often culled to suit the purpose of the argument. Inaccuracies are all the more surprising where Miller appears as coauthor and counterarguments are directed at radical behaviorism—in view of Miller (1951), at least.

4.3 The distinction between language and language behavior betrays the authors' formalistic commitments. Unfortunately, an outlook on language learning as a matter for abstract investigation and mathematical methods offers little promise of ever filling the gap between the specification of L and a characterization of its "users." As it turns out, little is added to that characterization besides verbal claims of adequacy (supported by a small corpus of convenient examples from syntax, as we have seen, and phonology, much more explicitly worked out at this point) or the reiterated insistence that "one can scarcely hope to develop a sensible theory of the actual use of language except on the basis of a serious and far-reaching account of what a language user knows" (p. 326). The remark about the existence of a rule and the possibly inconsistent "use" of it is to be understood in this light. (An analogy with "knowledge of arithmetic" versus actual performance of arithmetical operations is repeatedly made in this context, lest confusion arise between knowledge and performance.) Of course, it is also conceded that other "input data" having to do with the vagaries of performance may require empirical investigation, but their real status is never made clear. Behavioral science is anathema. The linguist, *qua* linguist, is concerned with linguistic competence. Nevertheless, "one task of the professional linguist is, in a sense, to make explicit the process that every normal child performs implicitly" (p. 276). Such a feat is possible by dint of a powerful metatheory.

We obviously cannot assume any predisposition to learn one language rather than another. Children learn the language of the community into which they happen to be born. The reasonable suggestion that environmental factors bear the burden, as they clearly do, say, with ethical behavior, must be discarded, however:

~ CHAPTER 4 ~

Mere exposure to the language for a remarkably short period, seems to be all that the normal child requires to develop the competence of the native speaker. There is actually very little support for the view that careful instruction and guidance, or careful arrangement of "reinforcement contingencies" (in any interesting sense of this phrase), are necessary for developing language skills in the young child. . . .

(Of course, nobody has suggested that contingencies of reinforcement are carefully arranged, or that "careful instruction and guidance" is what is at issue; in fact, the latter seem to describe instead Chomsky's own "corrections," and "indications that one item is to be considered a repetition of another, and perhaps other hints and helps." See below.) Instead, we are to gain insight into what goes on in language learning by constructing (in theory, that is) "a device capable of duplicating this performance, or certain aspects of it. The linguistic abilities of the mature speaker can in part be characterized by what we might call a 'formalized grammar' of his language." The remainder of the discussion then considers "only these aspects of linguistic competence."

Well in line with the discussion of evaluation procedures earlier, such a device would be a "machine," say the well-known "black box," whose input are sentences ("a sufficiently large and representative set," to be precise) and whose output is a formalized grammar. The device maps this set of observed sentences into the formalized grammar of the language of which they are a part. Such a device would have the form:

(1)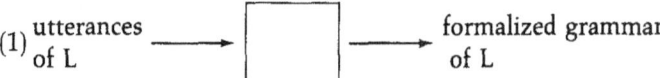

Its description amounts to a hypothesis about "the innate intellectual equipment that the child brings to bear in language learning." Of course, besides sequences of sentences, A, the child has other "data" available: B, nonsentences ("that is, corrections by the speech community"). He also has information

~ EXPLANATORY MODELS ~

about repetition of utterance tokens, C, the order of presentation of which may prove important, too, as well as other "hints and helps." We would want to revise the first diagram thus:

(2) A →
    B → ☐ → formalized grammar of L
    C →

Other relevant possibilities concerning inputs have to do with semantics. Chomsky admits that it is not implausible that semantic information "of some sort" plays an essential role, even though it plays no direct part in the output grammar. For example, it might be argued that with nonsense elements as inputs the principles of sentence formation might not be learned at all. Assuming this to be true, however, it would still be an irrelevant observation: "It may only indicate that meaningfulness and semantic function provide the motivation for language learning, while playing no necessary part in its mechanism, which is what concerns us here."

It would be interesting to push the analysis of "meaningfulness and semantic function" as far as possible in this light, and see whether indeed they play no necessary part in the mechanism of language. This can hardly be achieved, however, on the basis of vague generalizations like "semantic information of some sort." In connection with explanatory power (and the related justification of grammars), it is less than satisfactory to be flatly told that semantic function, whatever it may ultimately prove to be, plays no necessary part in the mechanism of language even though it provides the motivation for learning it in the first place.

Such an uncompromising commitment to the view that "the mechanism of language" is a strictly formal matter is possible only under the narrow definition of L quoted above (deviations from which amount, at most, to a paraphrase in Chomsky's subsequent writings) and assumes that verbal activity is a matter of linguistic rule. It also leads to rather farfetched arguments. Take, for example, the discussion of cases of parenthetical

~ CHAPTER 4 ~

embedding (pp. 286-287) like "(the rat(the cat(the dog chased) killed) ate the malt)" or, more illustrative of the complexities that a real grammar should be able to handle, the following "English sentence":

> Anyone$_1$ who feels that if$_2$ so-many$_3$ more$_4$ students$_5$ whom we$_6$ haven't$_6$ actually admitted are$_5$ sitting in on the course than$_4$ ones we have that$_3$ the room had to be changed, then$_2$ probably auditors will have to be excluded, is$_1$ likely to agree that the curriculum needs revision,

where identical subscripts indicate dependencies between words, the result being a system of nested dependencies involving a variety of constructions (when the same construction recurs we have self-embedding). We also have dependencies crossing those between "students" and "ones," between "haven't . . . admitted" and "have" ten words later ("admitted" has been deleted the second time, but it is understood).

The authors admit that such an utterance (and similar structures, presumably) is not likely ever to occur "except as an example" and contend that in this it is no different from "birds eat," "black crows are black," "black crows are white," "Tuesday follows Monday," and so on. These, like other utterances too obviously true, false, complex, inelegant, "or that fail in innumerable other ways to be of any use for ordinary human affairs," are not generally used. Even so, the dependency example above being a perfectly clear, unambiguous, and well-formed sentence, "a grammar of English must be able to account for it if the grammar is to have any psychological significance" (p. 287).

In fact, it is not difficult to imagine situations in which "Tuesday follows Monday" and the like (perhaps with varying degrees) would be perfectly likely to occur, unlike "Anyone who feels . . . ," which can occur only "as an example." Yet an adequate grammar must develop devices to account for artificially complicated structures such as these, even if they are not representative of the way people talk. It would seem that for psychological significance (say, explanatory power) the converse would be true. Of course, the defining characteristics of situa-

~ EXPLANATORY MODELS ~

tions which would give rise to examples like "Birds eat" have no place in a formally motivated approach. The qualifying "except as an example" sums up the matter rather effectively.

4.4 The formal import of the proposal is well synthesized as follows:

> Whatever such study might reveal, however, the problem of constructing a universal language-learning device cannot be stated clearly until we determine the properties of the formalized grammar that is to be its output. It is first of all clear that the formalized grammar, regarded as a predictive theory, is an idealization in at least two respects: first, in that it considers formal structure independently of use; and second, in that the items that it generates will not be the utterances of which actual discourse is composed, but rather they will be what the untutored native speaker knows to be well-formed sentences. Actual discourse consists of interrupted fragments, false starts, lapses, slurring, and other phenomena that can only be understood as distortions of an underlying idealized pattern.

The grammar, to be "successful and interesting," must be formally motivated. It must assign structure without recourse to *ad hoc* rules and it must point up appropriate ways to do so. It must contribute "seriously to the study of general features of linguistic structure or the study of the nature of a universal language-learning device that exhibits the intellectual abilities of the child." To do this, it must characterize such things as the mature speaker's ability to determine what is a grammatical sentence and other aspects of "what the speaker knows to be true of speech events"—which centers largely on disambiguation. The grammar incorporates information about "the units of which sentences are constructed, the grouping and arrangement of such units, the formal relations between sentences and their elements, and so on," in short, the notion of structural description in terms of which structure is assigned.

The specified relations are clearly kept within arbitrarily defined sentences, which Chomsky calls "speech events." This is

~ CHAPTER 4 ~

only consistent with the oft-mentioned "narrow definition of L"; the reference to distortions provides further indication. (Whether interrupted fragments, false starts, lapses, and the like can be so easily brushed aside as devoid of significance remains to be seen.) There is a tacit assumption that as long as semantic ambiguity is cleared up, one must expect a fixed assignment of structure for every sentence. One might argue that this is a complicating restriction and that relevant relations often disregard sentence boundaries, one of the several possible ways to challenge the sentence as an initial category.[2]

> What we seek, then, is a formalized grammar that specifies the correct structural descriptions with a fairly small number of general principles of sentence formation and that is embedded within a theory of linguistic structure that provides a justification for the choice of this grammar over alternatives. Such a grammar could properly be called an explanatory model, a theory of the linguistic intuition of the native speaker.

Well-formedness plays a central role, despite the obvious inherent difficulties involved. Chomsky argues that appeals to operational criteria for objectivity are based on a misconception: "Nothing is more simple than to construct a definition of 'grammaticalness' and an associated behavioral test that specifies the same set of events." (None is actually suggested; instead, a footnote meant to clarify the concept speaks of "equally absurd proposals.") Such measures would still have to be tested against the native speaker's intuition, just as a theory of linguistic structure would. Ideally, we might want to have both the theory and the test, but neither is prior to the other: they stand in a "perfectly symmetrical relation." But whereas an operational test specifies only the given set of events, the theory provides insights and hypotheses about the organization and structure of the specified system of sentences. This renders theory construction "the much more interesting" alternative. There is a strong implicit assumption made that this (infinite) set of sentences or system *is* specifiable (see chapter 5). This and similar unchallenged preconceptions have been pointed out at several points throughout this study. The following quotation appropriately synthesizes the a priori nature of the approach and suggests obvious inherent dangers:

> The linguist tries to discover the grammatical structure of some language, bringing to bear a selected array of concepts that give an implicit picture of what a natural language, in his view, *must* be like. He brings to bear, in other words, a more or less detailed general theory of linguistic structure, which *must*, furthermore, have the features of the language-learning device described above. (Italics added)

This is of course reminiscent of Hockett's preliminary proposal discussed in section 2.2. There is a serious, related question whether grammaticalness and related concepts would continue to occupy such a prominent position were we to abandon abstract strategy and face verbal data squarely. It all ultimately has to do with the unchallenged acceptance of traditional categories, which may or may not correspond to units reflecting the real dynamic properties of verbal performance. Greater formal sophistication may conceal but can do nothing to dispel these initial limitations.[3]

The following extended excerpt brings the various aspects of the proposal together in all its broad scope and implications:

> The theory of grammar must, therefore, precisely specify:
> (8)
> (a) a class $G_1, G_2, \ldots$ of potential grammars
> (b) a class $s_1, s_2, \ldots$ of potential sentences (in phonetic transcription)
> (c) the notion "structural description" and a function f that assigns the structural description $f(i,j)$ to the item s_i of (b) with respect to the grammar G_j of (a).
>
> We may suppose, in addition, that the ordering of grammars in (8a) is significant and indicates increasing complexity. That is, we assume that the general theory of linguistic structure provides an evaluation procedure that will justify the selection of a grammar over presented alternatives.

~ CHAPTER 4 ~

A particular grammar G, of (8a) can now be regarded as being, in effect, a theory of the language that it enumerates by means of the function f of (8c); a theory that accounts for certain aspects of the linguistic intuition of the native speaker.

With a general theory of the form (8), we could return to the problem of constructing a language-learning device, making the assumption that this device essentially incorporates the theory of linguistic structure. That is, corresponding to the specifications in (8), the device (2) has available to it an advance specification of

(a) the form that a grammar may assume and an evaluation procedure;
(b) a phonetic alphabet;
(c) a method for determining the structural description of an arbitrary sentence, given one of the permitted grammars.

This information is part of the internal structure of the device (2). [See section 4.3.] Suppose that this device is now presented with examples of sentences and nonsentences partitioned into conformity classes (classes of repetitions). The task for the language-learning device is to select the highest-valued grammar that is compatible with these data, in the sense that all sentences and no non-sentences are enumerated and nonrepetitions differ at the appropriate points in the structural descriptions assigned to them. Having selected this grammar, the language-learning device is capable, in principle, of assigning a structural description to each sentence, by virtue of its incorporation of the function f of (8c).

A general theory of linguistic structure of the sort just outlined would, in this way, provide an account of a hypothetical language-learning device and could thus be regarded as a theoretical model for the intellectual abilities that the child brings to language learning. . . .

To make this model realistic (that is, to make the language-learning device practical), we must supply it with some sort of heuristic or inductive principles that enable it, given input data, to make a rapid selection of several potential grammars to be submitted to the procedure of evaluation.

It is not clear, however, what the place of heuristic procedures actually is. Chomsky warns against excessive reliance on them. Even though we assume that a learning device must contain them if a recursive, formalized grammar is to be selected given fragmentary data as input, their role is bound to be reduced as the form of grammars is made more restrictive. Subsequent writings, indeed, eliminated their role progressively: "It seems to me that the relative suddenness, uniformity, and universality of language learning, the bewildering complexity of the resulting skills, and the subtlety and finesse with which they are exercised, all point to the conclusion that a primary and essential factor is the contribution of an organism with highly intricate and specific structure."

It would be foolish to deny that verbal activity is a complex phenomenon, but Chomsky's insistent emphasis on it has turned this complexity into something of a straw man among mainstream psycholinguists, who have often been led to make what are no doubt exaggerated claims (see chapter 1). It is not entirely unreasonable to suggest that this complexity is bound to appear all the more bewildering in the light of an initial "selected array of concepts that give an implicit picture of what a natural language [in the linguist's view] must be like," and in the light of the difficulty of reconciling this a priori view with the actual data. Were the linguist to do so without prior conceptual prejudice, the "relative suddenness" and "uniformity" of language acquisition would no doubt come under proper perspective;[4] he might want to reconsider also judgments about "subtlety" and "finesse" as well.

Relevant here are the special constraints that come to specify narrowly the range of natural languages, providing together a definition of this concept, "insofar as we are concerned with its formal properties." These are, in transcription:

(1) specification of the form of grammars excludes certain infinite sets of sentences from consideration as possible natural languages;

~ CHAPTER 4 ~

(2) a system of phonetic transcription limits the possible physical realization of the sentences of a language;

(3) procedures for evaluating grammars and determining structural descriptions impose strict conditions on the kinds of units that can be attributed to a natural language and the manner of their arrangement and interconnection.

4.5 There is a curious mixture of aggressive self-confidence and cautious self-restraint in Chomsky's writing of this period (the latter waned progressively in later years). Compare, for example, the following two statements in the 1962 paper: "The development of the theory of grammar and intensive application of this theory, is a necessary prerequisite to any serious study of the problems of language acquisition and many other problems of immediate psychological significance," and "Linguistics is, of course, far from being able to realize such an ambitious goal as this at present, and can only approach it in various aspects of the general theory" (a footnote to a discussion of an ultimate linguistic theory that would take the form of a system of definitions). Similarly, the compelling nature of many of the 1962 quotations transcribed above is countered by repeated warnings that a clear distinction must be made between description of L and the description of L-users (particularly in the 1963 papers).

According to Chomsky, severe constraints must be placed on the formulation in view of the fact that "no automaton with bounded memory can produce all and only the grammatical sentences of a natural language; every such device, man presumably included, will exhibit certain limitations" (p. 421). As elsewhere, the shortcomings of finite stochastic systems are pointed out. Thus, "in an effort to achieve a more appropriate level of complexity in our descriptions of the user, therefore, we turn next to models that take account of the underlying structure of natural languages—models that, for lack of a better name, we shall refer to here as algebraic" (p. 464). The incorporation of rewriting systems and a transformational component ultimately leads to what Miller and Chomsky call a "Theory of Complicated Behavior." Here the argument becomes bold

~ EXPLANATORY MODELS ~

again. One summarizing paragraph is particularly telling; it also illustrates once more the ease with which unchallenged preconceptions are incorporated into this sort of discourse.

> It should by now be apparent that only a complicated organism can exploit the advantages of symbolic organization. Subjectively, we seem to grasp meanings as integrated wholes, yet it is not often that we can express a whole thought by a single sound or a single word. Before they can be communicated, ideas must be analyzed and represented by sequences of symbols. To map the simultaneous complexities of thought into the sequential flow of language requires an organism with considerable power and subtlety to symbolize and process information. These complexities make linguistic theory a difficult subject. But there is an extra reward to be gained from working it through. If we are able to understand something about the nature of human language, the same concepts and methods should help us to understand other kinds of complicated behavior. (p. 483)

This indiscriminate use of terms from other fields is at great variance with the rigor and precision demanded where grammatical description is concerned. The preceding excerpt contains at least thirteen terms, fundamental to the statement, that would appear to demand prior careful examination. An operational definition might be available for a few of them, while others (along with some manners of phrasing) can only remain barren metaphors.

On the other hand, we also read: "In the present state of our understanding, the problem of constructing an input-output model for the speaker cannot even be formulated coherently" (p. 330). This is something of an anticlimax. It is perhaps consistent with the distinction between description of language and of the language user, but not with the slanted emphasis on the listener pointed out in chapter 3. The old argument recurs again, however: "models of linguistic performance can generally be interpreted interchangeably as depicting the behavior of either a speaker or a hearer. For concreteness . . . we shall concentrate

~ CHAPTER 4 ~

on the listener's task and frame our discussion largely in perceptual terms. This decision is, however, a matter of convenience, not of principle" (p. 465). It is such a view that allows Chomsky to write also: "though an explicit formulation of f of (8c) would show how, in principle, one who has mastered the grammar G_i can understand a sentence s_j (to the extent of recovering its structural description), a realistic perceptual model would have to incorporate some sort of heuristic principles to guarantee rapid selection of the structural description" (1962, fn. 12). It is on such grounds that strong claims about the innate equipment brought by the child to language learning are made.

The argument holds true, as it were, under the terms of an abstract formulation, but it is clearly at odds with the observed facts of language learning and use. The child becomes a speaker as soon as he begins to speak, and this obviously does not mean the production of well-formed sentences and derived formal concepts. Moreover, an abstract formulation is also incapable, by its very nature, of accounting for the intricate relations between speaking and understanding.[5] Performance variables immediately creep in, if one insists upon putting it that way (the child is presumably performing throughout the learning process). It is only reasonable to suggest that these variables should play a central rather than a peripheral role in any discussion of language behavior. In fact, they are neglected altogether. Subordinating the formulation of language users to the formal exigencies of the description of L does little to direct the required attention to the actual variables behind performance and can ultimately only cast doubt on the relevance of competence itself. Take, for example, the analogy between linguistic knowledge and arithmetic knowledge. In connection with the dependency example on page 72 above, Chomsky writes:

> In fact, such sentences . . . are quite incomprehensible on first hearing, but this has no bearing on the question whether those sentences are generated by the grammar that has been acquired, just as the inability of a person to multiply 18674 times 26521 in his head is no indication that he has failed to grasp the rules of multiplication. In either case an

artificial increase in memory aids, time, attention, etc., will probably lead the subject to the unique correct answer. In both cases there are problems that so exceed the user's memory and attention spans that the correct answer will never be approached, and in both cases there is no reasonable alternative to the conclusion that recursive rules specifying the correct solution are represented somehow in the brain despite the fact that (for quite extraneous reasons) this solution cannot be achieved in actual performance. (p. 327)

When first introduced, this dependency example was qualified as "perfectly clear," "unambiguous," and a "well-formed sentence," illustrative of the sorts of complexities that an adequate grammar must be able to account for. In any case, we meet again several features repeatedly pointed out about the sort of discourse under discussion. First, insistence on abstract formulation makes the empirical relation between competence and the behaviors of speaker and listener obscure, if not actually vacant. In view of the postulated infinity (productive and receptive) recursive means become obligatory; accordingly, models of language users become finitary. It is in terms of formal constraints (see points 1-3 on pages 77-78) that we ultimately speak of linguistic knowledge, intuition, or competence, versus actual performance in the untutored native speaker. Second, the uncritical appeal to prior conceptual frameworks extends to psychology as well. Notions like memory, attention, and the like, must be scrutinized before talking meaningfully about spans, (un)boundedness, and so on, in human beings, no matter how convenient they may prove for describing automata. What is more, what makes possible increases "artificial"? (Following this line of thought, any improvements in educational methods would then be deemed artificial, too.) Third, no suggestion is given about the real nature of the "quite extraneous reasons," which make theoretically possible performances impossible, or very unusual in fact. Their direct investigation can only throw light on the mechanism of language, empirically considered. Most

~ CHAPTER 4 ~

of the conclusions put forth above would then have to be revised accordingly.

We are told, instead, that the subject matter of the theory has to do with "innate or mature linguistic competence, ability to learn or knowledge of arithmetic, the nature of the physical world . . ." (p. 328, *sic*). There is no suggestion that such knowledge, which stands in sharp opposition to "actual or even potential behavior" (p. 421), is in any way overt. Indeed, Chomsky has argued repeatedly that it is unlikely that much of it *can* be made overt—it has taken linguists centuries to become aware of the real generative nature of the system of rules that determine the relation between sound and meaning. This is a problem for science. But then the analogy with arithmetic breaks down: the reasons lie in the behavioral history behind arithmetic learning and language learning. To go along with this terminology, arithmetic is not learned by mere exposure to an arithmetic environment. (This is not to say, of course, that the fundamental nature of the contingencies is essentially different.) No matter how complex an arithmetic computation, the rules can be and are recovered intraverbally as a matter of course.

The fundamental assumption that one and the same model accounts for both speaker and listener alike is made fully and pointedly explicit and deserves special mention: "Once a formal theory of communication or language has been constructed, it generally turns out to be equally useful for describing both sources and receivers; in order to describe one or the other we simply rename various components of the formal theory in an appropriate fashion. This is illustrated by the stochastic theories considered . . ." (p. 422). In the case of stochastic models, the mathematical argument is arbitrarily chosen to interpret the behavior of the source, "purely for expository purposes." By contrast, when it comes to algebraic models, the alternative strategy is adopted and the discussion is framed in terms of recognition and understanding, again as "a matter of convenience, not of principle." The heavy reliance on the listener pointed out several times before suggests, however, that there probably is more to this than mere expository convenience. It is not enough to state at the outset that "it is often assumed,

~ EXPLANATORY MODELS ~

usually by workers interested in only one aspect of communication, that our perceptual models for a listener will be rather different from any behavioral models we might need for a speaker. That assumption was not adopted in our discussion of formal aspects of linguistic competence, and it will not be adopted here in discussing empirical aspects of linguistic performance" (pp. 421-422). This kind of all-pervasive confidence is out of joint with the acknowledged difficulty of setting up a model of the speaker alluded to some pages back. Why should it then be declared so greatly out of reach?[6]

At any rate, the construction of perceptual models is overtly advocated. Under the terms of the formulation, it follows that the same grammar applies to both speaker and listener. Among other things, this places the problem of meaning (in some sense of the term) on a doubly awkward footing. Appeal to behavioral criteria is emphatically curtailed: "As a general designation for psychology, 'behavioral science' is about as apt as 'meter reading science' would be for physics" (p. 328). This is unfortunate in that much of the ensuing speculation about perceptual capacities must be reckoned as deceptively relevant and haphazard, pinned as it is on ill-founded perceptual theories.[7] This renders the related psychological constructs brought in to substantiate the construction of competence-based performance models virtually devoid of empirical content and, in turn, casts serious doubts about the validity of the corresponding formal contrivances (say, embedding, nesting, left-right symmetry, and so on) that they are called to support.

It should not, therefore, be surprising if subsequent research takes on the characteristics of theory testing (based on the description of final products, and aimed at inferred, though hardly demonstrable, cognitive activities). This research emphasizes the verification of an abstract proposal about a hypothetical speaker-listener rather than the direct exploration of the empirical variables through which human organisms become accomplished speakers and listeners.[8] There are other ways to do science.

Chomsky admits that "there is a certain irreducible vagueness in describing a formalized grammar as a theory of linguistic

~ CHAPTER 4 ~

intuition of the native speaker." Vagueness, however, is probably not the problem; we might rather want to speak of a certain circularity involved in developing a formal characterization of outputs, imputing such a characterization to "users" of natural languages (though granting that there is more to it), and then claiming that "performance" is what it is because of an initial "competence," a hypothesis about the internal structure responsible for language acquisition in the first place.

In a general sort of way, this is the procedure in model building elsewhere. But models are metaphors, particularly where the natural sciences are concerned, leading to the isolation of relevant properties, which can then be subjected to experimental analysis. Indeed, this is their only justification. But no matter how elegant from a formal point of view, the "input-output" hypothesis falls far short of making the nature of the inputs sufficiently explicit. In fact, it distorts the true behavioral nature of the oft-invoked notion of "verbal environment." Claims of explanatory power necessarily revert then to some form of nativism. As with black-box devices at large, the difficulty with the present model lies in the inaccessibility of the putative object of study.

4.6 The literature on models is of course extensive and unavoidably intricate. A particularly relevant coverage can be found in Turner (1967), whose major concern is with problems of explanation in the behavioral sciences. Despite, or perhaps because of, his adherence to a hypothetico-deductive methodology and a commitment to the reductionist thesis, some of his observations about the status of models in general, and the black box in particular, may prove useful in the present context. Indeed, they may help clarify the status of explanatory models in linguistics.

Turner's distinction between "formal" and "structural" models corresponds roughly to the distinction between "models in the formal sciences" and "models as representations of a physical process" referred to in note 1, this chapter, although he indicates that "this is a simplification for expository purposes only" (Turner, 1967, p. 237 and references cited there; unless otherwise indicated, quotations hereafter are from this work). Some underlying commonalities must be expected: "As remote as some discussions of logical models may be from the subject of concrete models, their relevance should not escape the theoretical scientist. For if he takes his own models seriously and holds out for them on the grounds of say their simplicity or microreductive potential, he must be sure that this model, as rigorously expressed, does in fact satisfy the requirements of isomorphic representations" (p. 237). Structural models are described as "those models whose entities in some sense are more palpable than those we find in formal models. . . . In the language of palpability, a structural model is something we can build, visualize, construct, put on paper, etc. Even though unconstructed in fact, the ultimate realization of such models entails a familiar space-time context. The problem of analogy, of course, remains open. One might have a mechanical analogue, say, of muscle action; it would be a structural model of the muscle but with limited analogy" (pp. 238-239).

Turner seems to find justification, however, for setting up a third type of model, namely, cybernetic models, relevant to model building in the behavioral sciences by virtue of their emphasis on functional units, feedback, and schematic functionalistic diagrams.[9] We are interested here in the relation between this third type of model and the black box. The schematic strategy of cybernetics is an elaboration on the old black-box principle, but some differences should be pointed out. The black box is characterized as "a mere substitute for the enclosed brackets of ignorance. Certain functional relations may be implemented by the black-box but details as to mechanics, process, and structure are missing. Thus the brain has suffered both the eminence and the indignity of being a black-box" (p. 240):

> If no simple laws are ascertainable as between input and output or as between stimulus and response, and if interposed between the observables there are mediating complications, then it is convenient to introduce the black-box analogue. Thus Woodsworth . . . interjected the organism, O, between stimulus and response as a catchall processing

CHAPTER 4

center for all those factors that make S-R psychology a more complicated discipline than pure reflexology. (p. 240)

Moreover, "black-boxes are, in logical terms, place-holders; they are the guarded lacunae to be filled in by future generations" (p. 240).

Cybernetic models, by contrast, are "structural and functional hypotheses which model the internal details of the boxes. In fact, the black-box must be partitioned according to the cybernetic hypothesis" (p. 240). As Turner puts it:

> Generally then the difference between black-box modeling and cybernetics is one of functional detail. But that difference is a significant one. Where black-box analysis simply indicates the presence of a mediating process of unspecified structure, cybernetics makes a functional analysis of mediating components such as to propose various structures sufficient to effect such functions. As Gregory has pointed out (1961) . . . black-box schemata have no explanatory power. They contain no hypotheses as to how the components work. A cybernetics model, on the other hand, being concerned with the structures and functional details of the components and even with the design of components, serves as an explanatory basis of control systems. (p. 241)

There is a broad difference of outlook, too, in that "the application of cybernetics exemplifies a pragmatic rather than ontological approach to modeling" (p. 240). So much for the limitations of the black box.

Whether a greater degree of specificity and an associated capacity to generate hypotheses of a more specific kind is all that is needed to provide explanatory power is open to question. Indeed, it is not quite clear why cybernetic models should be set apart from structural ones, particularly in view of that boasted specificity, a feature of paramount importance when the "truth status" of models is at issue. In any case, the relevance of the distinction between the black box and cybernetic models to the construction of explanatory models in linguistics should be immediately apparent.

~ EXPLANATORY MODELS ~

Chomsky's model is formally motivated. The logical aspects of his formulation are sound; to the extent that it provides a method of linguistic analysis (in the sense of characterizing structurally defined elements and their interrelations) it can probably be thought of as constructed on the formal pattern. The postulated syntactic relations were explicitly supplemented later, as we shall see, with rules that relate the meaning of the sentences generated to their acoustic reality. In a sense, the posited syntactic schemata are thus "interpreted" in ways that should make contact with, in principle at least, verbal performance. (The validity of these schemata is not at issue here.) What obtains is simply a descriptive proposal about L, that is, "what is learned."

But the theory of transformational-generative grammar is also offered as an explanatory model. This is done in ways that emphasize metatheoretical goals and constraints and try to minimize the role of heuristic devices. It is meant as a broad hypothesis about "the intellectual abilities which the child brings to language learning," a formulation, as we have seen, in terms of a formal system of rules (Chomsky called them "laws," it will be remembered) framed in terms of hypothetical constructs, certain a priori descriptive categories. The choice over alternative proposals is effected, so to speak, through the language of black-box conceptualization. As such, the model becomes "a mere substitute for the enclosed brackets of ignorance"; it glosses over what some, justifiably or not, would tend to look upon as a "catchall processing center," the seat of elusive "mediating complications."

In an attempt "to make this model realistic, that is, to make the language learning device practical," however, Chomsky is forced to go beyond vague hypothesis and endow the learning device, as it were, with heuristic or inductive principles that make possible "a rapid selection of several grammars" given certain input data. This is also part of the innate equipment that makes possible the internalization of the specific rules of the ambient language.[10] In other words, the L-user is quickly brought in, if only for the sake of significance. Questions as to how the speaker-listener puts his innate knowledge, intuition, or competence to use in actual performance immediately come up, lest the black box become an unassailable, well-rounded non sequitur.[11]

As a theoretician, Chomsky need not go beyond a convenient discussion in terms of analogies with automata. Whether constructed or not, the explanatory model comes to suggest specific details concerning "mechanics, process, and structure"; the "mediating process of unspecified structure" that a strict blackbox strategy leaves for future generations to fill in becomes "a proposal of various structures to effect such functions," which begin to seem palpable.[12] Although generally disavowed by "explanatory linguists," there is in all this a striking resemblance to the cybernetic strategy.

Terms of psychological significance are freely borrowed, as we have seen, and both concepts and the use they are put to are very much in line with those of the cyberneticist interested in setting up speculative neural networks or the possible design of machines capable of duplicating the performance of living organisms. The extensive literature on simulation processes finds its place here.[13]

The cyberneticist interested in "psychological" phenomena falls back on such issues as learning, categorical perception, generalization, and constancy effects. Hypotheses about memory function, attentional scansion, recognition, and perceptual variance are at the core of such formulations. Much of this is as old as cybernetics itself, designed as it was to cover "the entire field of control and communication, whether in the machine or in the animal" (Wiener, 1948, p. 19). The order is methodologically important. It is not for nothing that the new field grew out of the convergence of information theory and prediction theory, early computer technology, and considerations about neurophysiology and formal machines. Even so, "the need of including psychologists had indeed been obvious from the beginning. . . . Much of the psychology of the past has proved to be really nothing more than physiology of the organs of special sense and the whole weight of the body of ideas which cybernetics is introducing into psychology concerns the physiology and anatomy of the highly specialized cortical areas connecting with these organs of special sense" (ibid., p. 26).

A genuine interest in psychology should have made Wiener aware of alternative positions. He was limited, however, by his initial framework and naturally turned to brands of psychology emphasizing stimuli or, more exactly, the transformations suffered by stimuli once they have reached the organism—a view still prevalent among most students of perception and psychophysics. A preoccupation with perceptual mechanisms became and has remained the cornerstone of cybernetic psychologizing.[14] This is a particularly well suited approach for a framework in which "explanation" is understood as "accounting for" the internal equipment and function responsible for the processing of inputs. Great emphasis is then necessarily laid on the structural features of these inputs, the specification of which, however, is bound to rely heavily on prior information, available or hypothesized, about the internal mechanisms themselves. To say the least, various degrees of arbitrariness ensue.

There are serious restrictions associated with this kind of strategy. Concentration on the structure of "what is learned" neglects the learning process itself. The immediate outcome is the postulation of mental activities associated in one way or another with the posited components and functions—with the implicit (black box) or explicit (cybernetics) hope that neurophysiological justification will be found at some later date. After all, "he who studies the nervous system cannot forget the mind, and he who studies the mind cannot forget the nervous system" (ibid., p. 26).

To come closer home, an a priori conceptualization of L along the lines described above and the appeal to the black box for the rationalization of a theory of linguistic structure as an explanatory model have ultimately led Chomsky to propose for linguistics the status of a branch of theoretical (cognitive) psychology.[15] The properties of the presumed "catchall processing center" are thereby bound to come under closer scrutiny.

The special reliance on the listener in the course of formulating the descriptive theory has been pointed out. Explicit reference to the construction of perceptual models is offered by

~ CHAPTER 4 ~

Chomsky himself, as we have seen. It should not, therefore, be surprising if subsequent research reflects these initial biases and seems to be primarily designed to test some of the general assumptions underlying the abstract formulation. Witness, for example, the proliferation of studies on the perceptual cues of verbal stimuli for speech processing (which implies the existence of processing mechanisms); the extensive efforts to establish the psychological reality of linguistic segments and their interrelations on such a basis (perfectly in accord with a view of inputs as made up primarily of sentences and nonsentences); the place accorded to learning (see chapters 1 and 7) as a result of which developmental studies zero in, to a very large extent, on the emergence of formally defined structures, which are then duly related to cognitive activity and an unaccounted process of maturation. More generally, a growing concern over problems of neurological import, undoubtedly spurred by this latter-day nativist outlook, bears witness to a similarity with the broader pattern sketched before for cybernetic strategies, whatever their degree of specificity or sophistication.[16] In line with much reductionist thinking in psychology, many experts have come to look upon the formally recognized new field of neurolinguistics as the ultimate source of confirmation for the broader hypotheses of psycholinguistics. Curiously enough, the present standpoint makes contact with Hockett's 1948 proposal, discussed in chapter 2.

The present appeal to models stems largely from the extant methodological confusion over "explanation" as opposed to "mere description." The feeling that a formal characterization of language is at odds with the actual performance of real speakers and listeners is only too understandable. But a recourse to idealization of "what is learned" and the subsequent postulation of innate mechanisms on the assumption that mapping functions useful at the formal level have anything to do with the organism's makeup is not likely to provide the answer. Mathematical elegance and precision, and the related notion that verbal activity is a matter of linguistic rule, have little to contribute in this connection.

The analogy with automata turns the resulting theoretical constructions into a dangerous metaphor, unlikely to yield an explication of why organisms behave, and come to do so in the very specific ways they do. The entire notion of model building becomes suspect: models prove, at least at the present stage, an obstacle rather than a help in bringing out the relevant facts. There is no reason to believe that such operations as encoding, storage, processing, retrieval, and so on, real though they may be where actual hardware is involved, have a parallel in the living organism.

The proposed model entails, along with a number of initial preconceptions about the nature of language, a view of the interaction between organism and environment which finds little support in an experimental analysis. Among other things, it forces a conception of "knowledge" as rationalist, as opposed to (old-fashioned) empiricist, with which it is generally contrasted. But the distinction is based on philosophical preferences—on whether greater emphasis is laid on the organism or on the "impinging" environmental stimuli. These are independently described. In either case, the ensuing "action" is assumed to be some kind of mental process taking place, somehow, inside the organism.

What is called for is a thorough revision of the frequently invoked notion of "verbal environment." It is a great and common mistake to believe that its description has been accomplished once the linguistic "system" that the child is vaguely said to be exposed to has been characterized.[17] Nothing short of an analysis taking into account all the variables acting upon the single organism and responsible for the shaping and maintenance of its behavior will do (see, for example, Salzinger, 1979, 1980, and references cited there; see also McLeish and Martin, 1975, and notes 4 and 7, chapter 1). The distinction between "description" and "explanation" becomes redundant.

SUMMARY

The machine with inputs and outputs was not as aseptic as it looked. It eventually became a built-in evaluation procedure whereby the child learning to speak generates hypotheses about the variegated "data" he is exposed to and finally selects the highest-valued set of rules. Linguistics should now be concerned

CHAPTER 4

with competence, the underlying mental-innate apparatus that permits this feat. Without competence there would be no language learning, nor would verbal performance be possible. No evidence is given for such a view; instead, it is dogmatically asserted that the problem of constructing a language-learning device *cannot be stated clearly until we determine the properties of the formalized grammar that is to be its output*. This device is conceptualized as a black box. Language learning is reduced to an interplay between a largely redundant internalization of the rules of the ambient language and an unaccounted for maturational process. It is conceded that other "input" data having to do with the vagaries of performance may require empirical investigation. But their real status is never made clear. Thus, it is confidently stated that although "meaningfulness and semantic function" provide the motivation for language learning, *they play no necessary part in its mechanism*. Vague preference is given instead to such behaviorally dubious factors as time and memory limitations, attention spans, and the like. The analogy with automata should not be surprising: reference is made to the analysis and representation of ideas by sequences of symbols, the mapping of simultaneous complexity of thought, the processing of information, and so forth. These are hardly more than metaphors, however. Previous reliance on the listener finds now full expression: the general thrust is toward the construction of a "realistic perceptual model," which, it is explicitly stated, will describe the speaker as well. Clearly, this directly contravenes experience. A distinction of sorts is made between models of learning and models of performance. But is the child learning to speak not performing all along? Here as elsewhere, the black-box strategy is a synonym for ignorance—a place-holder eventually to be implemented with structural and functional properties. At fault is, of course, the view that what is needed for language learning is exposure to a verbal environment, by which is meant merely the acoustic effects of other people's speech. Concentration on "what is learned" neglects the learning process itself. The analysis of final products does little to suggest effective investigative strategy into the interaction between speakers and listeners, and the circumstances that bring their behavior about, in short, the real data.

~ CHAPTER 5 ~

Subsequent Refinements

5.1   Later technical modifications did not alter the basic nature of the explanatory power proposal. If anything, they strengthened it. The need to bring semantics—loosely identified so far, as we have seen, with the "use of language"—more intimately into the picture did much to consolidate previous built-in biases. It is customary to trace subsequent refinements to the explicit formulation of *Aspects of the Theory of Syntax* (Chomsky, 1965) and to refer to this version of TGG as the "standard theory." It is this formulation that has had a lasting impact among psycholinguists and psychologists. It will be well therefore to review schematically what these changes were and see the full extent of Chomsky's proposition. (Unless otherwise indicated, pages cited in this chapter are those of the 1965 book.)

Grammar has now become a *system of rules* that relate the meaning(s) of the generated sentences to their acoustic reality (sound structure). The syntactic component is made up of two combined systems of rules: the base component, roughly comparable to the PSG, generates an indefinitely large set of underlying phrase-markers, the deep structures of the sentences accounted for by the system; somewhat simplified transformational rules map the underlying phrase-markers onto associated derived phrase-markers, the surface structures of the language. In turn, the base component is composed of two parts: the categorial system and the lexicon. Aside from defining significant grammatical relations, the categorial system assigns an ideal order to underlying phrases, and determines the appropriate transformations to be applied. The lexicon is a set of lexical entries each characterized by a matrix of Jakobson-style phonological distinctive features (indexed for order and to indicate possible irregularities) and of semantic features, some of

~ CHAPTER 5 ~

which are necessarily abstract, recording individual characteristics of each entry much like a "dictionary definition." General regularities permit the inclusion of redundancy rules in the lexicon. Lexical insertion is effected by transformational rules. Since the grammar can overgenerate, an additional role of transformations is to rule out potentially unacceptable outcomes, formal and semantic, in what Chomsky calls a kind of "filtering effect."

The semantic and phonological components are simply representative. Deep structures contain the information necessary for semantic representation, which is carried out by the interpretive system of rules composing the semantic component. Similarly, a system of phonological rules maps the surface structures into their phonological representation. Thus paired deep and surface structures mediate the idealized semantic and phonological representation. This three-component system of rules is integrated in such a way that independent study of each must take the others into account. An unvaried feature of the approach is that the (infinite class of) objects of the syntactic component are abstract. (It should be noted that Chomsky acknowledged fairly early on that surface structures could also "contribute" to semantic interpretation, but for a long time he insisted that this was only so "in restrictive ways." The notion gathered momentum, however, as deep structures began to play a less prominent role in more recent revisions of his theory.)

The view that syntactic analysis should yield insight into semantics was already explicit in 1956 and 1957, but it was restricted, aside from an unclear and slanted association with understanding, to such general statements as "having determined the syntactic structure of the language, we can study the way in which this syntactic structure is put to use in the actual functioning of the language" (Chomsky, 1957, p. 102). The notion that systematic formal relations may sometimes correlate with significant semantic functions was not new, however. Harris (1952), for example, had shown rather striking examples, where the distinction between "distributional structure" and "interpretation" was drawn. Transformations emerged in this context as heuristic devices to help clear up prevailing relations

~ SUBSEQUENT REFINEMENTS ~

within long stretches of discourse, bringing to bear information from outside the text under analysis. Again, however, Chomsky's more abstract formulation, along with his sentence atomism and the general acceptance of preestablished schemes, was bound ultimately to force an even narrower range to "semantic interpretation."

The semantic absolutes referred to in 1957 have now become semantic features—say, male-female, agent-instrument, relational-absolute, and so forth—on the model of binary phonetic features. This is partly the result of descriptive convenience, brought about by the elaboration of the semantic component on a par with the much more highly developed (and reasonable) phonological component—largely the work of Halle—and its specific relation to the syntactic component (underlying phrase-markers constitute the basic "content elements"). Such a manner of specification of meaning, first worked out by some of Chomsky's more immediate colleagues (see, for example, Katz and Fodor, 1963; Katz and Postal, 1964), proves a *tour de force* altogether. Chomsky has repeatedly admitted that this is the weakest part of his proposal. This should not be surprising; technicalities (features, rules, and so on) aside, Chomsky's situation is remarkably reminiscent of what early generative grammarians used to say about the (ultimately also formalistic) Bloomfieldian approach. It may well remain so: semantic absolutes are to be shunned, of course, but it is doubtful whether the search for bundles of distinctive semantic features instead is the solution or even, in fact, a viable alternative. Significantly, TG grammarians have witnessed the first major split in their ranks precisely in connection with semantics (note the heated controversy between generative and interpretativist semanticists). Chomsky is aware that the notion "semantic interpretation" is far from clear. He believes, however, that there are enough "empirical" considerations supporting it to justify proceeding along the proposed course.

The general character of the criticism in Section 3.7 is also relevant here, where it seems to find actual confirmation. Take the examples, "John is eager to please" and "John is easy to please." Chomsky has repeatedly discussed their difference in terms of the availability of the nominalized form "John's eagerness to please" for the first but not the corresponding "John's easiness to please" for the second, as well as the relative closeness of their respective deep and surface structures (greater in the first case). Other frequent examples, for example, "I persuaded the doctor to examine John" and "I expected the doctor to examine John" (nearly identical as far as surface structure goes) are resolved more openly through recourse to semantic criteria, namely, the truth value ensuing from substitution of the passive "John to be examined by the doctor" for "The doctor to examine John." Corresponding active and passive mean the same where "expected," but not "persuaded," is concerned. There are, of course, many other (more formal) details in this search for differences in deep structure.

The introduction of the deep/surface structure distinction would be claimed as a formal refinement of the theory; as before, however, no possible discussion of actual examples is likely to show its relevance without taking meaning into account—not even a strategy involving the inspection of a vast amount of data, conceivable but ruled out on account of its unwieldiness. No English grammar had taken notice of the pertinent differences before; Chomsky (p. 22) points out that even his own efforts of 1955 and 1962b overlooked the formal implications of the (semantic) subtleties of "persuasion," "expectation," and the like. The long-term effects of the deep/surface distinction will depend, in part at least, on the availability of alternative methods of analysis flexible enough to disregard, among other things, the traditional commitment to sentence boundaries (see some of the current work in discourse analysis, text theory, and conversation analysis).[1] Theoretically, a generative formulation of grammar may not be restricted to a finite corpus, but the generative grammarian typically relies on a small number of theoretically suitable examples, the relevance to actual speech behavior of which is often far from clear.

An otherwise understandable preoccupation with the justification of grammars could hardly be expected to bring about a corresponding revision of fundamental concepts, formulated as this justification was in terms of metatheoretical evaluation criteria for descriptive and, by extension, explanatory adequacy.[2] Explanatory power, as discussed in 1957 and after, appealed inevitably to meaning and understanding. The special reliance on the listener is explicit again in 1965 (see, for example, pp. 4-5): "A fully adequate grammar must assign to each of an infinite range of sentences a structural description indicating how this sentence is understood by the ideal speaker-listener." This seems to be the extent of the "empirical conditions" to be met, repeatedly mentioned by Chomsky in this connection. Yet the nature of meaning remains obscure; dubbing it "intrinsic" to the sentences generated is too obviously uninformative. In line with the notion that grammar is "neutral" as between speaker and listener, meaning must now presumably be thought so too. But this directly contravenes experience.

Nevertheless, the inclusion of semantics as an integral part of grammar amounts to an important recognition, namely, the inseparability of meaning and form in language studies. As formulated, however, the fundamentally dualistic substance of the argument persists. This is particularly important in the light of explanatory power, however contrived. Moreover, the means proposed for the specification of meaning can scarcely be expected to cope with the full range of "semantic functions" characteristic of the "use of language," with which meaning was obliquely equated.[3]

5.2 Scientific theories aim at general statements, and this entails a degree of abstraction and, sometimes, idealization. The present theory, however, appears to do so by overruling a number of issues sufficiently tangible to first demand close empirical consideration. Consider the following statement: "Linguistic theory is concerned primarily with an ideal speaker-listener, in a completely homogeneous speech-community, who knows its language perfectly and is unaffected by such grammatically irrelevant conditions as memory limitations, distractions, shifts of attention and interest, and errors (random or characteristic) in applying his knowledge of the language in actual performance" (p. 4).

We have already had occasion to refer to the methodological

~ CHAPTER 5 ~

status of such behavioral phenomena and their assumed grammatical irrelevance. Distractions, shifts of attention, and the like are often the cause of errors, to which any speaker of a natural language is subject as a matter of course. One may question, however, the wisdom of ruling them out as mere "matters of performance," and of treating "random" and "characteristic" errors alike. The term 'error' covers a very wide range, and subtle variables may be at work (see also chapter 6). The line between certain kinds of errors and bona fide deviations may sometimes prove very thin, as any but the most theoretical concern with grammaticalness immediately shows.[4] The term 'error,' almost indiscriminately applied to deviations from a standard pattern, is not a description but a judgment relative to a well-defined set; but the status of languages as well-defined sets is suspect.[5] The language known "perfectly" by Chomsky's speaker-listener is not likely to be some natural language but L, the result of membership in a "completely homogeneous speech-community." This is a vacant state of affairs, which renders the status of the ideal speaker-listener highly dubious and the relevance of its description to real speakers, listeners, and their compliance with the contingencies of natural speech communities, extremely tenuous. There are (or should be) limits to idealization. (Chomsky, 1975, concedes that there are no homogeneous speech communities in the real world; he even goes so far as to admit that a speaker may control several grammars. Just what this admission does for his overall theory is far from clear.)

Perfect knowledge of a language is obviously an empty concept, too. The fundamental methodological distinction underlying this idealization is the competence/performance dichotomy: linguistic theory is about competence, a special kind of knowledge applied in performance. This "application" is of course metaphorical; but it is not quite clear just how metaphorical it is (see chapters 4 and 6). At any rate, it should not be taken literally. In Chomsky's view, only some such form of idealization can support the notion that performance is "a direct reflection of competence" (p. 4). The crucial question is, of course, whether it is, or whether competence is needed at all.

~ SUBSEQUENT REFINEMENTS ~

At one point the relative roles of speaker and listener are cast in somewhat more reasonable terms: "Thus an essential property of language is that it provides the means for expressing indefinitely many thoughts and for reacting appropriately in an indefinite range of new situations" (p. 5). This view presents problems of its own, however: to say that language serves to express thoughts immediately raises the further question of the origin of these thoughts, ideas, and the like, and what *is* the essence of their expression, in other words, their relation to verbal activity. The listener no doubt responds to the speaker's behavior; this is what *defines* him as such, but the term 'react' is too vague to suggest the full richness of his behavior or what *his* thoughts consist of. This is the essence of the dualism alluded to at several points above: language still retains the character of a self-contained instrument, independent of speaker, listener, and all that their qualified membership in a verbal community entails.

Chomsky continues to use the term 'knowledge' in a peculiar sense: as before, it does not refer to what people do when they behave verbally but to their underlying linguistic intuition. Neither does it have anything to do with awareness, even though introspection can play (in the hands of the linguist) an important role in the discovery of the initial tacit competence. The ability to talk about one's own behavior and/or the variables that give rise to it is obviously the result of additional and very special conditioning (Skinner, 1957, 1963)—and there may be a question of legitimacy as to the discriminations formed, for example, the notion that in actual performance repetition is the exception rather than the rule, that for purposes of analysis active and passive sentences are interchangeable, and so on. Assumptions of this sort guide subsequent research.

A formulation of the native speaker's innate competence still is, to Chomsky's mind, a prerequisite to the study of performance (the actual behavior), which cannot be taken as knowledge *per se*. But then either language is deemed a different kind of behavior, or else the same must be postulated for anything that organisms (human or otherwise) do. Chomsky is willing to go that far (see, for example, p. 34);[6] his commitment to ration-

~ CHAPTER 5 ~

alism was becoming explicit (see, for example, Chomsky, 1964, 1966) and has been subsequently strengthened without qualification (see, for example, Chomsky, 1972, 1976, and 1980; see especially chapter 7 below).

A recourse to full-fledged mentalism was only a logical next step:

> in the technical sense, linguistic theory is mentalistic, since it is concerned with discovering a mental reality underlying actual behavior. Observed use of language or hypothesized dispositions to respond, habits, and so on, may provide evidence as to the nature of this mental reality, but surely cannot constitute the actual subject matter of linguistics, if this is to be a serious discipline. (p. 4)

This is at least partly reminiscent of de Saussure's mentalism in the form of identification of concepts/meaning and mental images (see chapter 2 above). Chomsky, however, iterates the argument that de Saussure's view of *langue* as a "storehouse of signs" forced the assignment of creativity to *parole* and must be rejected in favor of Humboldt's conception, which comes closer to a view of creativity as a matter of systematic rule. (Humboldt frequently used the term *erzeugen* in a sense akin to Chomsky's 'generate.') The "open-endedness" of verbal systems is sometimes phrased, metaphorically, one must assume, as "the creative aspect of language," which amounts to more than mere reification of an abstraction: it suggests the attribution of creativity to "language" rather than to its "users." "A grammar of a language purports to be a description of the ideal speaker-hearer's intrinsic competence. If the grammar is, furthermore, perfectly explicit—in other words, if it does not rely on the intelligence of the understanding reader but rather provides an explicit analysis of his contribution—we may (somewhat redundantly) call it a *generative grammar*" (p. 4).

5.3 A generative grammar can be specified, however, by more than one system of rules. The justification of grammars is a two-level affair involving descriptive and explanatory adequacy; where deep questions of justification are concerned, the former implies the latter: "if he [the linguist] wishes to achieve descriptive adequacy in his account of language structure, he must concern himself with the problem of developing an explanatory theory of the form of grammar, since this provides one of the main tools for arriving at a descriptively adequate grammar in any particular case," (p. 41). Coverage of linguistic data alone will not do as a criterion. There is, as we have seen, a condition of generality: the theory must make available a descriptively adequate grammar for every natural language. Clearly, such a theory goes beyond mere provision of appropriate means; the selected system of rules matches the speaker-hearer's intrinsic competence, the new postulated object of linguistic theory. Descriptive adequacy has to do with justification on external grounds, matters of correspondence to "linguistic fact."

Justification on internal grounds involves descriptive adequacy plus selection of one principled adequate system over other alternatives with conceivably equal descriptive power: "Such a theory limits the choice of grammar by the dual method of imposing formal conditions on grammar and providing an evaluation procedure to be applied for the language L with which [the linguist] is now concerned. Both the formal conditions and the evaluation procedure can be empirically justified by their success in other cases" (p. 41). This selection is determined by their "relation to a linguistic theory that constitutes an explanatory hypothesis about the form of language as such" (p. 27). This is the metatheory discussed in preliminary fashion in chapters 3 and 4, which zeroes in on the *form* of language. Criteria are stringent indeed: internal justification or explanatory adequacy appeals to the construction, in abstract terms, of a model for the acquisition of language, a theory of language learning or grammar construction. Given its postulated universality, innate abilities are necessarily invoked.

We have seen the argument before. Citation of the formal requirements, as formulated in 1965, should provide an appropriate recapitulation of what we have labeled "strong explanatory claims" throughout. The theory should provide:

(i) an enumeration of the class $s_1, s_2, \ldots$ of possible sentences

CHAPTER 5

(ii) an enumeration of the class $SD_1, SD_2, \ldots$ of possible structural descriptions

(iii) an enumeration of the class $G_1, G_2, \ldots$ of possible generative grammars

(iv) specification of a function f such that $SD_f(i, j)$ is the structural description assigned to sentence s_i by grammar G_j for arbitrary i, j.

(v) specification of a function m such that $m(i)$ is an integer associated with the grammar G_i as its value (with, let us say, lower value indicated by higher number).

(The evaluation measure m has to do with "simplicity." This is not some measure understood in advance; rather, its determination is like the determination of a constant in physics. That the search for a numerical measure of simplicity is, even from a theory maker's point of view, so premature as to border on wishful thinking, hardly needs pointing out.)

The first four requirements cover the external conditions that a theory must meet to be "empirically significant"; the fifth is a matter of internal conditions. The child learning a language must have a "method of selecting one of the 'presumably infinitely many' hypotheses that are allowed by (iii) and are compatible with the given primary data" (p. 28). Like the child, the linguist must take (v) into account if he wants to endow his theory with explanatory power: Chomsky asserts that "the most serious problem that arises in the attempt to achieve explanatory adequacy is that of characterizing the notion 'generative grammar' in a sufficiently rich, detailed, and highly structured way" (p. 36). Proper selection and justification of specific grammars otherwise perfectly compatible with data would be impossible without some such evaluation measure. Moreoever, Chomsky states flatly, language learning could not take place. (For a more sober discussion of the relation between generative grammars and speculations on competence, see Matthews, 1979.)

In short, the linguist must determine, in the face of primary data, the underlying system of rules that, having been mastered by the native speaker, is then "put to use" to produce the data.

~ SUBSEQUENT REFINEMENTS ~

The child learning a language does essentially the same; that is, he develops an internal representation of precisely that set of rules determining "how sentences are to be formed, used, and understood." If successful, they both come up with a generative grammar of a very specific type. Chomsky writes:

> I am making the obvious comment that, wherever possible, general assumptions about the nature of language should be formulated from which particular features of the grammars of individual languages can be deduced. In this way, linguistic theory may move toward explanatory adequacy and contribute to the study of human mental processes and intellectual capacity—more specifically, to the determination of the abilities that make language learning possible under the empirically given limitations of time and data. (pp. 46-47)

5.4 To repeat, then, the grammar is a three-component system of rules that relate the meaning(s) of the generated sentences to their acoustic reality. Paired deep and surface structures mediate the idealized semantic and phonological representations. The system is so integrated that study of each of its components must take the others into account. A fundamental feature is the abstract nature of the infinite class of objects of the syntactic component.

Considerations of descriptive adequacy lean heavily on more stringent criteria of explanatory power. The justification of grammars is ultimately determined by a prior metatheoretical conception, a hypothesis about the form of language. The goal of linguistic theory is the characterization of the speaker-hearer's native intuition, a kind of knowledge of underlying forms and principles of manipulation which account not only for the creative characteristics of verbal performance but which are further postulated as innate concept-forming abilities responsible for language learning in the first place. In line with much traditional rationalist thinking, "experience" is assigned the exclusive role of activating this postulated mechanism and of determining the specific form of its actual manifestation.

~ CHAPTER 5 ~

For the present we cannot come at all close to making a hypothesis about innate schemata that is rich, detailed, and specific enough to account for the fact of language acquisition. Consequently, the main task of linguistic theory must be to develop an account of linguistic universals that, on the one hand, will not be falsified by the actual diversity of languages and, on the other, will be sufficiently rich and explicit to account for the rapidity and uniformity of language learning, and the remarkable complexity and range of generative grammars that are the product of language learning. (pp. 27-28)

In other words, if the obvious difficulties involved in the postulation of innate mechanisms on the exclusive basis of a strictly theoretical characterization of language must be taken as evidence of anything, it is an insufficient degree of formal specificity in the theory that must bear the burden: "Thus the major endeavor of the linguist must be to enrich the theory of linguistic form by formulating more specific constraints and conditions on the notion 'generative grammar' " (p. 35; see also chapter 4). The way to do this is through the establishment of linguistic universals: their study is the study of the properties of any generative grammar for natural language (p. 28), the principles by which child and linguist come to select the best grammar. (The need to impose stronger restrictions on grammars has become a sensitive issue, particularly since Peters and Ritchie, 1973, showed that the type of transformational grammars set forth in *Aspects* was too powerful, thus failing to narrowly delimit "the class of natural languages." For an interesting discussion, with implications for formal semantics, see Stern [1978]. Not everyone would agree, however, with Chomsky's psychologism.)

A distinction is also drawn at this point between formal and substantive universals in connection with all three components of the grammar and their interrelations. Substantive universals have to do with the metatheoretical descriptive vocabulary: the phonological component makes use of Jakobson's theory of distinctive features, "a small number of fixed, universal, phonetic features (perhaps on the order of fifteen or twenty), each of which has a substantive acoustic-articulatory characterization independent of any particular language." The semantic component might make use of such facts as the presence of "terms that designate persons or lexical items referring to certain kinds of objects, feelings, behavior, and so on" in every language. Likewise, certain syntactical categories play a central role in the description of all languages; it may be worth quoting Chomsky's remarks in full:

> Traditional universal grammar was also a theory of substantive universals, in this sense. It not only put forth interesting views as to the nature of universal phonetics, but also advanced the position that certain fixed syntactic categories (Noun, Verb, etc.) can be found in the syntactic representations of the sentences of any language, and that these provide the general underlying syntactic structure of each language. (p. 28)

Formal universals have to do with certain abstract conditions, again for each component, as long as they prove to be a general property of natural languages; they involve the nature of rules and their manner of interconnection. Phonological rules, for example, apply cyclically under certain conditions; conditions of designation, definition, and so on, are thus specified (e.g., "artifacts are defined in terms of certain human goals, needs, and function instead of solely in terms of physical qualities" [p. 29]). Transformational rules convert deep structures into surface structures in certain very specific ways. Notice that Chomsky appeals to a "fixed" set of available substantive universals for both phonology and syntax; this does not seem possible for semantics, however. (It is hardly necessary to point out that the empirical status of the semantic notions invoked remains unexplained.) At any rate, for both substantive and formal universals, syntax has been mentioned last on account of its central role in the grammar. As Hiż (1967) has pointed out, however:

> The distinction between substantive and formal universals does not seem sharp; if formulated more carefully it may easily disappear altogether. Verb, a supposed substantive

~ CHAPTER 5 ~

universal, is a concept used in such principles as: every sentence has a verb. But a verb is a part of a sentence which behaves in a characteristic way under transformations of the sentence. Therefore, what one wants to say is that in any sentence there is a part which in some specifiable ways remains invariant under transformations. But this is a formal universal.

The possible effect of some such thoroughgoing revision of all the concepts involved in the postulated tripartite structure of language (and the deep/surface structure distinction) is worth speculation. Whatever the ultimate place and form of transformations in linguistic analysis, the nature of Chomsky's framework would appear to preclude this sharper formulation: traditional grammatical categories are simply taken for granted, as we have seen. Far from even questioning their validity, Chomsky actively advocates their acceptance in many of his writings. They are the hypothetical constructs in terms of which rules ("laws") are framed (see section 3.2). The nature of the rules is itself in part determined by the assumption that the sentences of a language constitute a recursively enumerable set and by the nature of these constructs, which must remain hypothetical. Under Chomsky's conception of L they are actually hypostatized; a further distinction, for example, is made between "logical" and "grammatical" subjects, corresponding to deep and surface structure specifications. Despite repeated disclaimers to the contrary, distinctions of this sort would appear to be dangerously close to the assignment of "structural meaning" criticized in 1957. (For a discussion of deep structure and logical analysis, however, see Quine, 1972.)

The a priori search for universals is an important part of Chomsky's overall thrust toward universal grammar, in perfect accord with a rationalist epistemology, "if we take the essence of this view to be that the general character of knowledge, the categories in which it is expressed or internally represented, and the basic principles that underlie it, are determined by the nature of the mind" (Chomsky, 1967b). It also implies, to use his phrasing, that all languages are cut to the same pattern—though not necessarily the existence of a point by point correspondence among them. This has become something of a tenet amongst the vast majority of experts, highlighting one of the major differences between the original thrust of linguistic structuralism (which, for obvious reasons, attended to differences) and current theoretical claims.

The structuralist study of language, originally motivated (in part at least) by the need to overcome the limitations imposed by a single grammatical framework, comes full circle with the present emphasis on universal grammar. Abstract models aside, the analyst concerned with natural languages can hardly begin at zero. Descriptive statements demand a minimum of initial categories and the linguist bent on vindicating traditional modes of thinking can scarcely be expected to challenge the validity of conceptual frameworks that not even his more flexible predecessors managed to successfully abandon.

Hymes (1972) puts the story in a nutshell:

> Structuralism proper in linguistics began with phonology, wherein lies a story in itself. But surely an essential factor in Chomsky's impact is that he proposed a new orientation and role for syntax at a time when structural linguistics had reached *syntax,* so to speak, having elaborated methods and controversy successively in the sectors of phonology and morphology. . . .
>
> In Chomsky's successful introduction of the goal of generating all and only the grammatical sentences of a language, we can see the completion, or carrying through to syntax, of structuralist principle.

It is not obvious, however, whether this shift of emphasis regarding the broader goals of linguistic theory follows from the formal refinements themselves. Even if one must insist that the job of a grammar is to generate all and only the grammatical sentences of a language, one can still do transformational work without invading the psychologist's sphere of competence or claiming any special epistemological insights. The additional switch to competence is a philosophical, not a linguistic matter; and it is far from clear in what ways it turns the study of language into a more "serious discipline." (Hiż has appropriately called the presumed correlation of hypothesized formal structures, mental processes, and innate intellectual abilities a "genetic fallacy.")

It may very well be that the mechanisms of verbal performance are universal, that verbal activity everywhere shares certain essential properties. Human behavior being what it is, it would be surprising if the opposite held true. But the responsible mechanisms are functional, not formal, and it is highly questionable whether they are made more amenable to scientific study through the formulation of explanatory models via evaluation procedures, or whether any amount of rhetoric can lend a theory about innate intuitions the kind of empirical status its practitioners claim for it. The postulation of an underlying competence amounts, at best, to a grand hypothesis; but hypotheses are merely guesses, no matter how sophisticated the formal machinery in which they are couched. A more reasonable alternative is a more exacting adherence to a truly empirical outlook and a more critical regard for genuine and tangible data in all their functional complexity.

SUMMARY

Later technical refinements only strengthened the inherent biases of the initial proposal. Grammar has become a three-component system of rules (syntactic, phonological, and semantic), integrated in such a way that independent study of each must take the others into account. The inclusion of semantics as an integral part of linguistic descriptions amounts to an important recognition, namely, the inseparability of meaning and form. The linguist is now concerned with an ideal speaker-listener, who is a member of a completely homogeneous speech community and who knows his language perfectly well. This "knowledge" (which is the new object of linguist theory) is of course an idealization: it does not refer to what people do when they behave verbally, but to their supposed underlying intuition. The gap between competence and performance grows wider. Recourse to an even stronger mentalism was probably inescapable. The justification of grammars becomes a two-level affair involving descriptive and explanatory adequacy. This is only a more sophisticated version of the previous evaluation procedure and, we must assume, an attempt to endow the black box with specific internal properties. The appeal to innate mental processes and intellectual capacities has been called the "genetic fallacy." The principal task is to enrich the theory of linguistic form by formulating more specific constraints on the notion "generative grammar." Since it is assumed that all languages are cut to the same pattern, the establishment of linguistic universals appears to be the answer. The proposed distinction between formal and substantive universals (largely the categories of traditional grammar) can be challenged, however, on formal grounds alone. Proponents of the theory are not bothered by the obvious arbitrariness ensuing from this thoroughgoing apriorism: the formal means utilized ultimately determine the working conception of the subject matter rather than the other way around. The explicit view that meaning is intrinsic to the sentences generated by the grammar is unreasonable. Universals must be sought, if sought at all, in the shared practices of verbal communities, not in an abstraction from just one term of the contingencies which define them. No amount of idealization can change the fact that the mechanisms responsible for verbal performance are functional, not formal.

~ CHAPTER 6 ~

Performance and Competence

6.1 A brief quotation may serve as a fairly comprehensive summary of Chomsky's position and as a baseline for further examining the tenability of the competence/performance distinction:

> If the conclusions of this research are anywhere near correct, then humans must be endowed with a very rich and explicit set of mental attributes that determine a specific form of language on the basis of very slight and rather degenerate data. Furthermore, they make use of the mentally represented language in a highly creative way, constrained by its rules but free to express new thoughts that relate to past experience or present sensations only in a remote and abstract fashion. (Chomsky, 1972)

We have already seen that the basic difficulty with any formulation that appeals to the "expression of thoughts" is that it leaves the question of the origin of these thoughts and how they come to be expressed unanswered. Chomsky must be aware of this in some sense; hence the reference to past experience and present sensations. To say that the relation can only be "remote" and "abstract" is to dodge the issue entirely. Explanation of language use and acquisition in terms of a formal hypothesis about structure then necessarily becomes a matter of mental representation, creativity a matter of highly constrained rule, and mental attributes ultimately a question of native endowment.

The competence/performance distinction appears to be a form of compromise forced by an initial commitment to formal analysis on the one hand and the real nature of the data on the other. Not surprisingly, it has been the subject of widespread misunderstanding, much of which must be attributed to unavoidable methodological and expository contrivances associated with the construction of formally motivated models. For all its apparent conceptual rigor, the postulation of competence as the real subject matter of linguistic theory is couched in highly metaphorical language, as Hiż (1967) has pointed out. It should be added that when taken literally, metaphors have a way of becoming myths.

Confusion has arisen in particular around the relation between models of competence and models of performance. As Chomsky puts it, "a number of professional linguists have repeatedly confused what I refer to here as 'the creative aspect of language use' with the recursive property of generative grammars, a very different matter" (Chomsky, 1972, p. viii). The question is whether they are indeed so different.

We have seen that descriptive adequacy ultimately depends on explanatory adequacy. Given the conditions defining the latter, it is not difficult to see why confusion should arise. Waiving the question of whether verbal systems are well-defined, empirical adequacy for a grammar has to do with its capacity to make infinite use of finite means in coping with "linguistic facts." This forces the introduction of recursive properties into the descriptive system, specifically localized in the categorial component of the base. But then, the justification for this is to be found in the ability of native speakers to produce and understand an unlimited number of novel sentences: this is "the fundamental fact that must be faced in any investigation of language and linguistic behavior" (see p. 67 above). Selection of alternative generative grammars is effected through evaluation criteria—constraints on the form of grammars ultimately to match the speaker's native-intuitive knowledge of language. As we have seen, discussions of adequacy consistently fall back on understanding; the so-called empirical conditions are ultimately formulated as a function of listener responses, in particular those of the linguist. The appeal to perceptual devices has been a permanent feature in any discussion of explanatory models since their inception. The basic assumption is that mere exposure to a vaguely conceived "verbal environment" is all that the child needs to become an accomplished speaker and listener.

6.2 The standard misunderstanding that particularly bothers Chomsky is perhaps nowhere better synthesized than in a paper he wrote (1967a) for the benefit of psychologists and psycholinguists (unless otherwise indicated, quotations in this chapter are from this publication):

> We noted at the outset that performance and competence must be sharply distinguished if either is to be studied successfully. We have now discussed a certain model of competence. It would be tempting, but quite absurd, to regard it as a model of performance as well. Thus we might propose that to produce a sentence, the speaker goes through the successive steps of constructing a base-derivation, line by line from the initial symbol S, then inserting lexical items and applying grammatical transformations to form a surface structure, and finally applying the phonological rules in their given order, in accordance with the cyclic principle discussed above. There is not the slightest justification for any such assumption. In fact, in implying that the speaker selects the general properties of sentence structure before selecting lexical items (before deciding what he is going to talk about), such a proposal seems not only without justification but entirely counter to whatever vague intuitions one may have about the processes that underlie production.

Indeed, Chomsky is right. There is not the slightest justification for any such view.[1] Neither is there any reason to believe that the processes that underlie production are or must be a matter of vague intuitions, or that we can rest content merely with a sophisticated formal hypothesis about their nature and organization. Emphasis on competence adds nothing to solving the problem, if it is a problem, of the relation between form and content. Instead, it strengthens the far from obvious view that what the speaker says and how he says it can be easily separated.

This position is only tenable if we disregard the plain facts of actual speech and cling to an abstract view of language as strings of words forming sentences and of grammar as concerned with relations between phrases as determined by rules of the type proposed.

The general reference to selection of properties of sentence structure on the one hand and lexical items on the other steals the show completely and conveniently brings the pertinent facts together. Fortunately, selection and decision hardly cover the case for most speakers most of the time (including the self-conscious grammarian). Circumstances simply arise that cause the speaker to speak. No verbal event can be dissociated from the multiple variables that typically give rise to it. People do not simply go around "generating" sentences; in order to be effective they must speak, in sentences or not, in appropriate ways at appropriate times and places, a fact often conceded while missing its full implications (Julià, 1968b, 1974).[2] The alternative view is to put meanings and forms inside the organism and to decree speech production a joint matter of linguistic rule.

This is not to deny that people sometimes do "stop to think" before speaking, as when completely novel circumstances demand the composition of samples never uttered before. But except in very circumscribed cases, deliberation is bound to be brought about by reasons other than the grammatical structure of the forthcoming utterances. Given the functional nature and variability of the units manipulated, most of the features emphasized in a formal analysis simply follow as an integral part of the responses involved. Responses are uniquely determined. Selecting, deciding, and deliberating are well-defined behavioral processes that can help clear up speech performance. It is a case of self-deceit to vaguely assign to them an independent "pre-behavioral" status of some sort in order to support an a priori view of the subject matter (Julià, in preparation).

In any case, this is only a reiteration of an equally sharp statement to the effect that all the grammar does is characterize "in the most neutral possible terms" the knowledge of language that provides the basis for its actual use by a speaker-hearer. In itself, "generative grammar does not . . . prescribe the char-

~ CHAPTER 6 ~

acter or functioning of a perceptual model or a model of speech production"; in fact, such questions as how the speaker-listener might proceed, for example, to construct a derivation "in some practical or efficient way . . . belong to the theory of language use—the theory of performance" (Chomsky, 1965, p. 9). Interestingly enough, the reader is specifically referred for further clarification to Chomsky (1957) and Miller and Chomsky (1963). The quotation on page 79 above was extracted from the latter (the title, "Finitary models of language users," should be telling enough in itself); those on pages 55-56 and 58 are from the former; see also page 80 from Chomsky (1962a), the reference to processes of synthesis and analysis on page 56 and the statement that performance is a direct reflection of competence on page 98. Two pages after Chomsky's long disavowal quoted at the beginning of this section, we read: "For example, it was suggested earlier that in order to account for the perception of stress contours in English, we must suppose that the user of the language is making use of the principle of cyclic application." Contradictions of this sort are numerous indeed; some, besides the ones indicated above, can be found in many of the excerpts included throughout this study. It would be surprising if misunderstandings did not arise.

The clear-cut distinction between competence and performance is, in principle, only too reasonable and straightforward; yet one cannot help sensing that the overall proposal is somehow confounded. Chomsky begins at the wrong end; consequently, what he contrives as empirical evidence is not. It is also possible that models of competence are so insightful and overriding that not much of substance is left, despite repeated (though vague) warnings that many factors must be taken into account in performance besides competence as a necessary initial ingredient.

It is only reasonable to ask, then, what is the actual contribution of competence to performance; in other words, how are the principles, theoretically discovered and formally postulated, put to use, so to speak, in actual performance? As in 1963 (see chapter 4), this is never made clear. The linguist's task is to formulate competence ("the ability of the idealized speaker-hearer to associate sounds and meanings in accordance with the

~ PERFORMANCE AND COMPETENCE ~

rules of his language") and, it seems, to make it clear that performance—what people do when they behave verbally—includes much else besides. It is far from satisfactory, however, to be told that this "association" of sound and meaning takes place in accordance with the rules of the language.

The artificial character of the examples adduced in the abstract formulation of competence has been pointed out several times in this study. Chomsky is aware of this, but he has only this to say: "Actually, the unnaturalness of the examples we have used illustrates a simple but often neglected point, namely, that the intrinsic meaning of a sentence and its other grammatical properties are determined by rule, not by conditions of use, linguistic context, frequency of parts, etc." In any event:

> A grammar generates a certain set of pairs (s, I) where s is a phonetic representation and I its associated semantic representation. Similarly, we might think of a performance model as relating sound and meaning in a specific way. A perceptual model, PM, for example, might be described, as in 1, as a device that accepts a signal as input (along with much else) and assigns various grammatical representations as "output."

1

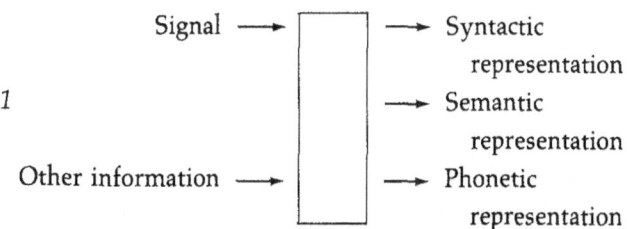

It is interesting to contrast this view with the disclaimers presented above. The "other information" has to do with such things as "extralinguistic beliefs concerning the speaker and the situation," which "play a fundamental role in determining how speech is produced, identified, and understood," although, one must understand, only "in a remote and abstract fashion." Moreover, linguistic performance is governed by "principles of

CHAPTER 6

cognitive structure (for example, by memory restrictions) that are not, properly speaking, aspects of language." We learn that "a central problem for psychology is to discover the characteristics of a system PM of this sort."

And this is precisely the point: an adequate competence model, to go along with the dichotomy, not only can help find out about such limitations as "constraints on memory, time, and organization of perceptual strategies "; by prescribing the outcome, it predetermines "the character or functioning" of the performance model as well:

> We would expect a system designed for the conditions of speech communication to be somehow adapted to the load on memory. In fact, grammatical transformations characteristically reduce the amount of grammatical structure in phrase-markers in a well-defined way, and it may be that one consequence of this is to facilitate the problem of speech perception by a short-term memory of a rather limited sort.

Following another statement about the absurdity of taking a description of rules and processes of grammar as the successive steps of a performance model, we read: "What we have said regarding perceptual models is equally applicable to production." Statements about memory spans, (un)boundedness, and the like, however, are phrased to suit the idealized hearer. One wonders about the relevance of perceptual strategies where the nonidealized *speaker* is concerned. (For further mention of the methodological status of such "variables," see Julià, 1968b; ch. 4.) Whatever the strategy employed, the behaviors of speaker and listener simply cannot be taken unequivocably as one and the same.

But then either models of competence are all that is needed to guide research, in which case genuine performance variables are all but obliterated, or else we must accept the responsibility for investigating such things as beliefs, intuitions, and so on (linguistic or not) as the behavioral phenomena they are—where the relevance of prior competence models becomes highly dubious.[3] There is no escape from a direct appeal to environmental factors like stimulus and reinforcement variables, an alternative that Chomsky rejects almost on grounds of principle. The only kind of psychological research worth the name seems to be, in his view, theory testing of the kind proposed, which means, in practice, speculation about cognitive processes with an appropriate fit.

The real contribution of competence is ultimately reduced to providing the innate linguistic intuition postulated as necessary for the child to discover "which of the possible languages he is being exposed to," that is, internalizing or "learning" its specific generative system of rules according to a preestablished general pattern, as formally defined: "The question, rather, is what range of possibilities may be within which experience can cause knowledge and belief to vary. If the range is quite narrow (as, it seems to me, is suggested by considerations of the sort mentioned above), then a first approximation of the sort suggested will be a prerequisite to any fruitful investigation of learning." There has been some confusion here, too. In reply to misunderstandings from philosophical quarters (Goodman, 1967), Chomsky (1968) writes: "it is misleading to speak of the innate schematism that has been proposed as merely providing 'limitations' for acquisition of language. Rather, what has been proposed is that this schematism *makes possible* the acquisition of a rich and highly specific system on the basis of limited data." The "limitations" alluded to are those imposed by the evaluation procedure, which provides grounds for selecting the highest valued grammar *and* the factual content of an explanatory theory.

6.3 To sum up, we can do no better than drink from the original source. The following excerpt constitutes an excellent example of strong, unsupported claims and of the clearly metaphorical nature of Chomsky's discourse:

> The child is presented with data, and he must inspect hypotheses (grammars) of a fairly restricted class to determine compatibility with these data. Having selected a grammar of the predetermined class, he will then have command of

the language generated by this grammar. Thus he will know a great deal more about phenomena to which he has never been exposed, and which are not "similar" or "analogous" in any well-defined sense to those to which he has been exposed. He will, for example, know the relations among the sentences 33 and 34 despite their novelty; he will know what stress contours to assign to utterances, despite the novelty and lack of physical basis for these phonetic representations; and so on, for innumerable other similar cases. This disparity between knowledge and experience is perhaps the most striking fact about human language. To account for it is the central problem of linguistic theory.

The examples referred to are again those on p. 96 above.

In the face of such powerful arguments, the reader has two courses open to him. He can follow the contemporary mainstream and take the formulation literally. For all intents and purposes, the differences between the postulated competence model and the proposed performance model seem to evaporate; the ensuing brand of psycholinguistics, within which "the fruitful investigation of learning" must be carried out has been labeled "experimental mentalism" (Fodor et al., 1974, and after). The expression would appear to be a contradiction in terms. Or else, he can take a closer look at some of the strong statements offered. This latter course inevitably leads to a critical appraisal of the assumptions on which the entire proposal rests.

For example, the assertion that the child knows a great deal about phenomena to which he has never been exposed constitutes a very strong statement, which has been accepted without further question. While it is true that the child will progressively come to say and understand utterances that he has never heard or said before, it does not necessarily follow that he does so primarily by virtue of the hypothesized rules of grammar. For that matter, it will similarly take an adult who changes subcommunities some time before he can be said to behave competently on a verbal (and nonverbal) level in accordance with the specific *Weltanschauung* that sets the new community apart. It would be unreasonable to ascribe the processes undergone by such a speaker to linguistic rule, for presumably he has already acquired the rules of the language before—at least if we subscribe to the notion of a uniform set of rules for the language, shared by all its native speakers. (It is perhaps fitting to point out that after twenty-five years of feverish activity, generative grammarians are nowhere near to providing anything like a reasonably complete grammar of English. Arguments still center largely on metatheory, and actual descriptions remain fragmentary and often at variance with one another. See Gross, 1979.)

The problem lies again in the definition of language, the corresponding view of grammar, and a misconception of knowledge. At stake in a central way is the problem of the units of analysis involved (Julià, 1968a, 1974). Casual observation shows that one is not necessarily able to say and understand Y just because one can do so with respect to X and Z. There are obviously questions of degree to be kept in mind in any discussion of the presumed "underdetermination of knowledge by experience." A "causal" account provides straightforward clarification through appeal to functional criteria. Availability of a given response under a given functional relation does not guarantee its availability under another—in sharp contrast to formalistic frameworks, where "knowledge of a word, phrase, or sentence" implies its universal "usability." (This view has long puzzled students of aphasia. For an extended discussion, see Skinner, 1957.) Ultimately, the problem is one of imputing a knowledge of something to an organism on the basis of its responses alone; clearly much else is needed. If responses are functionally determined, as they obviously are, their explanation lies in the determining variables; if the variables are different, the behaviors cannot be considered the same.

The disparity between "knowledge" and "experience" referred to by Chomsky becomes deceptively apparent in the light of the self-imposed conceptual apparatus within which his formulation is framed. Similarity of data is an empirical matter to be resolved by experimental analysis rather than by a priori arm-chair decision. It involves in a central way the notion of

~ CHAPTER 6 ~

response class, which cannot be dissociated from the independent variables giving rise to verbal activity.[4] These can hardly be treated vaguely as "other information" if we are to come to grips with such phenomena as "beliefs concerning the speaker and the situation." To dub them "extralinguistic" is misleading on several counts; in particular, it obscures the prevailing relations between behavior and its determining variables. Conditions of "use," linguistic context, frequency of parts, and the like *do* determine the meaning of sentences and, no doubt, their "other grammatical properties." Chomsky's assurances to the contrary run against the most casual, everyday observation and, what is more important, counter to the findings of many years of experimental research into the workings of verbal and nonverbal behavior alike. Chomsky is only looking at putative responses (actually their corresponding traces) and all he can do is compare them against each other. This is the essence of extreme formalism, the crystallization of a view of language as an abstraction.[5] Chomsky's assertions are based on the view that,

> The grammar of any language contains devices that make it possible to form sentences of arbitrary complexity, each with its intrinsic semantic interpretation. It is important to realize that this is no mere logical nicety. The normal use of language relies in an essential way on this unboundedness, on the fact that language contains devices for generating sentences of arbitrary complexity. Repetition of sentences is a rarity; innovation, in accordance with a grammar of the language, is the rule in ordinary day-to-day performance.

Even if we waive the implications of tacitly equating "grammar" and "language" (they both contain devices for generating sentences, of arbitrary complexity at that), it is not stretching the point to say that these claims about repetition and innovation are exaggerated and at great variance with observed fact. Creativity has been vastly overrated in the process of arguing for a descriptive-turned-explanatory system that capitalizes on the deft introduction of finite means to generate "all the sentences of the language." This infinity is, of course, a comfortable theoretical and technical assumption, but it collapses when the empirical facts are faced squarely (see, e.g., note 5, chapter 5).

For all their internalization of a given system of rules—say, those of English—perfectly normal speakers are not thereby in a position to understand, let alone produce, all the utterances generated by the grammar. Some, a small subset really, they will; others they will not. And the crucial question remains: "What accounts for the difference?" If speaking and understanding are equally a matter of linguistic rule, why should some pairings of sound and meaning come into effect and not others? It is obviously of little relevance to say that the grammar specifies all the sentences that *could* theoretically be considered well-formed sentences of English. Clearly, we must come out of the organism and turn to the environment—an exacting proposition. No appeal to a loose notion of "experience" can provide what is commonly felt to be a scientifically satisfying answer.[6]

6.4 The nature of performance is frequently misconstrued in yet another way. It is rarely discussed without some qualification as to its inherent "degeneracy." The cumulative effect of this is almost a view of "what the child is exposed to" as made up of a disproportionate amount of mistakes, interrupted fragments, false starts, lapses, slurring, slips of the tongue, changes in midcourse, nonsentences, and so forth, despite which, and in the face of limitations of time, amount of data, and cognitive structure, the child performs the mysterious task of learning to speak, that is, of becoming an acceptable native speaker. This view has become an unchallenged shibboleth among experts and an additional source of strength for the view that the real object of study of linguistics must recede to another level altogether. (Fodor and Katz, 1964, p. 8, for example, actually state that "almost all utterances are ungrammatical. . . .") Following this line of thought through, we must expect that for all his intrinsic knowledge of well-formedness the new speaker will now contribute to the general pool of slurring, mistakes, false starts, nonsentences, and so on, from which new children, making use of their initial competence will in turn become accomplished performers. And so on.

It is to a large extent due to this "degeneracy" that the linguist must idealize; he must work out his theory with nondegenerate data (i.e., paper-and-pencil examples).[7] Grammaticalness, which played such an essential role throughout, turns out to be a useful concept for discussing competence; when we come to performance we speak of "acceptability," which is (again in theory) amenable to "scaling" (Chomsky, 1965).[8] But acceptable utterances are not necessarily effective ones. Considerations of usefulness, which would appear to be of paramount importance in any theory having anything to do, however indirectly, with performance, only *occasionally* enter Chomsky's arguments (see, e.g., p. 72 above). The more recent appeal to "pragmatic competence" to supplement grammatical competence is primarily an effort to keep up with criticisms about the insufficiency of grammatical constructions as an explanation for verbal activity, without coming to grips with verbal performance as such.

Everyday speech does contain "anomalies," but as far as normal interaction is concerned, they must be reckoned as exceptions to the general flow. Even though they all occur for good behavioral reasons, a distinction should be made between formal distortions of the sort to interest the theoretical grammarian and the far more important kinds capable of thwarting effective verbal performance. It is not difficult to argue that methods of *scaling are of little relevance here (they are still too heavily tied* up with formal criteria) and that a great deal can be learned instead from an analysis of the variables that bring about real performance disruptions.[9] To eschew them all equally as mere "matters of performance" to be tolerantly put up with while seeking refuge in idealized patterns may be taken as an indication of how far the linguist in quest of explanatory power has gone from real data. (This is not to say, of course, that the study of verbal behavior should concentrate on "anomalies"; at any rate, *their discussion would take us too far afield into* the intricacies of verbal processes.)

6.5 All told, one inevitably asks, again, "What is the use of an entirely hypothetical competence model and the competence/performance distinction under the terms of the formulation?" Either the competence model is so powerful that, aside from trying to prove it right, there is little of substance left to look into, or else the gap between verbal behavior as it naturally occurs and the competence model presumably necessary to explain it is so wide that the maintenance of the distinction forces a number of methodological twists scarcely justifiable on any truly empirical grounds. It is not enough to assert that "the existence of innate mental structure is, obviously, not a matter of controversy" or that "what we may question is just what it is and to what extent it is specific to language." These supposed innate mental structures are the necessary *outcome* of the methodological standpoint underlying the formulation in the first place.

As pointed out in chapter 4, the fundamental problem lies with a strategy emphasizing first the characterization of "outputs" on their own grounds and then the postulation of a function relating them to "inputs." Concentration on final products rather than on how the organism got there may be consistent with given philosophical rather than scientific preferences, but it does little to suggest effective investigative strategy into the actual behavior of speaker, listener, or the real nature of the "inputs," in short, the real data. When these are faced squarely, we can easily dispense with the black-box metaphor altogether; we can proceed instead with the systematic investigation of the properties of verbal activity without the benefit of "models of performance" adapted to the exigencies of a priori "explanatory" competence restrictions. One major consequence of such an approach will be a characterization of "outputs" along entirely different lines.

Contrasting what he believes to be the modern version of the "empirical outlook" on mechanisms for the acquisition of (linguistic) knowledge with his own rationalist proposal, Chomsky (1967b and elsewhere) closes in on the procedures of segmentation and classification developed within the framework of pregenerative structural linguistics as the only clear and specific attempt to work out a system of inductive analytic procedures. (This is sometimes erroneously identified as the "taxonomic-behaviorist" point of view.) Chomsky concedes that these procedures could conceivably be improved upon to account for surface structures, but he deems it inconceivable that they could ever account for the abstract principles that generate deep structures and relate them to surface structures. He then adds: "This is not a matter of further refinement, but of an entirely different approach to the question." It is here submitted that as far as an empirical view of language as behavior is concerned, Chomsky's proposal *is* only a further refinement of previous trends: it has been forced by, and elaborated on the strength of, a number of unchallenged assumptions concerning language, grammar, categories, and formal means (for further discussion, see Julià, 1980a).

The initial descriptive thrust centered primarily on the formal nature (rather than the psychological defensibility) of the means employed; meanwhile, it left the rest of fundamental assumptions untouched. Should it be argued that Chomsky is more explicit than hitherto about the nature of both grammar and language, we would have to point out that, in view of the results, this too is damage wrought by the application of techniques far from suited to the matter at hand. Precision and suitability do not necessarily go together.[10]

Chomsky's apparently radical departure from previous trends amounts, in the last analysis, to a shift of emphasis from data manipulation to overall abstract theory. What he calls "an entirely different approach to the question" has to do with his explanatory claims and the eventual redefinition of the object of linguistic theory. A far more realistic role for descriptive linguistics will no doubt have to be considered.

SUMMARY

When language is taken as a formal object, claims of explanatory power necessarily lead to nativism. Some experts would forego, however, the epistemological claims; they would nonetheless retain "competence" to characterize the speaker-listener's knowledge of his language. With this goes the conviction that this knowledge must be approached through making explicit the underlying structure presumably inherent in all natural languages. Individual performance is simply discredited; it has been ruled out by decree. The disturbing fact is how readily this decree has been accepted. The much touted disparity between knowledge and performance (and the associated notion of "ceaseless creativity") rests on the view that language is constructed on the basis of a recursive principle; it also assumes the universal availability of linguistic forms once these have been learned. Involved here are decisions as to the similarity of data; but this is a matter for experimental investigation, not a priori decision. People simply do not go around "generating" sentences—a fact often conceded while missing its full implications: they must speak in appropriate ways at appropriate times. Such considerations lead directly to performance variables as the starting point. The prevailing view that grammar is at the core of verbal activity overestimates the importance of grammar and plays down the multiple determination, plasticity, and variability of the units of analysis at issue. Similarly, exotic claims have been made about the "degenerate" nature of performance; if taken seriously, the hypothesized knowledge of well-formedness becomes an obsolete mockery. The formulation is based on an unreasonable view of infinity (again, the effect of taking the descriptive means at face value); an unsupported emphasis on grammaticalness (based on artificial collocations of words); a monolithic view of language (nobody speaks a language in its totality; the proposed grammar becomes therefore an empty contraption); a fundamental confusion between speaker and listener (grammars, at best, refer to the latter); and the far from justifiable conclusion that speaking and understanding are a matter of rule. The supposed mental structures are merely an outcome of the position: assumptions and implications become confused in almost predictable ways. Models of this type guide research and become their own goal. But then either the proposed principles and rules describe the doings of speakers and listeners or the entire exercise is pointless.

~ CHAPTER 7 ~

Mentalism in Linguistics

7.1   While probably useful for demarcating the subject matter of linguistic theory as presently conceived, the notion of abstract study has relegated linguistics to the realm of speculative knowledge to an unprecedented degree. Chomsky (1972) writes:

> This process of abstraction is in no way illegitimate, but one must understand that it expresses a point of view, a hypothesis about the nature of mind, that is not a priori obvious. It expresses the working hypothesis that we can proceed with the study of "knowledge of language"—what is called "linguistic competence"—in abstraction from the problems of how language is used. The working hypothesis is justified by the success that is achieved when it is adopted. A great deal has been learned about the mechanisms of language, and, I would say, about the nature of mind, on the basis of this hypothesis. But we must be aware that, in part, at least, this approach is forced upon us by the fact that our concepts fail us when we try to study the use of language.

So we *are* concerned with performance, despite all the claims that it is about competence ("something else") that we must concern ourselves if we are ever to account for the true nature of language. That was never really denied, as we have seen. Indeed, what would be the sense of constructing a competence model at all that did not, somehow, make direct contact with the actual behavior of speakers and listeners? The fundamental qualms are methodological: they reduce to the simple question, "Are we in fact forced (wholly or in part) to veer radically away from the alleged *much else* that is "part of" performance and substitute "knowledge of language" in the above sense as the subject matter?"

To ask such a question at the present time may even sound naive. But then we must remember that the shift to competence has by no means left TGG proponents entirely at ease with respect to the empirical status of their position, as shown by (1) the frequency with which the question is brought up in their own literature and (2) the understandable preoccupation with the "psychological reality" of linguistic segments and operations. The essentially self-assertive nature of the answers usually put forth speaks for itself. At any rate, the hypothesis is only a proposal both about the *modus operandi* of linguistics and, Chomsky likes to think, the nature of mind. Its legitimacy depends not only upon a certain conception of the nature of language, the nature of knowledge, and their interrelations, but perhaps more important in the final analysis, upon one's view of scientific method—to which we return below. Chomsky admits that this hypothesis is not a priori obvious. What is more, he concedes that we may be facing "a problem of conflict between significance and feasibility." Although "caution is in order," his confidence is restored by the "many quite elegant results . . . obtained on the basis of this abstraction." Elegance, however, may not be the most appropriate criterion for evaluation: while it may meet questions of feasibility, it does not thereby answer questions of significance.

In fact, we might perhaps be permitted a second naive question as well, namely, what *has* been learned about the use of language (call it the "mechanism of language," if you will) or, for that matter, about the mind—even in the event that for some strangely compelling reason we might be inclined to retain the term to refer to the sum total of an organism's behavior? There is, for example, a question regarding the validity of the formal structures taken *ab initio* as well as the relevance of the formal operations (not necessarily their technical accuracy) postulated to relate them. We are at least entitled to a certain skepticism about the entities that make up our descriptive universe, the techniques employed for their manipulation, and the conclusions drawn from the resulting view of verbal data. It is

~ CHAPTER 7 ~

true that "our concepts fail us when we try to study the use of language," but it may well be that our concepts need to be reconsidered, not taken for granted.

Kuhn (1962, pp. 4-5) has put the matter succinctly for science in general as follows:

> Effective research scarcely begins before a scientific community thinks it has acquired firm answers to questions like the following: What are the fundamental entities of which the universe is composed? How do these interact with each other and with the senses? What questions may legitimately be asked about such entities and what techniques employed in seeking solutions?

It must be admitted that these conditions are clearly lacking here. If we are to pay verbal performance more than just lip service, we can hardly expect to find answers to these questions without a realistic reappraisal of what it is that we pretend to describe. The kind of reexamination called for is precluded by the pointed insistence on staying away (in theory at least) from performance criteria: 'knowledge of language' as a synonym for 'competence,' or vice versa, becomes less than palatable; and so does 'mind'—assuming that it must be brought in at all. Yet this seems to be what really interests Chomsky.

7.2 The difficulties besetting the study of "language use" are real enough, but it does not follow that the only alternative and best course lies in model building and the recourse to mental entities and structures. If we are seriously interested in a scientific analysis, nothing justifies shying away from the complexities of real data.[1] The comfort provided by any form of escape into a dream world of idealized entities is bound to be temporary: it can only yield spurious results, unfit for cumulative progress.

The study of behavior has known similar situations before. Skinner (1961) analyzed the sorts of contingencies that explain this tendency in the absence of an adequate experimental framework. The well-known behavioral process of extinction plays a fundamental role in the changeover to alternative approaches. Skinner groups short-term "solutions" of the sort into four different classes, which find a remarkable and all too natural parallel in the field of language behavior.

In broad outline, a "Flight to Laymanship" and a "Flight to Real People" can easily be identified, with proper adjustments, with the "language as it occurs" outlook associated in principle with modern structural linguistics. The emphasis on spoken language and the rejection of traditional straitjacketed academicisms was no doubt a step toward a more direct analysis of language as a natural phenomenon; but, for reasons pointed out in chapter 2, it could hardly be expected to go beyond the periphery of the real facts.

There are two other types of flights which prove even more directly relevant. They are intimately related, too. Let us first look at the "Flight to Mathematical Models": faced with seemingly chaotic data, psychologists invented "the ideal organism"—the Mathematical Model (on the pattern of the Political Man and the Economic Man elsewhere). Averaging data, whether from many trials or many subjects, did little to soothe the disturbing effects of variability in the "learning curves" of the period. Yet, order must be assumed to exist somewhere. As Skinner put it,

> The theoretical solution to this problem was to assume that an orderly learning process, which had always had the same properties regardless of the particular features of a given experiment, took place somewhere inside the organism. A given result was accounted for by making a distinction between learning and performance. Though the performance might be chaotic, the psychologist could continue to cherish the belief that learning was always orderly. Indeed, the mathematical organism seemed so orderly that model builders remained faithful to techniques which *consistently* yielded disorderly data. An examination of mathematical models in learning theory will show that no degree of disorder in the facts has placed any restriction on the elegance of the mathematical treatment.

It would misrepresent the facts to suggest that this approach has, for all *its* sterility, gone entirely out of practice among psychologists.

~ CHAPTER 7 ~

In any case, chaos and disorder are not, naturally, in the data but in the analyst's ineffective ways of going about their description. As intimated all along, there is no way around the development of a rigorous methodology appropriate to the behavior of the single organism. This is the core of an experimental analysis. There are some immediate questions for which a recourse to model building will simply not provide the necessary answers. Among others, what is verbal behavior? what are the relevant features of the environment to be controlled and measured? how are these independent variables to be related? To provide answers to these questions is indeed a laborious task, especially if contrasted with the construction of overall theories based on sweeping generalizations. But the record speaks for itself elsewhere, and there is no a priori reason why it should not cover the verbal case as well.

The remaining flight, the "Flight to the Inner Man," will not come as a surprise: it was only a short step for investigators who had begun with an honest concern for the *description* of behavior to claim an *explanatory* preoccupation with "what is going on inside the organism." The object of study receded again to mental and physiological processes. Although a distinction must obviously be made between their respective status, this is again the world of traditional "inner causes."

The similarities with the development of latter-day explanatory linguistic speculations could hardly be more striking.

7.3 The present criticism, like any other set of objections to the TGG-mainstream linguistic and psycholinguistic movement, probably reflects nothing but one more case of misunderstanding, and any alternatives intimated are no doubt a matter of triviality. One would, of course, like to make sure.

It was said in chapter 3 that the fundamental assumptions underlying Chomsky's proposal have varied little during the past two decades and that they are intimately related to his explicitly formulated goals for linguistic theory, which have permitted—if not actually motivated—the gradual shift of emphasis concerning explanatory claims. These initial assumptions, tentative on occasion at first, have in fact given way under the weight of the school's own polemic penchant. Supplied with ever more refined (though essentially inappropriate) means, assumptions and implications have become increasingly intertwined and more difficult to disentangle with the passage of time.

7.4 Chomsky has actually proposed for linguistics the status of a branch of theoretical (cognitive) psychology; characteristically, he has done so in ways that suggest that the latter cannot only profit from but must rather gear its course as the "new branch" dictates. As pointed out, a majority of psycholinguists and a surprising number of psychologists have come to accept the tenets and descriptive means of TGG at face value.[2] Nor has philosophy come out unscathed. The literature (pro and con) is also copious there. Juxtaposition of the terms 'language' and 'mind' (or some euphemism for it) is definitely on the rise again. Reference to Chomsky's speculations seems to have become, in one way or another, almost a permanent feature in philosophical writings wherever language is involved; interestingly enough, a concern with the semantics of natural languages seems to have been spurred among logicians.[3]

What has generally come to be called "The Chomskian Revolution" can be seen as an explicit turnabout demanding the abandonment of deep-rooted (though not necessarily well-established) empiricist principles in various fields. Curiously, however, latter-day mentalistic linguistics insistently asserts its empirical nature in the face of a rationalism that is at the same time vindicated and appealed to for historical support concerning the renewed interest in universal grammar. Self-justification sometimes leads to a convenient redefinition of terms (see, e.g., Katz and Bever, 1976).[4]

Chomsky's brand of mentalism is not strictly committed to the traditional dualism associated with rationalism, however. His position, as Lyons (1970, p. 108) has pointed out, would appear to be best characterized as an overt opposition to mechanistic determinism and, particularly, to behaviorism (which Chomsky seems to consider a more immediate danger and target). It has been suggested that, in contrast with philosophers

~ CHAPTER 7 ~

like Descartes or Plato, Chomsky could even be described as a "physicalist." It should not be difficult to see why: in his view, "the concept 'physical' has been extended step by step to cover anything we can understand" in the development of modern science, so that "when we ultimately begin to understand the properties of mind, we shall simply . . . extend the notion 'physical' to cover these properties as well." That day does not appear to be so far off as we might think; in fact, we may well be able to account for "mental phenomena" in terms of the "physiological processes and physical processes we now understand" (presumably with the aid of the proposed formulation of universal grammar).

These statements are reported by Lyons from a radio discussion with Stuart Hampshire (later published in *The Listener*, May 30, 1968) in the course of which Chomsky seems to have summed up the matter as follows: "The whole issue of whether there's a physical basis for mental structures is a rather empty issue"—a proposition one can only concur with, provided we place an entirely different interpretation on it.

These views foreshadowed subsequent developments. Chomsky (1976) offers a convenient elaboration of this new stage in his career as a psychologist and theorist of knowledge. A few choice examples provide a clear view of how far speculations of this type can lead. (Unless otherwise indicated, excerpts below will be from chapter one of this 1976 book, which sets the scenario for the slightly more technical chapters that follow it.)

7.5 Chomsky no longer argues for cognitive structures; he simply takes them for granted. The mind lurks behind it all. In fact, it justifies his technical interest in language by providing a more "general intellectual scope" to the task. In particular, "the possibility that by studying language we may discover abstract principles that govern its structure and use, principles that are universal by biological necessity and not merely historical accident, that derive from mental characteristics of the species. . . . Thus language is a mirror of mind in a deep and significant sense." The argument turns again around effortless acquisition of an intricate system of rules and guiding principles despite slight exposure to degenerate data, and so on; reference is made to the conveyance of thoughts and feelings, which arouse in others novel ideas, as well as subtle perceptions and judgments, and the like.

Some further refinements seem important; we also learn a few things about scientific method in the bargain: "I want to consider mind (in the narrower or broader sense) as an innate capacity to form cognitive structures, not first-order capacities to act. The cognitive structures attained enter into our first-order capacities to act, but should not be identified with them." Thus, "knowledge of English" enters into the capacity or ability exercised in using English, but it would be inappropriate to think of it as the "capacity" or "ability" itself—a mistake, Chomsky deplores, sometimes made by modern analytic philosophy. Such notions reveal "an unfortunate residue of empiricism" and, unlike cognitive structures (which are more abstract), they are too close to behavior to lead us "to inquire into the nature of the 'ghost in the machine,' . . . as normal scientific practice and intellectual curiosity would demand." (sic).

Chomsky believes that there is a more abstract level, the realm of "knowledge," "belief," "understanding," "expectation," "evaluation," and so forth, with which we must concern ourselves if we are ever to gain any real insight into human behavior. This is what the competence/performance distinction is all about. To sum up, "the proper way to exorcise the ghost in the machine is to determine the structure of the mind and its products." In practice, this reduces to speculation on the basis of the abstract study of "its products." In his view, "there is nothing essentially mysterious about the concept of an abstract cognitive structure, created by an innate faculty of mind, represented in some still unknown way in the brain, and entering into the system of capacities and dispositions to act and interpret."

In his concern to gain nontrivial insights into the nature of organisms (with a valid claim to the status of natural knowledge), Chomsky sees "no reason why cognitive structures should not be investigated rather in the way physical organs are studied." The purpose of qualifying insights as "nontrivial" is to

~ CHAPTER 7 ~

limit inquiry to (inferred) properties that will reveal uniform structure for members of a given species. It must be understood that "biological" concerns of this sort stand in sharp opposition to what Chomsky deems to be the findings of learning theory—which he calls "marginal phenomena."

Of course, science seeks uniformities, not differences—and this applies to experimental psychology as well. The fact that Chomsky assumes that the experimental psychologist must necessarily meet with variability as a matter of course suggests only that he is acquainted with the wrong literature. Science also proceeds in steps, approaching complex phenomena through the analysis of contributing simpler parts. This pattern seems to have been reversed by TGG-guided linguists, psycholinguists, and philosophers through their reiterated emphasis on accounting for that "enormously complicated system which a language is." Something like a "complexity syndrome" has set in.

In any case, the "language faculty" being a matter of cognitive structure we should not be taken aback to read that "the idea of regarding the growth of language as analogous to the development of a bodily organ is thus quite natural and plausible." The arm is especially mentioned in this connection. In Chomsky's words, "the language faculty, given appropriate stimulation, will construct a grammar; the person knows the language generated by the constructed grammar." The expression 'appropriate stimulation' is ambiguous, but we can safely assume that it refers to the earlier "exposure to a verbal environment." Following the analogy through, one wonders what the equivalent of this exposure or appropriate stimulation is for the growth of an arm.

It should be clear that what is really at issue here is the so-called innateness hypothesis, in its most extreme and most absurd form. The main point is that the language faculty is one of the faculties of the mind, common to the species. What is more, this language faculty, "serves the two basic functions of rationalist theory: it provides a sensory system for the preliminary analyses of linguistic data, and the schematism that determines, quite narrowly, a certain class of grammars." This is presumably what makes the critical difference. Though just as biologically determined as an arm's, language development is an "intellectual achievement"—although it is nowhere made clear what an intellectual achievement actually is. In any case, the grammar, as a system of rules and principles that determine the properties (formal and semantic) of sentences, "is put to use, interacting with other mechanisms of mind, in speaking and understanding language": "There are empirical assumptions and conceptual distinctions embedded in this account, and they might be wrong or misguided, but I think that it is not unreasonable, given present understanding, to proceed with them."

This is one of Chomsky's rare guarded moments. But *is* it reasonable to proceed with them, "given present understanding"? How can Chomsky be so firm nevertheless about structures created by an innate faculty of mind, represented in some still unknown way in the brain? Indeed, where does actual positive research of this kind begin? Does it have any future outside the speculative realm within which it is embedded? After all, once the *verbal* arguments in support of such a view are removed, all we are left with is an initial formal proposal, which is all that can be tested.

Performance includes "much else" besides competence; there was still some room earlier to ask whether it was totally out of place to suggest "giving the 'much else' a chance." But the question is all but irrelevant now: "I am insisting that the relation of experience to action be subdivided into two systems: LT (H, L), which relates experience to cognitive state attained, and Mcs, which relates current conditions to action, given cognitive state attained." The initials stand for various constructs introduced for the discussion of two simple, expositorily convenient little hypotheses, deceptively relevant at best to the present point. We are again reminded several times that "current conditions," "past experience," and the like have nothing to do with environmental variables and, again, that "the creative aspect of language use" and "the recursive property of grammars" are disjoint matters.

Chomsky condescendingly admits that experimental research of the type that centers on such variables may even develop

~ CHAPTER 7 ~

"laws of learning" with "some species validity." The problem is, however, that "it will, of necessity, avoid those domains in which an organism is especially designed to acquire rich cognitive structures that enter into its life in an intimate fashion," as a result of which we can only expect of it "to tell us little about the nature of the organism." There does not seem to be much point in asking where these cognitive structures come from; we are told beforehand that they are created by an innate faculty of mind.

It does not enter Chomsky's mind that the behavioral scientist, like any other natural scientist, avoids speculation wherever possible; he also tries to avoid circularity. His lack of interest in "rich cognitive structures" and the postulated "special designs" is not for him a matter "of necessity" but of elementary scientific hygiene. He can scarcely be satisfied to be told that these abstract structures are created by an innate faculty of mind, because he will in turn have to ask for evidence for this faculty. He will find it circular to say that human organisms *must* be endowed with such a faculty for otherwise they would not learn to speak. Until evidence other than sheer verbal argument turns up, he has no reason to prefer "ghosts in the machine" that enter the organism's life "in an intimate fashion" to the development of techniques for handling tangible data. All the more so, when these techniques have already proved extremely adequate in yielding an impressive degree of uniformity of data not only within but also across species.

The fact that Chomsky insists on disregarding the overwhelming evidence at hand may help explain his position, but it in no way excuses frequent *ex cathedra* proclamations such as:

> The discipline will be of virtually no intellectual interest. . . . The results and achievements of this perversely limited, rather suicidal discipline are largely an artifact. . . . It will be condemned in principle to investigation of peripheral matters such as rate and scope of acquisition of information, the relation between arrangement of reinforcers and response strength, control of behavior, and the like. The

discipline in question may continue indefinitely to amass information about these matters, but one may question the point or purpose of these efforts.[5]

These judgments, if valid, would be serious indeed. In point of fact, they are meaningless: they amount, again, to an ill-assorted array of terms loosely thrown together in ways that can easily lead the unprepared reader astray, a hodgepodge that suggests more than a *parti pris*. Some of these concepts have a very precise meaning in the operant literature, but Chomsky manages to mix them up in a way that makes them not only inaccurate but actually empty. What is more, he had repeatedly dismissed them as devoid of significance before, as we have had occasion to see. One wonders how he can concede now that such research, though limited to "peripheral matters," may develop laws of learning. In like manner, the "marginal phenomena" alluded to above have to do with "parameters of rapidity of learning," "scope of learning," and "rate of forgetting," which belong in a different context altogether. Hardly what one would call a sophisticated and balanced grasp of what behavior theory is all about.

So there is nothing left but to adhere to the notion that Chomsky's proposed "universal grammar" (UG) is "the system of principles, conditions and rules that are elements or properties of all human languages not merely by accident but by necessity." This is followed by the bizarre clarification, "I mean biological, not logical necessity." Is not Chomsky forgetting himself here? The system of principles, conditions, rules, and so on was formally worked out two decades ago on descriptive and logical grounds. His seminal work was about the *logical* bases of linguistic theory (Chomsky, 1955).[6] We saw on page 120 above that this system, though not a priori obvious, was "no mere logical nicety," either: the reason given in its support was the unboundedness of language and the need to cope with it through finite means. Yet it is now confidently stated that, "the 'innateness hypothesis,' . . . can be formulated as follows: Linguistic theory, the theory of UG, construed in the manner . . . outlined, is an innate property of the human mind. In

~ CHAPTER 7 ~

principle, we should be able to account for it in terms of human biology."

The entire discussion is still entrenched in formal criteria: although a concern with mind provides the more general intellectual scope for the technical study of language, it is the abstract formulation of UG that permits the most direct route to the study of mind. Biological "tangibility" is achieved, as it were, as follows: "In the case of human cognition, it is the study of the basic cognitive structures within cognitive capacity, their development and use, that should receive priority, I believe, if we are to attain a real understanding of the mind and its workings." One of the benefits of such an approach is that we may thereby gain "some insight into the class of humanly accessible sciences, possibly a small subset of those potential sciences that deal with matters concerning which we hope (vainly) to attain some insight and understanding." We must, presumably, take this as a contribution to epistemology.

It is here submitted that the argument has gotten slightly out of hand. We can only agree with Putnam (1967), for example, who, discussing an earlier and weaker version of the hypothesis, concludes that "invoking 'innateness' only postpones the problem of learning; it does not solve it." Chomsky's counterarguments (1968) remain still unconvincing as long as all he can do is reiterate that these abstract structures are represented in the brain in some unknown way. (Predictably, the debate continues. See, e.g., Piatelli-Palmarini, 1980.)

7.6 From the standpoint of natural science, there *is* something mysterious about abstract cognitive structures created by an innate faculty of mind and entering into the system of capacities and dispositions to act or interpret. Of course, there is nothing to prevent agreement to such a proposal, if one is ready to accept rhetoric as reality. Chomsky is obviously in no position to indicate specific ways to attach any kind of biological substance to the various constructs he juggles in order to support his explanatory claims. To the possible contention that his is only a hypothesis and that its potential empirical content is a matter of time one can only honestly reply that, indeed, time will tell.

Progress along these lines will be interesting to watch. (See note 6, chapter 1.)

The nature-nurture controversy is of course an old one. Chomsky's contribution to it is to have provided a formal framework that lends the proposal, at least for the case of language, a deceptive air of consistency and unassailability. It also makes for a rather peculiar view of scientific method. Two rather perplexing questions may serve to briefly illustrate the present point. In the process of arguing for his version of rationalism and against empirical studies, he asks: "What is a theory of learning? Is there such a theory as *the* theory of learning waiting to be discovered?" Surely this is a queer way of putting the matter. Theories of learning, their scope, nature, and relative merits have been the object of much (largely fruitless) discussion over the past several decades. In fact, their necessity has been seriously questioned altogether.[7] Nevertheless, this is probably the first time that the second of the above questions has been formulated in these terms. Since when are theories (of learning or anything else) out there, "waiting to be discovered"? Is that what the scientist expects to find when he sets out to investigate *nature*? Has Chomsky, from the lofty mist of his logical wonderland, not lost touch with the doings of natural scientists, among whom he now stakes out a claim to citizenship?

It will not do to appeal to old differences between deductivism and inductivism in science, or to the theoretician's license to introduce, redefine, or otherwise manipulate his constructs whenever greater insights into the workings of nature beckon, for here too certain restrictions must be respected.[8] It is true that hypotheses, models, theories, and so on, possibly disconnected from reality at first, eventually prove useful in furthering empirical knowledge—a historical fact of which we have often been reminded by explanatory linguists. But there is something fundamentally different in the present case. For one thing, there may be a question of maturity of the sciences involved; and it may well be that, against all appearances, linguistics is simply not ready for theoretical work at that level. The major problem lies, however, in the *use* made of abstract theoretical studies by Chomsky, in contrast to his predecessors' and (a few) illustrious

~ CHAPTER 7 ~

contemporaries' continued insistence on data manipulation. At the risk of triteness, the arch-theoretician's well-known observation that "pure logical thinking cannot yield us any knowledge of the empirical world; all knowledge of reality starts from experience and ends in it" (Einstein, 1934) is cited as particularly pertinent here.

The parallel with theoretical science at large cannot be upheld. Chomsky's original outlook and unquestionable expertise lies in the formal sciences—where metatheoretical concerns have been the object of a great deal of attention (for reasons not too dissimilar from those that have ultimately led linguistics to its present state). But in bringing this knowledge to bear on a would-be explanatory theory of language, Chomsky has failed to fully appraise the empirical nature of the subject matter. In fact, he has shifted his ground; as a result, conceptual and methodological contrivances have inevitably spiraled in the course of twenty years of self-defense. In his insistence on proceeding with the study of "knowledge of language" in abstraction from the problems of how language is "used," he has redefined the object of study in ways ever more remote from the well-established methodology of the empirical sciences.

Whatever the ultimate value of "experimental mentalism" may turn out to be, it is clear that what Chomsky proposes as present or potential knowledge of reality did not start with experience and it can scarcely be expected to end in it. As reasoned above (chapter 6), what Chomsky takes as empirical evidence is not. The rest follows from this initial false start.

Given an outlook on language as a mirror of mind (in a deep and significant way), it is not too farfetched to guess that the title of the book under discussion, *Reflections on Language*, is probably intended as a pun. Though consistent with the view that mind is what really matters and that language is a matter of mind, "Reflections on Language" falls short of its mark as a verbal response: it is in fact a wasted pun. Reflections (for lack of a better term) they are. But they are not reflections on language, let alone mind; they are only reflections on explanatory models in linguistics.

Aside from some excesses with regard to earlier claims, there is not really much new in Chomsky's 1976 (and subsequent) statements. The purpose of bringing some illustrative examples together was made clear earlier; the liberal use of direct quotations should be self-explanatory. Mindful readers can judge for themselves.

SUMMARY

The overall thrust is toward an even "deeper" explanation in terms of ever more remote abstract principles, a matter of exorcising the ghost in the machine. This is the realm of an ethereal world of knowledge, belief, evaluation, and so on, deemed the only way to gain nontrivial insights into the structure of the mind and its products. The frequent appeal to procedural elegance is a poor substitute for significance of results. In practice, it all reduces to large-scale speculation on the basis of products, not of the mind but of behavior. Language learning is still considered a matter of exposure; but the proposed analogy with the growth of a physical organ obviously breaks down. The universal fact of language learning is too broad, and vague, to justify this latest brainchild of the formalistic position. Despite all the claims that linguistic theory is concerned with competence, it is also concerned with performance; the facts show, however, that we cannot proceed with the study of "knowledge of language" in abstraction from language "use." The natural scientist has no need for cognitive structures created by a faculty of mind because there is a more direct route to account for the data: verbal forms do not merely occur; they occur at given times as a result of well-known environmental variables. Arguments to the contrary remain just that. The relevance of practical tasks should not be underestimated: any attempt to do something about the speech of concrete individuals involves modification of their behavior, hardly of their cognitive structures or faculty of mind. The initial interest in logical structure has become now a question of biological necessity. It is not easy to tell how much of this is due to bona fide internal demands of the theory itself and how much is an effort to defend a position in which much has been invested. Changes designed

~ CHAPTER 7 ~

to increase the generative power of the grammar construct are scarcely relevant. Related discussions on rules and representations, the range of possible grammars for human languages, or the degree of their learnability only show how far theoreticians have gone from the source of their data. They also reveal a fundamental confusion between the behavior of the analyst and the behavior under analysis. The problem lies ultimately with the hypostatical nature of linguistic data and the belief that these can be described in their own terms. What is taken as empirical evidence is not; everything else follows from this initial false start.

~ NOTES ~

Notes to Chapter 1

1. It is significant that a well-known textbook on the psychology of language, Fodor et al. (1974), should bear the subtitle "An Introduction to Psycholinguistics and Generative Grammar." Notice also such items as Block (1980), Fodor (1968), Katz (1971), Wexler and Culicover (1980).

2. Chomsky's standpoint has, of course, also been the object of widespread criticism from linguistic, philosophical, and psychological quarters. An extensive bibliography (generally centered on some partial aspect of the proposal) is readily on hand; although some token examples will be included or at least referred to at various points, it is no part of the present plan to review this aspect of the literature. References to Chomsky's own writings have been chosen with an eye to their conceptual representativeness and chronological relevance. While it is true, as Chomsky has repeatedly pointed out, that some of this criticism has been prompted by an inadequate appreciation of his position, it must also be recognized that TGG-advocates have often tended quickly to brush aside antagonistic views through the simple device of declaring them products of misunderstanding.

3. A definition of our subject matter as "behavior reinforced through the mediation of other persons conditioned precisely in order to reinforce the speaker" (Skinner, 1957, p. 224) clearly lays emphasis on the latter. Without the speaker there would be no verbal behavior for us to analyze. But then, without a listener there would be no reason for the speaker to emerge in the first place. Thus, both must be taken into account, even though much of the behavior of the listener as such is no different from the rest of his activity. The key terms are 'mediation' and 'conditioned precisely.' The latter makes provision for subtle differences that set verbal behavior apart from the rest of social repertoires; some of the most unique verbal functions to be accounted for derive from the fact that in time the speaker becomes his own listener. The former term, 'mediation,' points out that we are dealing with behavior which could not emerge from its direct effect upon the environment; therefore, it does not depend for its occurrence on a setting with specified physical properties. (The traditional "symbolic"

~ NOTES ~

value attributed to speech stems largely from this fact.) Here lie some of the most unique achievements of the verbal community.

The traditional domain is greatly enlarged: any movement, regardless of the musculature involved, perhaps in combination with an external medium, can become verbal. We are no longer restricted to vocal behavior alone. (To take an extreme example of bias, it is perplexing to see kinesic behavior consistently characterized in the literature as "nonverbal communication.") A clear distinction is made between the behavior and its traces, as independent physical entities. The definition is strictly functional and therefore nonarbitrary.

4. The differences are rather conspicuous. Operant behavior, which comprises the better part of the activity of the organism, is probabilistic. We move along a continuum ranging from complete certainty that a given bit of behavior cannot occur to virtual certainty that it will. Under laboratory conditions, we come close to the notion of probability of action through the study of frequency of occurrence over time. This is of course *rate*, Skinner's key methodological concept. Rate as a datum has made possible the systematic investigation of the major independent variables of which behavior, the dependent variable, is a function. The expert learns in time to extrapolate from observation and control in the laboratory to interpretation, prediction, and possibly control outside, where multiple variables usually come together in the generation of everyday phenomena, particularly where social behaviors are concerned.

Drawing mainly from a fairly recent, comprehensive restatement (Skinner, 1965), some of the more salient features of the position can be synthesized as follows:

Unlike stimulus-response psychologies or conditioned reflex formulations, which assign the stimulus an all-or-none eliciting value, the experimental analysis of behavior deals with the notion of stimulus control in more realistic terms: those aspects of the environment present when the organism is reinforced for a given bit of behavior acquire, to different extents, a degree of control over the behavior. The evidence for this is the behavior's increased frequency of occurrence in their presence but not otherwise. We can, and do, manipulate the range of effective stimulation. The discriminative stimulus, the well-known S^D, plays an important role as an independent variable.

Other independent variables have to do with the traditional fields of "motivation" and "emotion." The experimental analyst deals not with inner states, say thirst, but fluid intake; not with an inferred anxiety, but with the temporal sequence of preaversive and aversive

~ NOTES TO CHAPTER 1 ~

stimuli; and so on. In similar fashion, the age of an organism constitutes a more substantial variable than a supposed level of maturation; developmental studies follow suit.

We usually cannot manipulate inner states directly. But even if we could, the result would not be an explanation of how an organism comes under the control of obvious environmental variables. The conditions commonly associated, for example, with needs, wants, feelings, thoughts, purposes, states of mind, and so on, are not causes of behavior. They are themselves a product of antecedent events and are, therefore, of no avail in prediction or control. An experimental analysis accordingly dispenses with this inferred middle link (whether physiological, psychic, or mental) of a three-member chain and relates the relevant antecedent operations and the behavior directly. A similar treatment is accorded to the so-called cognitive activities, say, generalizing, concept formation, attention, memory, etc. There is no room either for related, essentially metaphorical concepts borrowed from other sciences, such as encoding, gating, reading out from storage, and so on.

Reinforcement, and especially social reinforcement, is often intermittent: its effects on various standard schedules are well known. It is not irrelevant to add that reinforcement can also be made contingent on rate itself, changes of rate, or specific patterns of change.

Contingencies of reinforcement play a preeminent role: they relate the conditions under which behavior occurs, the behavior itself, and its consequences. These interrelations can be extremely intricate, in the laboratory as outside of it. (The contingencies are external to the behaving organism and hence, strictly speaking, they do not include the behavior as such. They do include, however, some system upon which the behavior has an effect—the listener in the verbal case.)

These are all perfectly specifiable and replicable procedures. Out of systematic changes in rate brought about by systematic changes in the experimental operations emerges a view of behavior in terms of *processes* determined by environmental variables. (The joint operation of the experimental chamber and the cumulative recorder, which makes these processes visible, has been likened to the use of the microscope in biology.) Particularly important for our purposes is the possibility that the basic analysis affords us to interpret complex behavioral phenomena thus far considered inaccessible to direct treatment; the basic analysis allows us also to dispense with old concepts customarily assigned an ostensibly undemonstrated explanatory value. Among the general processes relevant to an extrapolation of basic findings to the

~ NOTES ~

verbal field are operant conditioning, extinction, forgetting, verbal memory, contingencies determining form, aversive control, motivation, and emotion. Some of these have, of course, been studied elsewhere, but a cogent formulation demands their reinterpretation in terms of changes in the strength of the behavior brought about by the interplay of well-known, specifiable variables.

It should be understood that, convenient though terms like 'motivation,' 'emotion,' or even 'learning' may be in bringing together possibly related groups of observations, we are in fact faced with specific contingencies—a much more useful and simple strategy than abiding by artificial boundaries sanctioned mainly by long-standing verbal habits. Traditionally, these terms have been assumed to mark distinct and separate fields, but their boundaries are often blurred. A science of behavior can only benefit from such a conceptual purge.

For a list of representative contingencies, see Skinner (1969, pp. 22-25); some basic contingencies in the verbal field are informally described as follows:

Mand: In the presence of a listener (S^D), the response *Water* is reinforced when the listener gives the speaker water.
Echoic behavior: When someone says *Water*, the speaker says *Water*, and reinforcement is contingent on the similarity of the two sounds.
Textual behavior: When looking at the printed word *Water*, the speaker is reinforced if he says *Water*.
Intraverbal behavior: Upon hearing or reading the word *Water*, the speaker is reinforced if he emits a thematically related response such as *Ice* or *Faucet*.
Tact: In the presence of a glass of water, a river, rain, and so on, the speaker is reinforced when he says *Water*.

An experimental analysis makes a clear distinction between behavior shaped and maintained by direct environmental contingencies and behavior dependent on instructions, what the subject has to say about the prevailing conditions (inside or outside the laboratory), and the like. Instructions, laws, rules, and so on often have an important place among the discriminative stimuli maximizing effective behavior. They must be understood, however, as the product of an analysis of relevant contingencies: they are statements about conditions and consequences and they are, therefore, different from those conditions and consequences themselves. So are the behaviors generated in either case. Laboratory research has made a direct analysis of the terms composing

~ NOTES TO CHAPTER 1 ~

such contingencies possible without a deceptive recourse to other dimensional systems (see, in particular, Skinner, 1969).

The special conditioning required for rule-following behavior is a particularly important point to keep in mind in any discussion of linguistic behavior, where "rules" enjoy an unusual prestige. Although we must assume speech to be as lawfully determined as the rest of behavioral repertoires, the assumption that the regularities commonly observed in most verbal activity are of a different, universally rule-determined sort, is clearly misleading and dangerous.

5. We are concerned here with the conditioning of verbal behavior. The available literature defies listing; the following general reviews provide, however, an entering wedge: Greenspoon, 1962; Holz and Azrin, 1966; Kanfer, 1968; Salzinger, 1959; Williams, 1964. Greenspoon and Brownstein, 1967, put the "problem" of awareness in proper perspective.

6. Whether ethology can provide anything but spurious support is worth considering. Its traditional emphasis on descriptive characterization, field study, and the appeal to models for investigating such problems as behavioral releasers, make ethology an especially convenient point of reference for psycholinguists committed to a view of language as species-specific behavior. But arguments along these lines are largely beside the point. It is customary to cite in this connection repeated failures to teach human language to members of other species. Premack's (1969, 1971) suggestion that the question "Can an organism other than a human acquire natural language?" should be rephrased as "What must an organism do in order to give evidence that it has language?" points at least in the right direction. It obviously entails a reconsideration of the status of natural languages.

Procedural similarities of a fairly general nature constitute a flimsy basis from which to gather support. Questions of ultimate relevance involve both a close examination of the more solid achievements of ethological theory and the real nature of the putative object of study of linguistic theory. Such achievements exist. Reporting on a conference designed to bring ethologists and experimental psychologists together, Schoenfeld and Baron (1965) write: "Ethological theory today is developing neurological and biochemical sectors of solid empirical character, in contrast with its earlier largely verbal and conceptual physiologizing about the bodily sources of behavior. This development was regarded by most conferees as encouraging, not only in itself but also because it may be a new basis for rapport between ethology and physiological psychology." Physiological psychology faces problems

~ NOTES ~

of its own, however, stemming primarily from a reluctance to base a "search for correlates" on a prior specification of well-established functional relations at the level of behavior (Skinner, 1938, and repeatedly after; cf., e.g., Schoenfeld, 1971). Much effort is bound to be wasted in a search for irrelevant conditions. The psychologist often finds himself trapped in a constellation of basically popular terms that he feels compelled to explain, frequently setting out to do so without further question. It goes without saying that all this applies to verbal behavior as well.

In an attempt to reconcile "the formal nature of language" with its "biological foundations," Lenneberg (1967) runs into difficulties. The underlying dogmatism (see, in particular, chs. 7, 8, and 9) stands in sharp contrast to the more reasonable introductory comment that "This book must be understood as a discussion rather than a presentation of the biological foundations of language. The exact foundations are still largely unknown" (p. viii). This being the case, how can he then go on to argue unreservedly for the innateness of some very specific modes of categorization and of actualization processes in language behavior? The contrived nature of the position can be clearly seen in one of the concluding paragraphs:

> The rules that underly syntax (which are the same for understanding and speaking) are of a very specific kind, and *unless man or mechanical devices do their processing of incoming sentences in accordance with these rules, the logical, formal analysis of the input will be deficient,* resulting in incorrect or random responses. When we say rules must have been built into the grammatical analyzer, we impute the existence of an apparatus with specific structural properties or, in other words, a specific internal organization. (p. 393, emphasis added)

In view of such a strong commitment to a prior logical and formal descriptive apparatus, the "evidence" brought to bear becomes suspect despite its bulk. Indeed, it is reminiscent of the "earlier largely verbal and conceptual physiologizing" mentioned by Schoenfeld and Baron.

7. Some leading statements from Skinner's *Verbal Behavior* are relevant. They bear on the overall scope of the formulation as well as the treatment accorded to some basic issues in any study of speech, namely, the notion of response class, its relation to specific instances, and the place of meaning. The concept of repertoire and the related notion of relative strength conveniently bring them all together and

~ NOTES TO CHAPTER 1 ~

point up the dynamic nature of the subject matter. The different roles of speaker and listener are brought into focus.

> The "understanding" of verbal behavior is something more than the use of a consistent vocabulary with which specific instances may be described. It is not to be confused with the confirmation of any set of theoretical principles. The criteria are more exacting than that. The extent to which we understand verbal behavior in a "causal" analysis is to be assessed from the extent to which we can predict the occurrence of specific instances and, eventually, from the extent to which we can produce or control such behavior by altering the conditions under which it occurs. (p. 3)

> For most purposes "operant" is interchangeable with the traditional "response," but the terms permit us to make the distinction between an *instance* of behavior ("So-and-so smoked a cigarette between 2:00 and 2:10 P.M. yesterday") and a *kind* of behavior ("Cigarette smoking"). . . . Although we observe only instances, we are concerned with laws which specify kinds. (p. 20)

> The distinction raises the issue of formalism. A response, as an instance, can be completely described as a form of behavior. An operant specifies at least one relation to a variable—the effect which the behavior characteristically, though perhaps not inevitably, has upon the environment—and is therefore not a purely formal unit. (pp. 20-21)

> What is needed for present purposes—and what the traditional "word" occasionally approximates–is a unit of behavior composed of a response of identifiable form functionally related to one or more independent variables. In traditional terms we might say that we need a unit of behavior defined in terms of both "form and meaning." (p. 20)

> meaning is not a property of behavior as such but of the conditions under which behavior occurs. Technically, meanings are to be found among the independent variables in a functional account, rather than as properties of the dependent variable. (pp. 13-14)

> We observe that a speaker possesses a *verbal repertoire* in the sense that responses of various forms appear in his behavior from time to time in relation to identifiable conditions. A repertoire, as a collection of verbal operants, describes the *potential* behavior of a speaker. To ask where a verbal operant is when a response is not in the course of being emitted is like asking where one's

~ NOTES ~

knee-jerk is when the physician is not tapping the patellar tendon. (p. 21)

Every verbal operant may be conceived of as having under specified circumstances an assignable probability of emission—conveniently called its "strength." We base the notion of strength upon several kinds of evidence. (p. 22)

We need separate but interlocking accounts of the behaviors of both speaker and listener if our explanation of verbal behavior is to be complete. In explaining the behavior of the speaker we assume a listener who will reinforce his behavior in certain ways. In accounting for the behavior of the listener we assume a speaker whose behavior bears a certain relation to environmental conditions thus assumed. The account of the whole episode is then complete. (p. 34)

The full scope of the proposal is summarized on pages 10-11 of *Verbal Behavior*. For a convenient summary statement, see Keller and Schoenfeld (1950) and MacCorquodale (1969); a systematic exposition can be found in Winokur (1976).

8. The behavior stream can only be "broken up" in nonarbitrary ways through appeal to the independent variables of which it is a function, notably its effects upon the environment. Once we do this, an operant class is defined and the notion of probability—meaningless in an analysis of isolated instances—becomes directly relevant.

One of the most important contributions of the experimental analysis of behavior has been the demonstration that, although topographical properties are necessarily lawful and thus amenable to scientific analysis, they are not central to the formulation. Failure to observe this fundamental principle leads to such embarrassing blind alleys as lumping together different instances of behavior on the grounds of their formal similarity alone or, conversely, of considering two or more formally different responses as unrelated when they are actually a function of the same variables.

This raises difficulties for the formalist who, by training, seeks *permanent and universal solutions easily integrated into an overall theoretical structure*. Witness, e.g., Chomsky's (1959) criticism: "Skinner recognizes the fundamental character of the problem of identification of a unit of verbal behavior, but is satisfied with an answer so vague and subjective that it does not really contribute to its solution. The unit of verbal behavior—the verbal operant—is defined as a class of responses of identifiable form functionally related to one or more controlling variables. No method is suggested for determining in a particular instance what are the controlling variables, how many such units have occurred, or where their boundaries are in the total response. Nor is any attempt made to specify how much or what kind of similarity in form or *control* is required for two physical events to be considered instances of the same operant." These are all, of course, empirical questions concerning the behavior of individual speakers at different times. The dynamic and topographical properties of repertoires change as an organism's behavioral history builds up. Insistence on a priori specification of the degree of similarity of form or control for membership of specific instances in the same operant class is to have missed the point of a functional approach altogether. It betrays a preoccupation with classification that is entirely alien, as formulated, to the spirit of a functional analysis. The theoretician's charge of vagueness and subjectivity regarding the definition must be judged in this same light (Julià, 1968a, 1975).

One possible objection to Chomsky's charge of insufficiency is the simple recall that extensive research with nonverbal repertoires has been successfully carried out for several decades—where no such considerations seemed to be of much consequence. Should they be considered so fundamental in verbal behavior?

Notes to Chapter 2

1. When we set out to study behavior we naturally respond first to its form or topography. There is in this something of a carry-over from our preprofessional days. We may then be tempted to explain this aspect of our data in its own terms. In the case of language we are led to a conception of the subject matter as a variety of self-contained systems of forms (the so-called languages), independent, as it were, of speakers, listeners, and their common environments.

De Saussure's characterization epitomizes this attitude. Concentration on segments of the *significant* leads to reasonably tight formal descriptions—the outcome being essentially a taxonomy of supposedly relevant types of elements. These are supplemented, at best, with rules describing their permissible combinations and thus adding a kind of predictive power to the description. But then, of course, there still remains the *signifié* to be accounted for. The multiplicity of the problems involved is matched only by their antiquity. The full range of its subtlety and complexity is all but irreducible in the light of available formal devices. Formalism entails dualism.

~ NOTES ~

2. A. P. Weiss is usually mentioned in this connection. Bloomfield's explicit adherence to mentalistic psychology (Wundtian variety) in his earlier book, *An Introduction to the Study of Language* (1914) is of more than just historical interest.

3. Kantor (1975, 1977) has recently reminded students of language of a variety of misconceptions that stand in the way of a naturalistic approach to the subject matter. He classifies them into three generic classes: the first of these he calls the "philological or textual tradition"; there is then a "mind-body tradition," which interprets language as "the expression of mental states by means of verbal utterances"; finally, a third class rejects mentalism but "reduces speech to verbal utterances on the model of physiological reflexes."

The philological tradition is particularly relevant in the present context. Steeped in old textual and literary practices, it construes language as made up of words. This view was especially enhanced by a transition period of historical and comparative studies. But words are the product of largely arbitrary efforts to leave a more or less permanent mark of an initial and genuine verbal response. Words are things; consequently language becomes a thing, too—a view that is thoroughly out of sorts with the behavioral nature of linguistic facts. Among other things, it disregards a great deal of the actual activity of human beings acting as speakers and listeners.

Kantor contrasts this vastly circumscribed point of view with his own treatment in terms of "interbehavioral fields," notably what he terms "speaking adjustments" and "symbolizing interbehavior." Kantor's efforts to dispel lingering "spooks" come at a much needed time: despite a conscious shift of emphasis toward spoken language, linguistic research during the last sixty years has not managed to extricate itself from the influence of the textual tradition. Spooks have continued to proliferate, reaching an unexpected peak during the last two decades.

Experts bound to think otherwise will do well to expose themselves to Kantor's brisk argument. His comprehensive survey of typological language functions can only prove salutary, whatever the ultimate form of behavioral treatment espoused (for an earlier indictment, see Kantor, 1936). It goes without saying that the present criticism is in fundamental agreement with Kantor's rejection of both mentalism and any form of physiological reductionism.

4. The notions of language as an abstraction, system, and structure are intimately related. They are all forced by the linguist's commitment to an analysis of speech phenomena in terms of topography alone. As

~ NOTES TO CHAPTER 2 ~

it is, linguistics (with the qualified exception of articulatory phonetics) does not even deal with actual responses but with their traces, graphic or acoustic.

Structuralism constitutes the culmination of the traditional practice of studying products of the behavior rather than the behavior itself. Early structural linguistics owes much of its development to the industrious experimentation with descriptive techniques on data gathered in (largely artificial) field work exercises. When put up for analysis, however, these data—usually in the medium of tape recordings—turn out to be nothing but mere records of the original response. (Direct phonetic transcription involves a different process, which comes to the same end.) The linguist's raw data are at least two steps removed from actual speech events in all their functional complexity. The heavy emphasis on analysis of unknown (and sometimes preferably remote) languages is more than symptomatic. More recent trends favor again written samples, usually (and more reasonably) from languages well known to the analyst. This procedural reversal is probably less explicit than it perhaps ought to be in view of simultaneous claims as to the nature of language. Indeed, only a minority of experts openly and systematically speak of "texts" as the immediate object of their grammatical studies.

It should not, therefore, be surprising if, when language is taken as a system of forms, descriptive efforts are often reminiscent of endless puzzle-solving exercises. The results are judged in terms of whether or not they comply with given preestablished criteria, themselves formally defined. Whether additional linguistic forms can be easily dissected in terms of previously isolated classes and formulated rules is, of course, another source of confirmation. But the predictive power derived from such rules is of an extremely limited sort: it constitutes a form of prediction of behavior from behavior alone.

There is an underlying, more or less implicit assumption: traditionally, language has not properly been thought of as a form of behavior and, when it is, it is generally believed to be behavior of a different kind, i.e., not a function of the same variables as the rest of human repertoires. The vast majority of psycholinguists, and a surprising number of psychologists, share the linguist's view of language as a series of entities which can somehow be tracked down and described independently of the variables that give rise to them. The title of publications like *Language and Language Behavior Abstracts* is telling enough; such periodicals as the *Journal of Verbal Learning and Verbal*

~ NOTES ~

Behavior make matters even more explicit. Psychologists have not wholly exorcised the spell of deep-rooted, comfortable descriptive and explanatory fictions. The plain fact is that a long tradition and the consequent wealth of conceptual systems blocks the way to any attempt to look at verbal behavior simply as behavior that is verbal.

5. The implication is, of course, that certain features are somehow secondary. Intonation is a good case in point. Even as sober a writer as Bolinger can call an interesting article on it "Around the edge of language: Intonation" (Bolinger, 1964).

The notion that linguists zero in on topography or, rather, its traces, needs further qualification yet. Prosodic features are part and parcel of the response, not something to be taken into account in order to "complete," reluctantly as it were, the description of the segmental phonemes on which the higher levels of morphology and syntax rest— hence Hockett's *when* clause. (Subsequent level-mixing developments whereby grammatical analysis takes place "from the top down" have not done much to change the priorities in any fundamental ways, either.)

The way had been paved by the preliminary development of systems of phonetic transcription. Although structural linguistics emphasized the spoken rather than written language, the influence of the textual tradition has made itself felt even in such areas as phonetics. Many of its more obvious culs-de-sac can indeed be traced to the inherent biases of early transcriptive work.

6. The reader may want to check Koutsoudas' (1963) searching paper about the morpheme, where both IA and IP come again under close scrutiny. Among other things, the role of rules in IP receives a more pointed attention. Writing from the standpoint of TGG, Koutsoudas naturally favors IP and takes the notion of model for granted. He is also unaware of other inherent dangers in structure-centered analysis at large.

It may not be altogether irrelevant to cite Koutsoudas' conclusion:

> the definition as it now stands results in a concept which is unjustifiably independent from syntax. Since the morpheme eventually is to be used as a tool for syntactic analysis (i.e., traditionally it is the basic unit of grammar and without it a syntactic analysis cannot be carried out), then why attribute morphemic status to units which may prove to be irrelevant to syntactic analysis. In other words, why not let the syntactic analysis determine the morphemes of the language under consideration?

~ NOTES TO CHAPTER 2 ~

A redefinition is then significantly phrased as "that unit of grammar the arrangement of which is specified by the syntax and the resulting sequences of which are used to predict the physical form of utterances."

7. See, however, Harris (1976). Following a long line of research dating back to 1952 (the notion of transformation grew out of it), Harris continues to refine techniques aimed at bringing out structural relations that will not betray "semantic reality." Subtlety has undeniably been gained through the years, and "a view of language" emerges at this point.

The basic contention is that "language is related to meaning distinctions in its basic structure, but at the same time is not committed to any particular set of meanings or view of meaning." Harris concludes that "we need not appeal to a structure existing independently of language or prior to language." There are two reasons for this, one negative and one positive: the first is that there is no way of demonstrating its existence; the second is that the structure of language, when properly handled, reveals closely enough "the conditions of language" to render the search for such an independent structure superfluous.

It would seem that with such precautions any form of ontological commitment would be avoided and, one might expect, all varieties of dualism as well. But a structural treatment affords at best a half-way success. Thus, when we inquire into the resulting view of language, we find that "language turns out to be an instrument for transmission, and, in the light of the present theory, one might say in the first place transmission of information." What is more, language ("the set of sentences") is unbounded, while speakers are finite beings; therefore, its characterization, grammar, must also be finite. This is reminiscent of arguments to set up "explanatory models." Sentencehood constitutes a central concern.

Language continues to stand alone. What is more, it consists of sentences, i.e., combinations of words; words are made up of discrete objects, phonemes. The creation of discrete elements (forced by "transmission conditions") sets language apart as a special object. It is not 0.25like other behaviors. But then we are still entitled to ask what the origin of the transmitted information is, why and how it comes to be transmitted, and what its fate is once it has reached the listener or, perhaps more a propos here, the "receiver."

There appears to be an insurmountable gap between concern with theory and the more modest goal of improving descriptive methods, which need not be necessarily *ad hoc*.

~ NOTES ~

NOTES TO CHAPTER 3

1. The present conception of grammar postulates that speakers and listeners can produce and understand an infinite number of grammatical sentences. These sentences (and many more) presumably make up the sum total of the language; they are what the grammar generates. But is the relation between the two sets so clear? This is an empirical question, not a theoretical one. Examples brought to bear on infinity and the related concept of grammaticalness generally share the same artificial character.

The argument for infinity runs as follows: it is impossible to assign a limit to the number of acceptable word combinations in a language; therefore, the number of grammatical sentences must be infinite. The argument is then usually framed in terms of length of the sentences themselves: since we cannot give an upper bound for sentence length, it is concluded that perfectly grammatical sentences can be expanded indefinitely (e.g., through such devices as conjunction, embedding, the insertion of constructions like "I know that . . . ," "You believe that . . . ," and so on). Grammar must then be constructed to account for this fact. As one linguist has put it, "It is always a few rules reapplicable indefinitely that make natural languages infinite" (Gross, 1972).

There is a difference, however, between a strictly theoretical formulation of what *could* be in a language (conceived as an object) and the actual behavior of speakers and listeners. It is to them that the linguist must turn for empirical support—at least as long as claims of explanatory power are made. No one believes, of course, that one can expand a sentence indefinitely and still come up with another sentence that an ordinary native listener will consider good English. The natural consequence of including even a moderate example of such a sentence (say, those mentioned in 4.3) in a text intended for publication is to have the text rejected as insufficiently edited (except when the sentence is offered as an example in a discussion on grammatical theory). Presumably the expression 'practical limitations,' often encountered in connection with discussions on infinity, is meant to cover this disparity between theory and the realities of everyday speech and writing. The concept of sentence, thus formally defined, becomes itself suspect. It is in the nature of behavioral repertoires that they expand in response to changing circumstances, but it is also in the nature of the dynamics of behavior that this expansion take place in terms of well-established patterns and relations. And these are not what the generative grammarian suggests.

~ NOTES TO CHAPTER 3 ~

In point of fact, presented with numberless well-formed and *real* English sentences, all the average listener can probably say is that they are English (though the not infrequent remark, "This is Greek to me," is symptomatic). Verbal communities are defined by commonality of practices. Environmental contingencies determine the various speech varieties within which people usually operate and account for the formation of horizontal and vertical dialects and (sub)languages. (The relevant variables are the sort of thing to interest the empirical sociolinguist.) The notion of intelligibility or, more precisely, effectiveness comes to the fore: speakers speak for their effects on their listeners, who must at least partially share their verbal history. Common classificatory criteria generally zero in on formal cues, but thematic differences are at least equally important. E.g., the switch to a different "universe of discourse" requires the concurrence of effective contingencies somewhere along the line (as in entering a new field, learning a new trade, changing social classes, etc.). We are inevitably back among the independent variables.

Finally, the claim that the theoretical grammarian's task is somehow related to the child's process of language acquisition relies heavily also on this false notion of infinity. At the core is the postulated relation between the set of observed sentences and the set of grammatical sentences, based on the assumption that a natural language is a well-defined system valid for "all its speakers." Recourse to nativist explanatory schemes should not be surprising. There is little justification for such an analogy: the conditions governing each kind of performance are not even remotely the same; therefore, neither are the resulting behaviors.

A conception of grammar as a device that generates all and only the grammatical sentences of a language is an elegant construct. The TG proposal amounts to an attempt to import into linguistics such commonplace concepts in logic as formation rules, well-formedness, and so on; it adapts, in the process, Harris' notion of transformation. But a treatment of infinity, e.g., on the pattern of the formal sciences, makes the strong assumption that natural languages *can* be effectively described in primarily formal terms. The fundamental problem lies in a view of language as made up of things—say, words that are put together to form sentences or pulled apart in order to understand them. The notion of a single description for a language epitomizes the textual tradition. (We return to the concept of infinity in chapter 6; see also note 5, chapter 5.)

2. Much of what has been said about infinity applies to grammat-

icalness as well. The pseudoproblem of grammaticalness is bound to remain a merely theoretical issue. People do make mistakes, but a division of utterances into perfectly grammatical and perfectly ungrammatical sentences is an oversimplification and the assignment of degrees to intermediate cases, as suggested some fifteen or twenty years ago, is bound to prove an impossible task. (A more sober treatment casts the issue in terms of partial ordering.) At any rate, the technical interest in the problem seems to have dwindled and for good reason. It is now generally taken for granted that the job of grammar is to specify the well-formed sentences of a language.

In actual practice well-formedness is a fuzzy issue, as anyone will agree who is ready to face real verbal data rather than the typical cases usually employed in technical discussions. Examples are frequently farfetched and artificial and rarely reflect the sorts of deviations found in actual verbal performance: such favorite polar examples as "John ate a sandwich" vs. "Sandwich a ate John" are possible only under a conception of language as made up of discrete independent parts, say, words.

As we have seen, the operational tests proposed involve such observations as the correct intonation with which grammatical sentences will be read and the ease with which they will be remembered in contrast with their ungrammatical counterparts. Ungrammatical sentences, and nonsense examples frequently put forth in discussions on grammaticalness, are usually described as "sequences of unrelated words." Questions about their relevance immediately come up. Linguists and psycholinguists concerned with the description of real verbal behavior are likely to ask, "What does the notion of related words suggest?" and "Why should some words be usually related and not others?" (Indeed, they are likely to realize that if they say "Sandwich a ate John" often enough as an example, they end up uttering it with virtually normal intonation; also, many a native speaker falters after "green" or "ideas" in "colorless green ideas sleep furiously" the first time around.) Familiarity of co-occurrence provides the answer: it suggests behavioral processes at work. In everyday speech "words" do not occur together by chance, but for sound functional reasons. Such facts as contiguity of use, intraverbal linkages, and the like, ultimately explain why certain patterns "feel right," "make sense," are quickly responded to and remembered, and so on. If anything, this is what grammaticalness is all about.

In recent years much has been made of the native speaker-listener's intuition, in keeping with efforts to construct grammars describing

~ NOTES TO CHAPTER 3 ~

idealized underlying patterns. His linguistic sensitivity has been overemphasized, however, and his role has been vitiated by the extreme formalistic argument in relation to which he is generally referred to. Where the truly naive native listener is concerned, the really important thing is whether the speaker's (or the linguist's) verbal responses "say something." In the absence of grossly distorted phonological features, it does not make much difference whether ideas are "colorless green" or "green colorless." If asked about less than fully clear examples taken from everyday speech, the more sophisticated listener may reply "Oh, it depends on the circumstances!"; of a foreigner with a full command of the grammar he may well say something like, "Yes, he makes himself understood but he says things I wouldn't quite put that way"; he may come up with a similar remark about a native's expression which "doesn't sound quite right." (The fully ungrammatical and many of the relatively ungrammatical examples brought up by the linguist rarely, if ever, occur outside the community of linguists.) Unlike some students of language, the ordinary listener-speaker has little use for nonsense: he is bound to dismiss it or, if patient enough, he may give it a second chance. (He may prove more patient if he is getting paid for acting as an S in an experiment on grammaticalness.)

As formulated, the notion of "grammatical sentence" becomes suspect. At issue are the units of analysis taken into account: utterances are not necessarily sentences, and, at any rate, they are effective or ineffective. As MacCorquodale has pointed out, we usually expect a listener to understand rather than pass judgment. (See also note 4, chapter 5, and note 8, chapter 6.)

3. The assignment of different readings to ambiguous sentences emerges as one of the principle functions of grammatical analysis. But the TG-grammarian proceeds to elaborate techniques on the strength of isolated textual cases. This is by no means the only available alternative. The real question is whether the analytical measures proposed are relevant to real cases of ambiguity where everyday language, spoken or written, is concerned—in other words, whether formal analysis will do even as a basis.

In his recent effort to reconcile formal and empirical studies, Catania (1973) provides a relevant discussion:

> The written sentence "Dropping bombs can be dangerous" has one of two structures, depending on whether the speaker is concerned with the people in the air or those on the ground. . . . But the structural account cannot help us to choose between the two structures. The choice must be based on functional considerations:

~ NOTES ~

the conditions under which the sentence is generated. But say instead that the words are spoken. Now the two sentences can be distinguished by different patterns of stress. Once both phonological and grammatical analyses are available, an account can be given of the relation between the two types of structure. The problem is not surmounted, however; even at this point the structural account cannot tell us about the circumstances under which a sentence with one or the other structure will be uttered. That issue is again functional.

In developing analytical techniques, the linguist brings to bear his full active repertoire as a reader-listener and, to that extent, as a speaker. Whether he likes to admit it or not, he necessarily falls back on the independent variables of which responses are a function, as Catania's example (restricted to an isolated sentence though it is) makes all too clear: in this case, through appeal to the stimulus control of the sentence.

It might be pointed out that the notion of "context," often invoked in this connection, is too vague to suggest useful lines of investigation. (We come back to the problem of ambiguity below.)

4. Linguists performing the analysis of a verbal system are listeners or readers of a very special sort. They respond to traces of verbal responses and assign structure to them. They are likely to make the unwarranted assumption, however, that their descriptive statements and, more generally, their analytical categories at large, are relevant to the activity of speaker and listener alike. The construction of formal models does little to dispel such assumptions; in fact, it only strengthens them. Verbal behavior is reified as L. Much confusion ensues.

Discussing, significantly enough, the problem of the unit of analysis, Sapon (1971) offers some very pertinent remarks. The basic issue is one of "parts" as opposed to "processes." Sapon points out that linguistics runs into difficulties because it relies primarily upon the speaker as the only source of data, which "leaves us in the odd position of describing, analyzing and predicting the performance of agents in a communication system on the basis of the *formal* properties of *one half of the system.*"

It is the speaker who provides the raw data to be subjected to fragmentation. Linguistic analysis centers on the determination of discrete parts and their interrelations. The listener in this analytical scheme is, at best, a hypothetical character called upon for judgments of grammaticalness, the existence of minimal pairs, and the like. But this scarcely corresponds to the actual activity of the ordinary listener, whose behavior (verbal and nonverbal) ultimately accounts for the existence of speakers. As Sapon points out,

> The performance of the listener . . . *qua* listener does *not* present to the observer the kinds of performance that can be fragmented according to the analytical scheme applied to the performance of the speaker. *The listener who displays his "understanding" by following my directions to* "Bring me the third book from the left on the top shelf" *certainly does not display any "parts" of a sentence*. He does display a good deal of movement, but none of this movement is transcribable in linguistic terms. It is only when he begins to talk that the listener acquires linguistic reality and existence.

Much of the behavior of the listener is of the sort described by Sapon; a good deal of it, however, is verbal, and then the listener's active repertoire as a speaker must also be taken into account. Indeed, some of the more interesting aspects of the process of "understanding" demand this kind of analysis. Verbal humor provides a particularly revealing reference: how else do we account for the listener who gets or misses the point of a pun, joke, etc.? But even here the two behaviors have to be studied for what they are—each in terms of its determining variables. Investigation into the "use of language" requires a far closer scrutiny of the characteristic behaviors of speaker and listener, neither of which can be studied in isolation. (The relevant processes in understanding are also fundamental to the student of speech perception.)

Notes to Chapter 4

1. This was Chomsky's contribution to the "Symposium on Models in Linguistics" held under the auspices of the 1960 Congress of Logic, Methodology, and Philosophy of Science (Nagel et al., eds., 1962). A far from casual interest in models had been building up for some time. There had been at least one collective precedent: a "Symposium on Operational Models in Synchronic Linguistics" had taken place in 1958 (cf. the first issue of *Anthropological Linguistics*). But Chomsky's proposal added an entirely new dimension to the problems on hand. In Chao's phrasing, "The importance of a transformational model is that it not only is powerful for analysis but also functions as an explanatory theory of grammar." The question is, of course, whether this is so. Serious methodological considerations are at issue.

It *is* common knowledge that the concept of "model" is by no means

~ NOTES ~

clear among experts. Discussions inevitably center on the relation between models and the things modeled. After an interesting survey of the use of the term by linguists and some nonlinguists, Chao (1962) comments: "We see here that things synonymous with the same thing are not always synonymous with each other, and that sometimes the same thing is not synonymous with itself." This synthesis by one of the 1960 participants should be telling enough; it is also indicative of the greater variety extant in the literature on models at large.

A basic distinction is usually drawn between models in the formal sciences, where their function is to realize or interpret some formal axiomatic system, and models as representations of some physical process. Here methodological considerations are framed in terms of degrees and manner of similarity, concreteness, abstractness, or their plain metaphorical nature. Terms like 'iconic,' 'analogic,' 'theoretical,' and so on are common in this connection.

As Chao points out, "The term 'model' in linguistics is mainly modeled after models in mathematics." But then he proceeds to cite Hiż's pertinent observation that "the usage among mathematicians seems to be almost the exact opposite of that of the social sciences, if linguistics is called a social science. In mathematics a model is more concrete than what it is a model of, while in the social sciences a model is more of an abstraction" (oral communication). This should not be surprising. The confusion is quickly dispelled once the notion of "social science" is clarified. A proper treatment points to the behavioral nature of the phenomena under description, i.e., the contingencies that account for the interaction of organisms with one another and with a common environment. Verbal behavior must be reckoned a subdivision of social behavior and therefore a natural process.

The risks involved in model-building based on standard abstractions are immediately apparent. A characterization of language on the mathematical model pattern may afford formal elegance and concreteness, but it is bound to do even greater violence to the subject as a natural phenomenon. It should not be difficult to see why. As Chao puts it, "In linguistics . . . one does not deal with tokens . . . but primarily with types, and so there is that much abstraction to start with already. A model for any phase of linguistics is at least of that degree of abstraction." Questions arise about the origin of these types. Among the dangers involved are a hypostatization of entities and ultimately a reification of *traces* of verbal behavior into L.

The reader is invited to examine Chao's carefully constructed list of synonyms and nonsynonyms for 'model.' It is interesting to note, in

~ NOTES TO CHAPTER 4 ~

particular, the three different senses he registers of Chomsky's use of the term prior to 1960. These are: (1) "a conception of linguistic structure (to provide a grammar that generates all and only the sentences of English)," (2) "a grammar," and (3) "a theory."

2. Hiż has repeatedly argued against this sentence atomism on the grounds that the linguistic context within which a sentence is embedded can alter our interpretation of the sentence. In his review of Chomsky (1965), he writes:

> To the present reviewer this sentence atomism does not seem justifiable. A two-sentence text often is a paraphrase of a one-sentence text, and this fact often is directly relevant to the structure of the three sentences involved. And there is still the most important linguistic problem: how does it happen that an ambiguous sentence ceases to be ambiguous when placed in the context of other sentences? How do these other sentences contribute to the elimination or diminution of ambiguity? (Hiż, 1967.)

Taking Chomsky's broader epistemological and psychological claims into account, Hiż concludes that "it should be easier to explain why we assign such-and-such a structure to a sentence by pointing out how this sentence changes the readings of neighboring sentences than by referring to innate universal ideas and mental reality." For a more technical discussion, see Hiż (1968), where he actually stretches the point and convincingly points out that a plurality of structural interpretations proves useful even where there is no question of ambiguity in the usual sense.

3. In an interesting discussion of the range and problems of mathematical linguistics, Plath (1961) appropriately warns:

> If language models are considered as abstract systems of discrete elements, a variety of mathematical concepts and techniques, ranging from elementary ideas of number to complex logical, statistical and set-theoretical operations, may be applied to them. However, the idea that the mere attachment of numbers or mathematical operations to the elements of a system makes statements expressed in terms of the system either more "exact" or "scientific" is completely erroneous. What has to be demonstrated is that the new system so obtained is in some sense a more satisfactory model than the original system, either in that it makes possible the formulation of simpler or more general theoretical statements about certain aspects of the modelled domain or in that operations on the model give new insights into the results of corresponding

operations in the modelled domain. One of the greatest dangers involved in the construction of mathematical models of language, particularly quantitative ones, is that indiscriminate introduction of mathematical apparatus inevitably leads to the generation of meaningless and misleading results. It should therefore be clear that the prerequisites for significant contributions to linguistics from this quarter include not only knowledge of the pertinent branches of mathematics, but, in addition, a thorough comprehension of the nature of the linguistic problems to which the mathematical methods are to be applied.

In a related footnote, he writes: "Chomsky (1957) has emphasized the importance of criteria of this type in connection with the evaluation of the relative merits of various types of grammars."

Plath aptly classifies linguistic models into "statistical" and "structural." The former, based primarily on data obtained from counts (hence also called "quantitative") have sometimes proved useful in such studies as the overall regularities in vocabulary distribution, whether in individual languages or authors, and measures of degree of genetic kinship between natural languages—generically labeled "large scale language phenomena." More directly relevant to the present discussion, he writes: "Much of modern linguistics is concerned with the construction of models which represent languages in terms of the possible structural configurations and interrelations of elements defined on a number of different levels (phonology, morphology, syntax)." The two types need not be entirely unrelated.

At any rate, the practicability of models depends on their being "abstract systems of discrete elements" in some sense isomorphic, one must assume, with the modeled languages—which are then construed as *things*. There is, however, no behavioral evidence to support such a view. It is extremely doubtful whether constructions emphasizing structural configurations and interrelations of predefined elements can capture the nature of verbal repertoires. It may well be the case that some of the active features of verbal performance can best be accounted for by techniques of an essentially statistical nature. It does not follow, however, that these must conform to the model pattern or, for that matter, that they have anything to do with their application to the study of large-scale language phenomena.

While we can only agree about the futility involved in the "mere attachment of numbers or mathematical operations to the elements of a system," we must take exception to Plath's statement that risks are greater where quantitative properties are concerned. In fact, one could

~ NOTES TO CHAPTER 4 ~

argue to the contrary: structural models are by their very nature the more likely to generate "meaningless and misleading results" in view of their inherent arbitrariness. Indeed, there may be no such thing as a "system" to be modeled at all. It may well be that linguistics has not reached that stage of "thorough comprehension" of its real problems which is a "prerequisite for significant contributions." Until that time comes, any introduction of mathematical apparatus is bound to prove more or less "indiscriminate," and the construction of models (structural or statistical) likely to remain a hazardous endeavor, contemporary claims to the contrary notwithstanding.

4. Militating against any such view is the considerable latitude revealed by any unprejudiced look at developmental data, particularly when an element of genetic homogeneity is implied. There is no need to expatiate. Sapon (1965) brings the principal facts together as follows:

> A child . . . in the absence of incapacitating abnormality, has at least the potential for producing the human speech sounds under whose control he is likely to come, and there is obviously also the potential of acquiring a repertoire of controlling language. I speak in so guarded a fashion about *potentials* because I want to avoid the snare of assuming the inevitability of productive language, or of looking on it as a natural, maturational process. It is true that the potential is realized in almost all children, but the variability of performance level, *age of inception, and rate of progress is so* great that many aspects of normative development data are vague beyond value. Two examples of this can be seen in "size of vocabulary," variously reported as ranging, at age two, from two words to two thousand, and in the summary statement given by McCarthy, "a basic mastery of spoken language is normally acquired very rapidly . . . usually between the ages of one and five years."

(See also note 6 below.)

5. The differences between the corresponding repertoires have long been recognized, as indicated by distinctions such as "active" vs. "passive" or "productive" vs. "receptive" language. After a careful exploration of different modes of "communication" in a very specific setting, Sapon (1965) proposes a useful redefinition of these terms in perfect accord with the definition of verbal behavior given in note 3, chapter 1:

> A promising way of looking at these behaviors and their function is in terms of "control." . . . An individual can be said to dem-

~ NOTES ~

onstrate receptive language, or to understand, when his behavior can be shown to be under the control of another's . . . verbal output. "Understanding," then, is the evidence of verbally *controlled* behavior. Productive language, or "speaking" can be looked upon as evidence of an individual's attempts to control his environment through his own verbal output. Speaking is seen, then, as *controlling* behavior.

The reader will do well to examine Sapon's description of "speaking" and "understanding" behaviors in all its unprejudiced scope.

6. Sapon (1965) has discussed the fallacy of considering speaking and understanding as two sides of the same coin, or two manifestations of the same system, in the context of language development as follows:

> When two repertoires normally co-exist it is inevitable that they come to be considered parts of one complex repertoire, and thus conversely, when one repertoire exists without the other, that it be looked upon as an abnormal situation. . . . Yet there is agreement that in the normal developmental process "understanding" precedes "speaking," presenting thus a transitory phase in which normal children "understand without speaking." Even on into adult years there is a commonly observed disparity of levels of performance between the two behaviors, with receptive language showing a marked lead over productive language in most individuals as seen, for example, in measurements of "active" versus "passive" vocabulary.

Yet these differences extend far beyond the limits imposed by static orthographic criteria steeped in a view of language as made up of inanimate word objects amenable to structural analysis, a fact that any description (call it "theory," if you will) will have to take into account to be considered adequate.

The speaker's behavior can be more or less effective, and though by no means irrelevant, it would be difficult to argue that in such a gradation grammaticalness plays the major role; correspondingly, a proper analysis of "degrees of understanding" obviously goes beyond mere lexical and structural characterization and brings to the fore some of the most interesting aspects of the dynamic nature of verbal activity or performance (see note 4, chapter 3).

7. For a classic discussion about the relation between perception and behavior, see Schoenfeld and Cumming (1963).

8. This kind of steadfast adherence to a preliminary theory has sometimes led writers, in their enthusiasm, to take positions which

~ NOTES TO CHAPTER 4 ~

can scarcely be said to find room within the established canons of empirical science (see note 4, chapter 3; also, Julià, 1980b). Thus Saporta (1965) writes:

> If one adopts the view that such notions [say, the initial descriptive categories] constitute terms in an overall theory of considerable abstraction, it is difficult to know how one would go about asking for behavioral correlates for a given part of such a theory, in any way that could be said to constitute a crucial test. . . . If a test designed to demonstrate behavioral correlates fails to yield the predicted results, one feels obligated to modify the test, not the theory.

9. The temptation, occasionally detected, to theorize about behavioral findings in cybernetic terms should be resisted. The "functional units" of the cyberneticist rarely correspond to those discovered in the course of an experimental analysis. Feedback is not necessarily reinforcement and, by and large, the true nature of the contingencies is obscured. Functionalistic diagrams become superfluous.

10. The often invoked notion of "internalization of rules" must be deemed little more than a figure of speech. Under the terms of the formulation, the rules are already there, as are the substantive universals (see chapter 5) presumably brought into play. It is simply a matter of human biological endowment.

Language acquisition is assumed to be a matter of letting the internal mechanisms draw up hypotheses about the "incoming data." Success in coming up with the right grammar is guaranteed, however: these internal operators function in accordance with the general theory of linguistic structure, which is based on the prior characterization of outputs. The fact that everywhere people learn to speak is taken as ample (empirical) proof of the correctness of the position; all languages are constructed on the same generative pattern. The theoretician can then confidently turn the black box into LAD, a pun on the language acquisition device. Learning to speak and understand is reduced to letting developmental processes make the best of these innate dispositions, or vice versa. One important drawback of the position is that nothing of substance is thereby added to these developmental processes or, for that matter, the presumed innate dispositions—which, as formulated, stand outside the scope of empirical reach anyway. (As Skinner, 1969, p. 124, has pointed out, "To say that 'the child who learns a language has in some sense constructed the grammar for himself' is as misleading as to say that a dog which has learned to catch a ball has in some sense constructed the relevant parts of the science of mechanics." See also Quine's [1970] distinction between "fitting" and "guiding" rules.)

There are different, though, in the last analysis, negligible, degrees of orthodoxy among psycholinguists of the content persuasion: where Katz (1964 and repeatedly after) neglects learning in any behavioral sense altogether, McNeill (1970), e.g., would make some allowances. A more reasonable view can be found, e.g. in Schlesinger (1971). (For a record of growing dissatisfaction with the position, cf., e.g., various contributions in Aaronson and Rieber, 1980.)

The only available evidence is the fact that the child's verbal behavior (like its nonverbal counterparts) comes progressively to conform to the standards of the community into which it happens to be born. It is hardly necessary to point out that this obviously implies a great deal more than the production of acceptable utterances.

It may not be out of place to observe that a similar process may be repeated many times throughout life, whenever the speaker is compelled to change (sub)communities and adjust—where appeal to developmental processes would appear to be less than appropriate. The conceivable "hypotheses" that would be made in such a situation are obviously dependent on the speaker's degree of sophistication about verbal matters and thus amenable, if necessary, to overt analysis.

11. Much of the early confusion about the relation between generative devices and machine translation (which Chomsky disowned) owes much to this fact. It was sometimes fostered by proposals explicitly worked out in the context of automatic translation, which made them mechanizable. It is in this connection, for example, that Yngve (1960) developed his model of sentence analysis, drew up the distinction between "regressive" and "progressive" structural types, and framed his well-known "depth hypothesis." The depth of a sentence is determined by the number of intermediate stages stored in a temporary memory in the course of producing the sentence.

Working with sentence generating devices with a necessarily finite temporary storage and operating on a left-to-right expansion principle (PS-representations, included for each sentence along with its component words, are framed in terms of Łukasiewicz's parenthesis-free notation) Yngve found a direct relation between the tree structure of sentences and the maximum amount of required temporary storage. The assigned depth is closely related to the direction of the associated branching (relatively large depth for left branching, small for right

~ NOTES TO CHAPTER 4 ~

branching). Further investigation led to the conclusion that there is an upper bound on sentence length in English.

Yngve was encouraged to generalize these findings in a comprehensive hypothesis, a prediction that similar results with respect to depth will be found in other languages. The approximate correspondence with the results reported by Miller (1956) about immediate memory spans in human subjects added strength to this contention. It was eventually suggested that if this hypothesis could be verified, sentence generating devices of this sort could then be taken as models of human language production. Early psychologizing of this sort must be held as timid in the light of later developments. The formulation of more abstract proposals seems to have blurred all sense of proportion. Thus Katz (1964), for example, writes:

> Given that both speaker and hearer are equipped with a linguistic description and procedures for sentence production and recognition . . . [the speaker] uses the sentence production procedure to obtain an abstract syntactic structure having the proper conceptualization of his thought. . . . After he has a suitable syntactic structure, the speaker utilizes the phonological component of his linguistic description to produce a phonetic shape for it. This phonetic shape is encoded into a signal that causes the speaker's articulatory system to vocalize an utterance of the sentence.

It must be understood that in the beginning there are "ideas," which the speaker "wishes" to "express."

12. Although we will have occasion to return to the relation between competence and performance in the chapters to follow, a preliminary reference is probably appropriate at this point.

Fromkin (1968) has argued for the construction of abstract performance models on a par with, and incorporating, a model of competence. She rejects Katz's model of performance (see note 11, this chapter) on the grounds that "when people speak they do not speak in 'grammatical' sentences, or sentences which they know to be grammatical. Actual speech is replete with false starts, grammatical deviations, slips of the tongue, etc." This observation falls far short of giving the reasons for the inadequacy of any such proposal. Fromkin's own speculations about performance models are too intimately tied up with the conviction that models of competence constitute a necessary prerequisite to permit raising questions about the need for either, or, for that matter, the model strategy itself. Broadly representative of the contemporary outlook, Fromkin's speculations deserve to be treated in some detail.

~ NOTES ~

According to Fromkin, a model of performance can be "just as formal a system as a model of competence, with its own axioms and rules and its own theorems derived from them." Moreover, the system of "performance rules" is also internalized (the problems posed by rule ordering recur several times) and aimed to describe what *an idealized speaker does in an idealized situation*. Such a standpoint is all the more surprising in an experimental phonetician dealing with tangible data at every step and aware that people do not usually talk in grammatical sentences. In view of the complexities of the problem, Fromkin concentrates on the "processes" involved in the "active" part of communication, the encoding of linguistic units into neural commands, although "we must . . . assume that at some previous level of brain activity some grammatical and semantic unit of sentence . . . has been encoded into a series of discrete elements."

Bringing to bear some very interesting data from her own work with electromyography and relying heavily on the investigations of the Leningrad group led by Kozhevnikov, Fromkin discusses several outlines for a model of performance capable of generating nontrivial research. Just what light these admittedly limited data (the activity of the orbicularis oris involved in the articulation of CVC utterances, where C = /b,d/ and V = /i,ʋ,u/, and some considerations on voicing) can ultimately throw on the kinds of linguistic units dictated by theory is not clear: discussion "comes down" from noun phrases, nouns, verb phrases, and so on, to the relevance of distinctive features, phonetic vs. phonemic criteria, extrinsic vs. intrinsic allophones, and the importance of the syllable, for purposes of efficient storage. Whatever its undeniable intrinsic interest, phonetic research of this sort inevitably suffers from well-known dimensional restrictions (cf., e.g., Julià, 1973). The construction of performance models along these lines may prove little more than a *tour de force*.

Fromkin makes reference to the work of the Haskins team, whose primary preoccupation with the listener's recovery of phoneme segments given a semicontinuous signal led to the motor theory of speech perception. (Witness, however, the impact of syntax-centered philosophies. Cf., e.g., Liberman, 1970.) The Halle-Stevens type of analysis-by-synthesis approach is also brought into focus, mainly as regards the need to "take physiological factors into consideration more directly" (although in Fromkin's view, "neurological data are important only in so far as they can confirm or negate, or lead to linguistic hypotheses"). Fromkin reaches the not altogether expected conclusion that "Whereas hearing and understanding may not be the reverse

~ NOTES TO CHAPTER 4 ~

decoding process of the speaker's encoding, there is still too little known about each stage of the system to assume either to be the case." (Hearing and understanding, though apparently equated here, are of course two very different matters.)

Of special interest here is the unabashed recourse to one or another variety of functionalistic diagrams, the introduction of feedback mechanisms whenever convenient, and the fact that the discussion centers on brain storage capacity, messages, processes of encoding and decoding, and so on. Fromkin's graphic representation of Katz's model is revealing enough, as are her own diagrams seeking the simplest possible model for operations leading from stored message to motor commands. The reader may want to inspect directly also those diagrams offered by Halle and Stevens (1964). It may be worth pointing out, however, that whereas Fromkin's model centers on encoding alone and is primarily speculative, analysis-by-synthesis approaches are aimed at a "generalized model for both speech production and recognition" and have sometimes been implemented, at least in part. It is not entirely a digression to note that Fodor and Katz included this paper by Halle and Stevens in the section "Psychological Implications" of their well-known 1964 *Readings in the Philosophy of Language*. The full process of "communication" is assumed to be the entire "chain" from ideas to acoustic output and back again. (See also Miller, et al., 1960, and Miller and Chomsky, 1963.)

A final observation is in order: in practice, performance is here taken to be the activity of the articulatory system in the speaker and/or discriminative responses on the part of the listener. At any rate, this is where actual experimentation stops. Why then add anything else to the formulation? As a phonetician, Fromkin need not go any "deeper" than she does in her research work; it is as a linguist committed to a prior competence model that she feels compelled to do so. Still, the question can be asked, "In what ways does the inclusion of such factors as brain storage capacity and neural commands make the 'performance models' proposed more complete and explanatory?" To ask such questions is not to advocate concentration on the response alone. A long tradition in the name of "objectivity" in psychology is sufficient to disallow all forms of muscle twitchism. Surely something else is needed to account for performance.

It should be pointed out that Chomsky himself fluctuates in his view of the relation between competence and performance. Sometimes his position is akin to that of Katz, as we have seen, while at other times he limits himself to an insistence that competence constitutes a *sine*

~ NOTES ~

qua non for the study of performance, which incorporates a vaguely conceived "much else" besides, as we shall see. But what can this "much else" be, however, if not the effect of environmental variables?

13. Thus Miller et al. (1960, p. 46) write: "the attempts to simulate . . . processes with machines are motivated in large measure by the desire to test—or to demonstrate—the designer's understanding of the theory he espouses. History suggests that man can create almost anything he can visualize clearly. The creation of a model is proof enough of the clarity of the vision." There are obvious inherent risks involved, however. Theories of the kind alluded to reduce largely to a form of dignified guesswork. In the absence of an appropriate conceptualization of the subject matter and techniques for addressing relevant questions, frameworks of this sort immediately acquire a peculiar status: they both guide research and become their own goal. They appear to be there mainly to be proved or disproved. As Skinner (1938, p. 44) has pointed out, "There are doubtless many men whose curiosity about nature is less than their curiosity about the accuracy of their guesses."

14. "From the beginning, we have anticipated that the problem of the perception of Gestalt, or of the perceptual formation of universals, would prove to be of this nature. What is the mechanism by which we recognize 'a square as square' irrespective of its position, its size, and its orientation?" (Wiener, 1948, p. 26). Group scanning operations, the formation of group spaces through a uniformly distributed set of samples, sets of parameters to be processed through appropriate transformations, and so on are invoked, over and above difficulties arising from whether we are dealing with a two- or three-dimensional space. Wiener seems to have thought some aspects of the traditional empiricist doctrine of the "association of ideas" relevant and mechanizable.

The processes involved "can be summed up in one sentence": "we tend to bring any object that attracts our attention into a standard position and orientation, so that the visual image that we form of it varies within as small a range as possible. This does not exhaust the processes which are involved in *perceiving the form and meaning* of the object, but it certainly facilitates all later processes tending to this end" (ibid., p. 158; italics mine). An alternative explanation is of course available: there is no reason whatsoever why the organism should react to any object (or property of an object) as special or different unless there are some consequences attached to such a response. That one should respond to large numbers of squares as squares, for example, despite differences such as those mentioned by Wiener simply suggests that there have been reinforcing consequences at work. As a result, we can treat the class of squares involved as a topographical set of stimuli (Goldiamond, 1966) controlling similar responses. What is more, this appeal to contingencies of reinforcement can also explain why an organism with a more limited history might not be able to recognize a square as square, a possibility, which Wiener overlooks.

It is revealing that he should speak of the "perception of meaning" of stimuli as well. But meaning, like novelty, familiarity, and so forth is a meaningless concept if reference is restricted to stimuli alone. Appeal to the organism's history with respect to these stimuli or similar ones is mandatory. Explanation demands that all the terms in the contingencies, past and present, be taken into consideration. Similar remarks apply where we say that the organism "identifies," "observes," "classifies" or, when a certain time has elapsed, that it "remembers," "recalls," and so on. The notion of "re-cognition," which is as frequent in cybernetic as in explanatory linguistic writings, is indicative of the unnecessary and fallacious inferences to which a less than straightforward approach is bound to lead. The fields of "concept formation," "attention," "memory," and certain types of problem solving can thus be put in good empirical order (Skinner, 1953, and repeatedly after; see, in particular, Skinner, 1969).

Finally, Wiener's observations about the ideal computing machine are worth considering. They provide further evidence of the ways in which an original commitment influenced his entire outlook on models of the type discussed:

> The ideal computing machine must then have all its data inserted at the beginning, and must be as free as possible from human interference to the very end. This means that not only must the numerical data be inserted at the beginning but also all the rules for combining them, in the form of instructions covering every situation which may arise in the course of the computation. Thus the computing machine must be a logical machine as well as an arithmetic machine, and must combine contingencies in accordance with a systematic algorithm. (Wiener, 1948, p. 139)

In a different but not unrelated vein, Wiener was faced with problems much like those posed by the construction of explanatory models expected to lead to explanatory hypotheses. At issue here, in particular, is the problem of accounting for infinity through finite means. A mathematical solution (recourse to recursive devices) may prove adequate in the case of computers, but under the terms of his formulation, Wiener was also concerned with how logic impinges on psychology,

~ NOTES ~

or vice versa. Whether the effort involved in an empirical analysis can be circumvented in this way, where natural phenomena, say behavior, are at stake, is seriously open to question. Some of the assumptions and consequences to be guarded against have already been suggested; they apply just as well to contemporary, and not wholly unrelated, research on artificial intelligence.

15. For an outstanding example of how the competence/performance distinction provides a measure of much needed direction and cogency to psychologists with a particular outlook on their subject matter, see, e.g., Pylyshyn (1972), who writes:

> In trying to understand the nature of intelligence it is useful to distinguish two aspects of the problem. One has to do with what people know and with how this knowledge may be represented in the mind. The other has to do with how people can, in spite of a number of cognitive limitations, use this knowledge to get along in the world. While there is no doubt that these two aspects are intimately related, there are some important differences between them which suggest that it may be strategic to drive a wedge between these two aspects in the task of understanding cognition.

Furthermore,

> Although the above discussion, as well as many of the examples which will be used later, deals with linguistic competence, it should be apparent that the same remarks apply to all other cognitive abilities. Thus we could have theories of perceptual competence, of reasoning competence, of spatial competence, or any other cognitive competence.

16. Thus Katz (1964) unreservedly writes:

> every aspect of the mentalistic theory involves psychological reality. The linguistic description and procedures of sentence production and recognition must correspond to independent mechanisms in the brain. Componential distinction between the syntactic, phonological, and semantic components must rest on relevant differences between three neural submechanisms of the mechanism which stores the linguistic description. The rules of each component must have their psychological reality in the input-output operations of the computing machinery of this mechanism. The ordering of rules within a component must . . . have its psychological reality in those features of this computing machinery which group such input-output operations and make the per-

~ NOTES TO CHAPTER 4 ~

formance of operations of one group a precondition for those in another to be performed.

Though perhaps not all equally extreme in their claims, statements of this sort are numerous in the literature. For further discussion of linguistic theory and computational and processing mechanisms, see, e.g., Chomsky (1977, 1980), Cooper and Walker (1979), Fodor et al. (1974), Fodor (1975), Halle et al. (1978).

17. Psycholinguists and psychologists share this view of their subject matter when they speak of a child's "acquisition" of language, how many phonemes the child "possesses" after so many months, how he learns to use words, noun phrases, verbs, and so on. Expressions of the sort suggest the independent existence of a set of forms: the child is exposed to them and, somehow, he avails himself of these forms and their interrelations. The evidence is the progressively more skillful "use" he makes of them. But this still does not explain why the child should bother to learn to speak or what is exactly the "use" he puts speech to once he has "acquired it."

A nativist outlook is probably the only course open to experts committed to a formulation of language as an object. Here, too, Chomsky has some extreme opinions to offer: "The problem of language acquisition now is to discover sufficiently powerful principles about the universal form of language that compensate for the impoverished input to the child's language acquisition mechanism." Such an outlook can lead to absurd forms of reasoning: for example, Miller et al. (1960, pp. 146, 147) argue that "a child must hear 2^{100} sentences before he can speak and understand English. That is about 10^{30} sentences." Since there are about 3.15×10^9 seconds in a century, "the child would have to hear about 3×10^{20} sentences per second in order to be exposed to all the information necessary for the planner to produce sentences according to . . . left-to-right rules of grammar." Assuming an upper limit of sentence-length of twenty words ("we had to set it somewhere") and "perfect retention of every string of twenty words after one presentation" this would mean "a childhood 100 years long with no interruptions for sleeping, eating, etc."

These (much cited) computations were offered as evidence against any attempt to use "simple stochastic chains of behavioral events as a general description of human behavior" and in favor of a language acquisition device based on the TG model of sentence structure. Typically, the argument erroneously identifies the so-called "chaining hypothesis" with a behavioral account of language. It is a false but widespread view that all behaviorists take the emission of verbal behavior to be a matter of stimulus-response chains, where each response acts as a stimulus for the next; it also shows a lack of discrimination to assume that all behavioral formulations can or must be similarly identified with left-to-right devices or, indeed, that such translation exercises serve any useful purpose. Some basic issues are distorted or neglected. To cite but two, the size of the units revealed by an operant analysis varies widely and only occasionally approximates the linguist's "word," on which these outlandish computations are based; generalization plays a fundamental role in the overall economy of behavioral repertoires, yet no reference is made to it or, for that matter, to the rest of processes revealed by an experimental analysis.

Generally, research on "language development" concentrates on recording the appearance of novel responses, which are then attributed to some maturational process or, more recently, taken as evidence of innate rules at work (or a mixture of both). Thus Menyuk (1969, p. viii) summarized her work on "sentences children use" as "concerned with the acquisition and development of syntactic rules, although children's acquisition of phonological and semantic rules is touched upon, primarily to indicate how little has been done in those areas of grammar acquisition." Bellugi and Brown (1964) offer the following example of such a rule to account for a structure observed in the speech of two children: "In order to form a noun phrase select first one word from the small class of modifiers and select, second, one word from the large class of nouns." This would presumably explain a response like "My hand." As Skinner (1969, p. 90) points out, no reference is made to the conditions under which the response first appeared or is subsequently emitted. Skinner goes on to comment as follows:

> How often has the child echoed the verbal stimulus *my hand*? How often has he heard stories in which characters referred to their hands? How often has he heard *hand* when his own hand has been important as a stimulus—when, for example, it has been hurt, touched, washed, or shaken? What verbal history has sharpened the distinction between *my* and *your*? How many other responses containing *hand* and *my* has the child already learned? It seems safe to overlook all this material if the child selects words and puts them together to compose phrases or sentences by applying rules with the help of a mental mechanism. But selection and composition in that sense are rare forms of verbal behavior, characteristic mainly of logicians, linguists, and psycholinguists.

~ NOTES TO CHAPTER 4 ~

Children become normal adults as they control and are controlled by their physical and social environments more effectively, in accordance with the standards of their community. A large part of this process is verbal. Albeit a function of the same types of variables, every speaker has his own peculiar history. There is, of course, overlap between the repertoires of different members of a community; indeed, this is what defines them as such. Quine (1960, p. 8) offers a useful metaphor: "Different persons growing up in the same language are like different bushes trimmed and trained to take the shape of identical elephants. The anatomical details of twigs and branches will fulfill the elephantine form differently from bush to bush, but the over-all outward results are alike." Quine's phrasing comes close to a naturalistic outlook. It is interesting to note his use of the term 'language': he speaks of people "growing up *in* the language," i.e., it is people who develop in it, not "the language" that develops in them. Emphasis is laid upon the verbal environment, the practices of the community rather than on the child. It is to the environment that we turn for an explanation of nonverbal behavior, and there is no reason not to do the same where (to keep close to the customary restrictive treatment in the literature) the articulatory musculature is involved.

(Some linguists, and particularly sociolinguists, have been aware all along that formal analysis, even if supplemented with semantic interpretation, is far from sufficient to account for the facts of language as social behavior. For example, Hymes has argued for what he calls "ethnographies of communication" for more than a decade (Hymes, 1964); he would retain the concept of competence, what he terms "communicative competence," to cover the abilities displayed by people who function verbally in a social context (e.g., Hymes, 1974). An anthropologist as well as a linguist, he states his case in a nutshell when he says that "the study of language as human activity calls for ethnography as well as logic" (Hymes, 1972). The order is important. There is a question, however, as to whether ethnography can provide the necessary tools to account for the occurrence of this activity in truly functional terms. Cf., e.g., Bauman and Sherzer, 1974. The argument runs parallel in some of the current work in so-called functional syntax. See, e.g., Kuno, 1980.)

In recent years, developmental research has been primarily concerned with substantiation of theory rather than with a naturalistic account of processes. Chomsky's reluctance to face environmental factors squarely places a severe limitation on the range of phenomena

~ NOTES ~

that verbal activity has to offer for meaningful empirical investigation. It should not be surprising if disaffection follows. Some writers have begun to take a more reasonable view of the language learning process. Thus Bloom (1970) applies a "method of rich interpretation" to get at the nonlinguistic context of a child's behavior; a unique structural representation seems inadequate if the "same" utterance has occurred under different circumstances. Brown (1973), though interested in morpheme combinations and using length of utterance as a primary criterion for dividing several years' data into "stages," takes such things as "semantic relations" and "context of reference" into consideration. This does not, of course, cover the full range of relevant factors or show the best way of taking them into account, but it points in the right direction. Such a study as Horner (1968), which concentrates on contingent relations and functionally defined units recorded on a continuous basis for several days, yields a great deal more insight into what goes on in language learning than the exhaustive analysis of responses alone, discontinuously recorded over a period of months or years, even when (as is sometimes done) the properties of adult ambient speech are also subjected to structural analysis.

Notes to Chapter 5

1. Here is what Chomsky has to say about his sentence atomism. In his reply to Hiż's criticism (see note 2, chapter 4), he writes:

> Here he [Hiż] is confusing two entirely different kinds of explanation. If I want to explain why, yesterday afternoon at three o'clock, John Smith understood "the shooting of the hunters" as referring to the act of shooting the hunter, rather than the hunter's act of shooting, I will of course bring into consideration the situational context (not limiting myself to "the readings of neighboring sentences"). If I am interested in explaining why this phrase is susceptible to these two interpretations . . . I will appeal first to the particular grammar of English, and more deeply, to the linguistic universals that led to the construction of this grammar by a child exposed to certain data. Since entirely different things are being explained, it is senseless to claim that one manner of explanation is "easier" than the other. (Chomsky, 1968)

This reply begins with a distinction between what Chomsky calls the "presystematic level," the realm of "models of use and understanding" within which competence is formulated, and the "systematic level,"

NOTES TO CHAPTER 5

in which "that competence is expressed by a generative grammar that recursively enumerates structural descriptions of sentences."

If there is any confusion, it lies in a formulation that typically permits a retreat to the "presystematic level" whenever the wherewithal of the "systematic level" is under attack, or vice versa. Thus Chomsky ignores Hiż's suggestion about more effective techniques of disambiguation, a matter presumably pertaining to the "systematic level," charging misunderstanding at the same time, despite the fact that it is by virtue of innate competence that the speaker-listener selects the best grammar in acquisition and continues to assign adequate structural descriptions in later "use." Thus John Smith understood who was doing the shooting because he disentangled the ambiguity in accordance with the generative grammar that expresses his competence and is therefore the best grammar.

Chomsky is right in pointing out that the readings of neighboring sentences are not (always) enough to disambiguate ambiguous sentences. But it is disingenious on his part to say that he would take "situational context" into consideration. For one thing, he would be hard put to spell out with any degree of specificity what this "situational context" is without yielding to behavioral variables, which he will do under no condition. (As we shall see, what Chomsky usually calls "other conditions" entering performance besides competence is never made clear in his writings.) For another, he is not meeting Hiż on the same formal grounds on which the objection is made; Hiż is talking about texts and, unlike Chomsky, makes this clear and consistently keeps to them in his arguments. Chomsky does not give a reason why his own approach to ambiguity through appeal to the grammar of English first and, more deeply, to the linguistic universals that led John Smith to construct it for himself, is the better of the two methods. Chomsky, in fact, does not answer Hiż's broader criticism, nor does he show that two entirely different things are being explained.

At the basis lies the fundamental flaw of Chomsky's speculations, namely, his "psychologism"—the notion that grammatical descriptions have psychological import, which, he argues, justifies his specific form of grammar. In fact, he has nothing to go by in the way of empirical checkpoints except more grammatical examples, like everybody else.

2. More data-oriented linguists are sometimes aware of the prevailing conceptual limitations. Thus Harris (1962) writes at the beginning of his book on string analysis: "A prefatory remark about sentences may be in order here. There are many difficulties in describing empirically what is to be included in the set of sentences of a language.

~ NOTES ~

For one thing, there is the problem of deciding what are utterances of the language." Furthermore, "Given the decision as to what are utterances of the language, there are further problems as to what are the sentences." Linguists should presumably be clear about the nature of utterances before going on to establish their analytical categories. Harris goes about it in an indirect way, namely, through appeal to sentences. Particular types of sentences are "those segments of speech (or writing) over which certain intonations occur or within which certain structures occur." An utterance can be then described as "a sequence or fragment of sentences." The decomposition of utterances proceeds in terms of centers and adjuncts. This does not solve the "further problems as to what are sentences," however.

Earlier, Harris (1952) had put forth a method of analysis that made it possible for descriptive linguistics to range "beyond the limits of a single sentence at a time." Discourse analysis was a milestone in linguistic analysis in that it permitted a statement of distributional relations among the sentences composing long stretches of discourse. Among other things, it respected such facts as that "definite patterns may be discovered for particular texts, or for particular persons, styles, or subject matters." Despite its desirability, however, Harris immediately qualified this departure from earlier practices, saying that "in every language it turns out that almost all the results of analysis lie within a relatively short stretch, which we may call a sentence," thereby falling back on the formally defined sentence, with subjects, predicates, and the traditional parts of speech.

Special reference has been made to sentences on account of their central role in recent trends. It is not too farfetched to say that in spite of the structuralist language in which it is dressed, the concept is still reminiscent of the old definition in terms of "expression of complete thoughts," which presents the problem of having to say what a complete thought consists of. Words, of course, deserve special mention, too. Reliance on texts or possibly transcribed protocols of spoken language may be to a large extent responsible for the apparent impossibility of giving up old schemes. A commitment to structural analysis may well be at the basis of the entire problem. It is clearly illustrated in Joos' entry for 'Word' in his "Comments on Certain Technical Terms": "Words are needed in IC analysis . . . attempts to define [words] universally have not survived" (Joos, 1957).

It is just possible that analysis of forms alone, and textual ones at that, simply does not provide the necessary means to overcome such conceptual limitations. In this, Chomsky is not alone; he shares the

~ NOTES TO CHAPTER 5 ~

biases of structural analysis at large. The difference between him and other writers is that he claims explanatory power for his descriptive statements, whereas others, more reasonably, do not. (For a discussion of the three basic approaches to grouping linguistic segments into grammatical categories, see Hiż, 1960.)

3. That arguments usually reduce to the old notion of reference has already been noted. This is roughly the field of discriminative behavior, which schemes of denotation, designation, and the like, do not successfully cover (among other things, they do not account for so-called multiple meaning). They do not exhaust the full range of types of meaning, either: equally important are those aspects arising from, broadly speaking, "motivational" and "emotional" variables. (Cf. e.g., Akmajian et al., 1979, for an updated discussion as well as an effort to catch up with and incorporate recent work in pragmatics. Significantly enough, the chapter on semantics bears the subtitle "Meaning and Reference," the one on pragmatics "Language Use and Linguistic Communication"; the references cited there attest to the struggle to find a way out of the inevitable blind alleys to which the formulation leads. See also note 3, chapter 7.)

4. The suspicious similarity between discussions on grammaticalness and prescriptivism has been repeatedly pointed out. They suggest a regression to the earlier, primarily normativist, outlook of the philological tradition with regard to the role of grammar.

Speakers of natural languages often exhibit a considerable latitude in their verbal patterns: to zero in on the more obvious, dialectology, much of the data of the sociolinguist, the specialized languages of various fields, and so on, provide inexhaustible sources of "deviance" from a fabricated standard; personal idiosyncrasies are not necessarily mistakes, either (see, e.g., Carden, 1976; Gumperz and Tannen, 1979; Labov, 1972; Ross, 1979). Any theory with empirical aspirations should at least show respect for facts of this sort. Ideally, it should incorporate them: the outcome would be a very different treatment of language.

The alternative practice of brushing them aside as merely tangential (to be perhaps reckoned with at some later stage) accounts for the great discrepancy between theory and real data: competence, with which grammaticalness (absolute or relative) is associated, remains the idealized form of knowledge it is posited to be, while performance is typically characterized as full of anomalies. Where the relevance of the former becomes dubious, the characterization of the latter is obviously out of sorts with observed fact. (One is tempted to ask, "What becomes of

~ NOTES ~

the overriding uniformity suggested by the notion of innate knowledge of well-formedness?" See also chapter 6.)

The formalistic outlook renders judgments of grammaticality highly subjective; it is not very clear, either, how consensus could be ever reached beyond the most artificial and (largely trivial) collocations of words offered as examples for theoretical argumentation. Bowers (1969) illustrates the present point when he discusses Chomsky's arbitrariness in saying that "His criticism of the book before he read it" is ungrammatical, while "His criticizing the book before he read it" is not. Bowers sums up the matter as follows: "Empiricism is an odd term to use for a method which leads to the conclusion that another native speaker's acceptance of an expression unacceptable by Chomsky is a result of the speaker's failure to note criteria of grammaticalness which are derived from Chomsky's private area of acceptability" (Cited in Kantor, 1977).

5. The definition of (boundaries for) natural languages is a well-known problem in linguistic geography, particularly in the case of as yet unwritten languages, where there is lack of historical information, or where otherwise supporting socio-political conditions are unclear. We are concerned here, however, with recent efforts to cope with the notion of language in formally rigorous terms. The issue comes up, to a large extent, as a result of Chomsky's extreme formulation of language as a well-defined system. Some experts have argued to the contrary. Hockett (1968) believes that the basic assumption of current work on algebraic grammar, namely, that "a language can be viewed as a well-defined subset of the set of all finite strings over a well-defined finite alphabet" is false; natural languages are ill-defined:

> As one attempts a longer and longer sentence of the kind shown [perfectly grammatical collocations of the type "One," "One and one," etc.] or the kind defined by any other open-ended pattern, one encounters *flexible constraints*, that are, in my opinion, *parts of language*, just as the time limits of a football game are part of football. Moreover, it seems that *all* constraints in a language are of this more or less rubbery sort, yielding no definite boundary to the "set of all possible sentences" of the language; and just for these reasons languages are ill-defined. (p. 61)

If this is the case, the mathematical machinery brought to bear on natural languages (which was developed for well-defined systems) ceases to be relevant for linguistics. Hockett argues that Chomsky's entire proposal hinges on the notion of well-definition for natural languages:

NOTES TO CHAPTER 5

"Chomsky nowhere says so explicitly, but I believe this point is absolutely crucial for his whole theory. If this is true, or if one accepts it on faith, then all that Chomsky says is rendered at least plausible. If it is false, then everything falls to pieces" (p. 57).

Hockett goes on to discuss well-definition in relation to such fundamental concepts in Chomsky's framework as idealization, completeness of description, and rules—all of which are dependent on it. In connection with the view that language behavior is rule-governed, he pointedly writes: "if one believes, as I do and argue in extenso in the text, that the rules for a human language are ill-defined, then the whole rule terminology becomes a bad one: it is merely misleading, overly cumbersome, and (in some circles) a dishonestly prestigious substitute for the simpler traditional terminology" (p. 87). We can only agree with Hockett's observations. This is not to lend support, however, to his alternative proposal that language is "a set of habits in stability," for which he seems to settle, probably because he (surprisingly) shares Chomsky's view that "the vast majority of the sentences encountered throughout life by any user (= speaker-hearer) of a language are encountered only once," a fact "for which any linguistic theory must provide."

For all his preoccupation with the "open-endedness of language" in acquisition and use, Hockett's argument is basically formal: it is still based on a view of language as a single system of structurally defined entities (see his parallel excursions into historical linguistics). His general statements are nonetheless a powerful indictment of Chomsky's position. The following quotation illustrates both Hockett's reliance on formalistic criteria and his more empirical penchant: "A language, as a set of habits, is a fragile thing, subject to minor modification in the slightest breeze of circumstance; this, indeed, is its greatest source of power. But this is also why the transformationalists (like the rest of us!), using themselves as informants, have such a hard time deciding whether certain candidates for sentencehood are really 'in their dialect' or not" (p. 90). Dialectal differences are only one of the sources of legitimate variance militating against a monolithic view of language. Reference has already been made to individual idiosyncrasies (see preceding note); one could also mention different stylistic properties or, for that matter, the need to reinterpret texts from earlier periods, written, as the expression goes, in the same language.

Institutional idiosyncrasies have been pointed out elsewhere. In an illuminating paper, Hiż (1975) gives elegant formal expression to the otherwise functionally well-established fact that different audiences

~ NOTES ~

control different sublanguages with no obvious interdependence among them. He writes:

> To know, to speak, to understand, and to process the language of biology one does not, in general, have to know the language of jurisprudence or of maritime engineering. On some occasions these sublanguages must function together, however, for instance in a deposition filed in litigation concerning a poisoning on a ship. A man masters no more than a very few of such specialized sublanguages. Since English is composed of many particular ways of talking, nobody really speaks the English language in its totality.

These sublanguages are to be distinguished from dialects in the sense of local variations: whereas dialects are characterized by special phonetic properties beside lexical and grammatical differences, the various sublanguages differ from each other in their vocabulary and syntactic restrictions alone. Switching sublanguages in this sense seldom involves changes in pronunciation.

Hiż brings forth an array of carefully selected examples from various fields to show that "a sublanguage is not only a selection of words, but also a set of restrictions on the grammatical forms in which these words can occur." Some interesting interrelations obtain among the various sublanguages, but they are difficult to track down formally; it would be easier to formalize each particular sublanguage. (The switch from one speech variety to another is a functional matter; so are, ultimately, their interrelations.)

Hiż, a linguist and a logician, goes as far as to say: "If in a sublanguage an expression cannot occur in all its forms, or if an expression cannot take all the modifiers it takes elsewhere in the language, then for the sublanguage we must have a different grammar than for the totality of the language." To cite but one example, he points out that "for arithmetic the comparative and the superlative *greater, greatest* . . . cannot be derived from the positive form *great*, as is usually done in English grammars." Hiż concludes: "Not only the vocabulary but also the content of the grammar rules for a sublanguage differ in important respects from English in general." We are not yet sensitive enough to differences of this sort; yet they are at the basis of all concerns with grammaticalness, infinity, language comprehension, and the role of rules. The proposal to deal with sublanguages as more realistic constructs seems to be gathering momentum and it is reassuring to have, for once, functional justification for it (Julià, 1979, 1980a).

The notion of one-language one-grammar calls for revision; indeed, the entire concept of grammatical study (its goals, limits, etc.) demands careful reappraisal. The recognition that nobody speaks or understands a natural language in its totality (whatever this may be) adds strength to the above criticism of natural languages as well-defined systems. A single grammar for this totality becomes a vacuous contraption.

It is somewhat ironic that such a conception of language should have been given explicit form by a school of linguists who not only aim at descriptive adequacy but at explanatory adequacy as well, on the strength of a presumably valid universal descriptive scheme, which assigns unique structural analyses to isolated sentences through a unique set of recursive rules.

6. Elsewhere (cf., e.g., Chomsky, 1972), Chomsky seems to endorse the view that verbal creativity is different in kind from creativity in other areas, such as the arts (music is specifically mentioned in this connection). What makes language unique is that "as an expression of the human mind rather than as a product of nature, [it] is boundless in scope and is constructed on the basis of a recursive principle."

Notes to Chapter 6

1. It is of some interest to note that in his review of Skinner (1957) Chomsky comes close to adopting precisely the view he criticizes here:

> The study of hesitation pauses has shown that these tend to occur before the large categories—noun, verb, adjective; this finding is usually described by the statement that the pauses occur where there is maximum uncertainty or information. Insofar as hesitation indicates on-going composition (if it does at all), it would appear that the key responses are chosen only after the "grammatical frames." (Chomsky, 1959, fn. 45)

2. This point has repeatedly been made in the literature. For example, Cofer (1968) makes the following, related observation: "I often think that despite possession, presumably, of linguistic competence, I have nothing to say. Our interest in communication arises in the first instance from a desire to say something, rather than from the pleasure that exercising syntactic structures may provide us." Discussing Chomsky's reluctance to admit the action of stimulus and motivational variables, MacCorquodale (1970) makes a similar point:

~ NOTES ~

> Chomsky is totally silent . . . about what might be the form of input which would . . . engage the grammar construct when speech is to be produced, and tell it what to be grammatical about, and how to select a possible transformation to say it in, and so forth. . . . Sooner or later something must *enter* the system. Guthrie complained that Tolman had left the rat "lost in thought" because he provided no relation between the expectancy and behavior. Chomsky leaves the speaker lost in thought with nothing whatsoever to say.

Kantor (1977) fittingly sums the matter up as "autistic speculations."

3. This is also the conclusion naturally reached by Salzinger (1975), who ends his insightful discussion with the puzzle, "When is behavior not performance?" He then proceeds:

> The answer that Chomsky and his colleagues give us is, "When it is competence." I believe that behavior theory can more meaningfully deal with the problem that underlies the distinction between competence and performance. The distinction came about because people behave differently on different occasions; they speak differently and they respond to speech differently. My suggestion is that we study the conditions that provide us with differences in behavior, without worrying about which one reveals the real underlying ability of the individual.

In his excellent reply to Chomsky's review of Skinner (1957), MacCorquodale (1970) had earlier argued in similar fashion:

> So far as one can tell, Chomsky's one controlling variable for speech production—grammar, rules, competence—rests locked away in the brain somewhere, inert and entirely isolated from any input variables which could ever get it to say something. Unless some external input is permitted one must suppose that the grammar construct regulates itself, a repugnant notion. No one speaks pure grammar. All sentences have grammatically irrelevant properties; they are, in addition, about something. . . . The behavior of the grammar construct must now be explained. Until it is we are no further along than we were without it. It is simply that which controls grammatical behavior. But that, of course, is the question, not the answer. The speaker's cognitions will not do, since they too are theoretical constructions and must in turn be explained.

Although the statement that all sentences are about something probably demands closer scrutiny, MacCorquodale effectively brings all the pertinent issues together. See also Julià (1968b) and Richelle (1973).

~ NOTES TO CHAPTER 6 ~

4. For an extended and penetrating essay on the problem of response class in verbal behavior, see Salzinger (1967). An interesting discussion on the provenance of operants can be found, e.g., in Segal (1972), who, bringing to bear primarily a wealth of evidence from the animal laboratory, aptly sums up the problem as "an open experimental question." Skinner (1969) provides a full treatment of the fundamental nature and general scope of contingencies of reinforcement.

5. The study of ambiguity is a good case in point. It highlights some of the more glaring biases of extreme formalism. As Salzinger (1975) has pointed out, whereas the ordinary speaker and listener can always ask "what?" or "What do you mean?," the generative grammarian "can only reread the same isolated puzzling sentence." If this were all, linguistics would only be a puzzle-solving exercise. Many grammarians, however, do more than that: they assign structure and purport to say something about speakers and listeners at the same time. Yet in the process of arguing for a formalistic approach, they forget the real facts of verbal performance. We can hardly expect the result of analysis to reflect the behavioral nature of speech.

The preestablished frame of reference makes several important assumptions. In particular, it assumes that spoken language can be described on the basis of textual study (see Catania's example in note 3, chapter 3), even though merely textual responses would be insufficient in clearing up various kinds of meaning differences. It also assumes that sentences occur in isolation, which is only rarely the case: under normal circumstances a multiplicity of cues work together to offset possible misunderstanding. When available, adjacent verbal behavior may prove useful in dispelling some of the sources of ambiguity; but "linguistic context" is only a restricted source of information, only one of the independent variables. There is no alternative to a full-fledged appeal to "conditions of use." Furthermore, the formulation indirectly implies, to be consistent with the notion of a single model, that ambiguity applies equally to speaker and listener. But surely there is no ambiguity for the *speaker*, if such there be, of classical examples like "They are flying planes" or "The shooting of the hunters."

This is not to deny the existence of ambiguity, which ultimately reduces to a matter of "understanding" and degrees thereof. As such, it applies uniquely to the listener, who may fail to respond to one or more of the variables responsible for the speaker's responses. But we must distinguish between the various possible sources of ambiguity—in broad outline, the clarity of verbal behavior as a stimulus and other sources of weakness to be found in the listener's own repertoire. A

~ NOTES ~

very different kind of investigative strategy immediately suggests itself.

Formally defined, ambiguity does not generally match actual cases of functional ambiguity. The psycholinguist in search of ambiguity (see, e.g., MacKay and Bever, 1967, or even Wales and Toner, 1979) cuts a very different figure from the analyst concerned with sources of misunderstanding in the empirical sense (for an extended discussion of the behavioral status of ambiguity, cf. Julià, 1980b).

6. In this same context Chomsky goes on to say:

> The idea that a person has a "behavioral repertoire"—a stock of utterances that he produces by "habit" on an appropriate occasion—is a myth, totally at variance with the observed use of language. Nor is it possible to attach any substance to the view that the speaker has a stock of "patterns" in which he inserts words or morphemes. Such conceptions would apply to greetings, a few clichés, and so on, but they completely misrepresent the normal use of language, as the reader can easily convince himself by unprejudiced observation.

People do say and (sometimes) understand things they have never heard before, of course. But to conclude that this is the rule of ordinary day-to-day performance is to completely misrepresent the normal "use" of language. Indeed, one shudders to think how difficult life might become if this were the case. It is a great mistake (which intellectuals are particularly prone to make) to generalize, if not "project," to the population at large conditions obtaining in their very special community. The contingencies are simply not the same.

It goes without saying that great caution is in order when speaking about academia as well. Without any desire to belabor the point, recourse to environmental variables becomes inevitable. What, for example, if not behavioral history, can account for misunderstandings among people all equally equipped with the innate intellectual ability to say and understand an unbounded number of sentences and who "speak the same language" besides? Take, for example, the above rendition of a behavioral view of language. Its author's behavioral history has not equipped him to speak about verbal performance in performance terms. In fact, Chomsky would no doubt admit, if not boast, an inability to "bring himself to saying" the sorts of things a behaviorist has to say about speech.

The plain fact is that we all speak in ways far more set than some, perhaps for other than scientific reasons, are ready to acknowledge. A chronological revision of Chomsky's writings and the TGG-inspired psycholinguistic literature at large, for instance, provides an excellent source of data to put the notion of ceaseless creativity to the test and gives a chance to learn a thing or two about "stocks of frames," "clichés," "habits," and so on, as the reader can easily convince himself by unprejudiced observation. (Learning about behavioral repertoires is a slightly more complicated matter.)

7. We seem to live in a degenerate world. In a more recent book, to which we will have occasion to refer more extensively in chapter 7, Chomsky (1976, pp. 21-22) discusses this issue within a broader context. Assumptions and conclusions become blurred in almost predictable ways:

> Investigating the cognitive capacity of humans, we might consider, say, the ability to recognize and identify faces on exposure to a few presentations, determine the personality structure of another person on brief account . . . to recognize a melody under transposition and other modifications, to handle those branches of mathematics that build on numerical or spatial intuition, to create art forms resting on certain principles of structure and organization, and so on. Humans appear to have characteristic and remarkable abilities in these domains, in that they construct a complex and intricate intellectual system, rapidly and uniformly, on the basis of degenerate evidence.

How such widely different stimulus situations as "a man's face" and "an outline drawing of it" can be similarly responded to was one of the numerous things that mystified Wiener (1948), too. He spoke of "recognition," with all that the term implies. So does Chomsky, who is not to be mystified. Chomsky goes further and confidently hypothesizes not only abilities and cognitive capacities but the organism's construction of intellectual systems—which are complex and intricate. His system encourages the assumption that cognitive domains are well-defined and the assertion that these intellectual systems are constructed with rapidity and uniformity. This is obviously at variance with closely observed fact, no matter how convenient from a model-builder's viewpoint. It is difficult to see what is gained by the introduction of such mystifying notions or, for that matter, why different forms of stimulation, eventually responded to in similar fashion (under certain circumstances), should thereby be branded "degenerate."

A less judicial approach suggests that what we are really faced with is a wealth of empirical data awaiting experimental investigation, where

~ NOTES ~

the existence of a model may well prove more a hindrance than a help. Our only evidence is that some people, sometimes, behave similarly (or differently) in the presence of similar (or different) aspects of the environment. All the observations made with respect to the related problem of accounting for the "recognition of a square as square irrespective of its position, its size, and its orientation" apply here as well. (See note 14, chapter 4).

8. This is not to be confused with Harris' notion of "acceptability grading." There are profound differences, stemming from the two writers' fundamentally different standpoints with regard to the nature and goals of grammatical theory. Harris' view of grammatical rules as a way to systematize co-occurrence relations places a realistic (though not necessarily easy) treatment on the inherent complexity of the data—hence the notion of a continuum of "intermediate cases" between fully grammatical and fully ungrammatical sentences encountered in everyday language. Distributional properties necessarily reflect inescapable effects of grammatically extraneous constraints upon the "use" of language.

This stands in sharp contrast with Chomsky's clear-cut separation of sentences into "two exclusive and jointly exhaustive sets," made possible by his conception of natural languages as well-defined systems on the one hand and his appeal to idealization (and all that follows from it) on the other. As we saw in chapter 3, a complete and adequate generative grammar, constructed on the basis of strictly grammatical sentences and excluding all the ungrammatical ones, should handle the "undecidable" cases in a systematic fashion. Explication involves absolute categories: ungrammatical strings will be assigned a "degree of grammaticalness" in accordance with the nature of their formal deviance (cf. especially Chomsky, 1961). If we are forced to talk about "acceptability" at all, it is because there are factors of various sorts to be taken into account when facing real performance data. But these have nothing to do with pure grammar, competence, and so on.

Katz and Bever (1976) have discussed this issue in terms of empiricism vs. rationalism. These writers attribute the difficulties associated with Harris' formulation to his empiricist leanings (at one point we read that Harris construed his model "in empiricist and behaviorist terms"), and, in particular, to his stand on "explication" and "absolute formulations," two of the major topics which differentiate, in their view, his methodology from Chomsky's rationalism—under which these difficulties are more easily (one might say "lightly") done away

~ NOTES TO CHAPTER 6 ~

with. (The remaining topics are "novelty," "explanation," and "transformational levels.")

Katz and Bever also use their interesting systematic comparison of the two formulations to make a strong case for the view that Harris' pernicious empiricist criteria are being reintroduced into the TGG conception of grammar through the emphasis on "relative grammaticality," which is central to the work of the splinter group of "generative semanticists."

9. Curiously enough, most of Chomsky's cases of "degeneracy" belong in the latter class, even though he is obviously making the point for the sake of the former. It is easy to declare that interrupted fragments, lapses, false starts, and the like can only be understood as distortions; but no understanding of these phenomena follows in fact from the comfortable concentration on idealized patterns. What little research has been derived from such a view becomes, primarily, an indirect justification for the idealized pattern itself.

10. Take, for example, the notion of rule. In a formalistic approach rules are used to relate forms; this is generally the case in linguistics and logic. It is one of Chomsky's academic achievements to have given the notion "rule of grammar" a degree of specificity unknown in linguistics before.

But this specificity cuts two ways. We have seen that serious difficulties arise when the resulting characterization of L is brought to bear on the actual behavior of speakers. On a strictly speculative level, the possible relations among constructs presumably making up language can be described in any of a variety of ways; hence the room for controversy over competing grammars. Recourse to "explanatory power" as the final arbiter, however, places linguistic analysis outside the scope of the (strictly) formal sciences, and the postulation of rules as inherent features of language, to say the least, on an awkward empirical footing. Under such a view, rules are necessarily imputed to the organism.

Yet Chomsky construes rules as counterparts of laws in other sciences. As a result, rules have become a central concern in any attempt to develop methods of grammatical analysis, including those worked out in opposition to TGG. Linguistic behavior has been turned into a matter of rule. The question is whether a theory of linguistic structure that pretends to explain the "mechanisms" of speakers and listeners as well should not reconsider its methodology in the light of the natural sciences. If this is done, the entire outlook changes. Laws are convenient descriptions of the subject matter under analysis: they reflect the current state of knowledge in a given field: they are not in nature, but in the behavior of the analysts concerned. Nature remains the same while laws describing it change. Research takes place on an entirely different plane: it concentrates on the direct development of techniques for getting at the only thing we can expect from nature, i.e., order, rather than on metatheoretical arguments having to do more with the behavior of the analyst than with the "facts" he is after. (Even historical and comparative linguistics, that most stable of linguistic enterprises, is not without related difficulties. See Hoenigswald, 1977.)

NOTES TO CHAPTER 7

1. After a detailed study of Chomsky's writings and an admirable coverage of the available literature, Derwing (1973, p. 322) aptly concludes:

> Our current generation of linguists . . . at least that portion of it which has been heavily influenced by Chomsky, wants to travel a good deal farther than their methodology will permit. They have taste for the fruits of scientific labor, but none for the labor itself. One of these tastes will have to be adjusted. One does not make an empirical science out of a discipline merely by wishing or proclaiming it to be so. We can hope to extend the range of our scientific interests . . . only if we are prepared to deal with new problems which have no simple solutions, and especially not solutions which are accessible by "thought experimentation" alone.

Derwing is generous with regard to the changes in taste to be envisioned. Though keenly aware of many of the dangers involved in aprioristic approaches of the type epitomized by Chomsky, he is not bothered, as a linguist, by a recourse to cognitive research; in fact, this is the road he openly advocates, in conjunction with the construction of performance *models*. A proper reappraisal of the subject matter as operant behavior, and therefore amenable to an extension of principles effectively worked out and applied elsewhere, shows that adjustments in taste are bound to be not one but many.

2. For obvious reasons, special reference has been made throughout to psychologists already committed to a cognitive outlook. More surprising is the case of another group of writers. Catania (1972) inaugurated the trend to translate formalistic proposals into behavioral terms. Despite the obvious inherent dangers involved, the argument seems to have taken root (see, in particular, Robinson, 1977; Segal,

~ NOTES TO CHAPTER 7 ~

1975, 1977; for a different perspective, see also Staats, 1974). The argument runs essentially as follows: whereas function has to do with the circumstances of emission of verbal behavior, structure has to do with its internal organization, the ways in which sentences or parts thereof are interrelated. It is said that these are different dimensions of verbal behavior and that although they are orthogonally related, the study of each throws light on the other (in the manner of biological structure and biological function, Catania says).

Conciliatory efforts of this sort, no matter how accurate the translation (where translation is feasible) are fraught with difficulties. Catania's extension of this proposal to psychology at large (Catania, 1973) is revealing. He points out that, changes in matters of detail aside, the history of psychology in the past century has really centered on the problem of developing psychologies of structure (prominently, Gestalt psychology) and of function (the study of contingencies of reinforcement), which need not stand in opposition. In his concern with conciliation, Catania endorses the possibility of a "psychology of structure" just as explanatory as a psychology of function in its own domain, which concentrates on the description of the properties of complex stimuli (what is learned). This is especially surprising, coming from an experimental analyst of behavior whose task is to deal with the dependent variable *as a function of* the independent variables giving rise to it.

The question comes up, "What does a psychology of structure amount to and where does some such compromise lead?" In the verbal field it clearly reintroduces "language" as an object. In so doing, the approach neglects the fundamental nature of verbal stimuli as speaker responses and the variables which bring them about; among the latter are nonverbal stimuli, which remain outside the scope of the characterization. It also promotes the view that a "psychology of structure" accounts for the behavior of both speaker and listener. What looks in principle like conciliation never really materializes.

Sometimes it becomes difficult to draw the line between conciliatory efforts and impractical or harmful subservience. Catania's efforts to accurately appraise the structuralist position smack of the latter:

> At issue is the question of whether cognitive and behavioral approaches are inappropriately interpreted, respectively, as structural and functional psychologies.
>
> It is not unfashionable these days to be a mentalist; only dualism is reprehensible. . . . In fact, the possibility of an internally

~ NOTES ~

consistent mentalism is implicit in the notion that a behavioral translation of mental or cognitive vocabularies is feasible.

psychogenesis must deal with the development of the organism's behavioral or mental capacities; this is what the psychology of learning is supposed to be about.

A measure of preoccupation with the formal properties of verbal behavior is perhaps justified. But psychologists concerned with complementation should be aware of the inherent arbitrariness in their choice of alternative methods of structural description. The parallel with biology does not quite work. In the present instance, the adoption of Chomsky's framework and not, say, Harris' transformational grammar, must probably be attributed to the former's current popularity or else, more seriously, to a (presumably conscious) acceptance of implications attendant to the resulting blend—a difficult possibility to imagine in view of these researchers' initial outlook. After all, arguments for the descriptive adequacy of TGG are framed in terms of explanatory adequacy; ironically, its popularity stems primarily from its invasion of the psychologist's sphere of expertise. (It is true that Chomsky's speculations have generated a considerable amount of research along cognitive lines, but this can hardly be taken as a proof of their correctness. The only arbiter is the value of the research generated.) It is doubtful whether, as formulated, any of the available systems of linguistic analysis is fit to service the interests of the behavioral scientist. For reasons discussed above, TGG turns out to rank low among the various candidates.

Attempts at rapprochement rather than Balkanization are always laudable, as long as they do not betray fundamentally well established facts and promise long-term results beyond immediately gratifying "solutions." In particular, psychologists should not be lured by the linguist's superficially neat formulations: their own work may thereby be deflected in essentially unproductive directions, dictated by the linguist's conceptual armamentarium. The zeal for compromise can lead to bizarre conclusions.

Segal (1975) marshals arguments akin to Catania's on somewhat dissimilar grounds. Toward the end of her review of Brown (1973), she writes: "I will not dwell on the epistemological implications of this unexpected convergence of disparate theoretical and pretheoretical viewpoints, but I do want to suggest that there is something of value in the current cognitive and psycholinguistic literature, even though some culling, some paraphrasing and interpreting, and some granting the benefit of the doubt, may be necessary to get to it." But *are* we entitled to this light treatment of the underlying methodological assumptions and implications? Indeed, what is the nature of this "unexpected convergence"? And will the suggested culling, paraphrasing, and interpreting suffice in case the convergence is less real than it appears to be? Perhaps a distinction must be made between coincidence and convergence. The fact that translation is sometimes possible (as both Catania and Segal ably show) does not alter the fact that, as Segal puts it, differences in manner of speaking influence "the direction of research on verbal behavior, the different kinds of data that behaviorists and psycholinguists collect, the different methods of collecting them, and the different conclusions drawn from them." Segal points out that certain general observations in Brown's analysis of grammatical morphemes are reminiscent of Skinner's treatment of autoclitic responses in terms of stimulus control and effects upon the listener. Brown, however, a "mentalist" and "intentionalist," speaks of the child's "semantic intentions" in order to account for the facts. This is more than a terminological difference. One cannot but take exception to such statements as, "One may be excused . . . for doubting the deep significance of this difference, for both theories attempt roughly the same job." The fact that they attempt the same job is a feeble basis on which to speak of a convergence: the two approaches emphasize different if not incompatible aspects of the data; among other things, Brown's allows for an analysis of responses in TGG terms, which Skinner's does not.

Along with some very insightful observations about Skinner's formulation of verbal behavior, Segal (1977) assumes the validity of Chomsky's framework. In particular, she feels that the deep/surface structure distinction is better suited to account for "grammatical behavior" than Skinner's interpretation in terms of the autoclitic formula. But surely such a matter must be decided by empirical inquiry, not by the simple expedient of adopting an essentially formal distinction with explanatory overtones. Segal's statement that "the two languages, the linguistic and the behavioral, are roughly equivalent, that is they display comparable respect for the phenomenal complexity of grammatical processes," raises the question of whether respect for the "phenomenal complexity of grammatical processes" is all that counts to make two radically different approaches roughly equivalent. (As already pointed out, linguists seem to be bent on looking at these complexities as being more phenomenal than does the behaviorist—which would presumably mean that they have more respect for them.)

~ NOTES ~

In adopting a formal framework, behavioral scientists explicitly commit themselves to a conceptual framework that rarely coincides with the kinds of problems presented by a functional analysis (cf., e.g., Robinson's adaptation of the generative outlook to formulate what he calls the "syntax crystal model." In particular, confusion ensues between the behavior of the analyst and that of the language learner, as the title of his paper, "Strategies for the acquisition of syntax," clearly shows). The adoption of a formal framework entails immediate decisions as to what constitute relevant questions (say, a concern with grammaticalness, formal ambiguity, etc.), what are pertinent answers, and how one must proceed to relate the former with the latter.

To zero in on the more obvious, take, e.g., the problem of the unit of analysis. The superimposition of formally determined analytical schemata *ipso facto* obliterates one of the most important contributions of a causal approach, namely, the great variability revealed by functionally determined units. No presently available descriptive frame of reference, as noted above, comes near to providing the kind of flexibility demanded for the demarcation of simple units, let alone their interrelations. (In one way or another the above writers unnecessarily speak of hierarchical structure, in kind with the TG grammarian's dictates, which in turn leads to a convenient though inaccurate interpretation of experimental strategies on hand.) Yet in the study of verbal behavior, as in the study of any other natural phenomenon, a clear conception of the units involved constitutes a prerequisite to subsequent measurement. Discussion of this problem would be beyond the bounds of the present study (cf., e.g., Salzinger, 1973b, 1975, and references cited there; Sapon, 1971).

In similar fashion, to reinterpret "meaning" as a matter of discriminative stimuli and reinforcement, though superficially helpful in keeping up the basic operant outlook, does not really add anything. (Note Robinson's further distinctions of stimulus-determined "meanings.") A commitment to the analysis of sentences and parts thereof leads to a concentration on the response term of the contingencies and indirectly supports the view that responses can still be analyzed as independent objects, indeed, that there are steadfast means to do so. Under the circumstances, whatever may be said about "semantics" and "reference" as opposed to "pragmatics" does less than full justice to the full complexity characteristic of the multiple determination of verbal behavior.

3. To cite but a few representative examples, witness the symposia in *Synthese*, Vol. 17, and in *Journal of Philosophy*, Vol. 44; Hook,

~ NOTES TO CHAPTER 7 ~

1969; Davidson and Harman, 1972; Hintikka et al., 1973; various contributions in Harman, 1974; Gunderson, 1975; Guttenplan, 1975; French et al., 1977; the series of volumes titled *Syntax and Semantics*. Meaning is where the action is now. Linguists and philosophers are converging on precisely this issue and for good reason: a common concern with form, treated without regard for the contingent relations of actual speech, forces them later to seek substantiation for the posited formal relations. (Quine [1970] has pointedly discussed some of the more pertinent issues as "philosophical progress in language theory.")

Theories of semantics proliferate. The venerable thoughts and ideas handed down by tradition have long been replaced, in some quarters at least, by no less mentalistic meanings, concepts, propositions, beliefs, and so on. Progress is expected to follow from the development of ever more refined formal schemes to deal with distinctions like meaning vs. reference, meaning vs. use, use vs. mention, lexical vs. grammatical meaning, speaker meaning vs. linguistic meaning, and so forth; others are concerned, in one way or another, with criteria of meaningfulness, truth, verifiability, and the like; distinctions of older vintage, like the synthetic-analytic or sense vs. reference, keep cropping up. The resulting dualism (which not even so-called ordinary language philosophy can escape) bears witness only to the inherent sterility of formalism.

Pragmatics (whether in the strictly theoretical context or in more recent developmental studies) finds itself in basically similar disarray for similar reasons: the three-fold distinction of which it partakes, along with syntax and semantics, cannot be upheld. This is not the place to go into greater detail beyond pointing out that to the extent that it counteracts the unreasonable view that meaning is intrinsic to the sentences generated by the grammar, pragmatics can be seen as a healthy trend. Some current work in this area comes close to a behavioral outlook in that it at least appeals to speakers and listeners. By and large, however, it does so with an eye toward fixed structure, what is or is not "acceptable in the language" (as a system), and rules that presumably describe what people "do" with sentences. Such notions as "context," "information," and "intention" are brought in uncritically; logicians and linguists alike appeal to "intuition" with abandon—a notion too close to competence for comfort.

4. Reference has already been made to Katz's and Bever's systematic comparison of Harris' and Chomsky's work. The following quotations provide a view of the full scope of the rationalist revolution, along with a measure of historical perspective and a glimpse of the future.

~ NOTES ~

The profound contribution of the Chomskian revolution was to reinterpret Harris' formal innovations, to see them from the opposite philosophical perspective, and to derive the important philosophical and psychological implications that follow from this change in the interpretation of the formal model. Chomsky thus turned Harris' formalism against Harris' empiricist conception of linguistic structure.

within the Chomskian framework, transformations took on a new and revolutionary character. Because linguistic rules were interpreted as representations of a mental rather than a phonetic or orthographic reality, the postulation of transformations constituted the discovery of a new level of psychological structure. On Chomsky's interpretation, the existence of transformations constitutes for linguistics a discovery of roughly the same magnitude as the discovery in physics that matter has an atomic structure.

Curiously enough, Katz and Bever claim a concern with "how empiricism could make a comeback." One suspects that, in real truth, they seek to obstruct the widening gap between "generative" and "interpretive" semanticists.

Problems have arisen in connection with the manner in which the formal model of grammar is to be interpreted in order to make contact with reality. Chomsky's theory, even his "extended standard version," is incomplete in that respect: "nothing in the theory tells us how such formal systems are construed as empirical theories that make specific claims about linguistic behavior." This makes room for more than just terminological or notational differences.

Generative semanticists would appear to be, in principle, more realistic about the nature of speech events than their more orthodox interpretive colleagues. Whether this makes them empiricists is a moot question: their work is larded with difficulties arising from an unshaken commitment to the formal model itself, as shown by their concern with well-formedness and their dependence on ill-defined notions of belief, knowledge, and so forth. But the tendency to relativize the concept of grammaticalness suggests that much else is forthcoming. As Katz and Bever point out, after undermining explication and absolute formulation (see note 8, chapter 6), "an important secondary target of an empiricist counterrevolution must be the absolute concepts of synonymy, analyticity, and entailment, at the semantic level." In fact, they actually anticipate a threat to the competence/performance distinction itself. It is only reasonable then that these old-guard revolutionaries should want to expose the roots of recent deviationist tendencies and try to restore the unity once prevalent among the ranks of TGG devotees. (But perhaps, to go along with their dialectical reasoning, such efforts are bound to be wasted. History must follow its course.) These authors write: "The absence of even a fairly well-developed theory of interpretation makes it easy for the empiricist to attack these notions, for without such a theory there is no rationalistic criterion for what is linguistic and what is not, what belongs in the grammar and what is extragrammatical." But then, it is precisely this precarious state of the theory that makes the comeback of empiricism possible, "through the backdoor." The solution is to complete the interpretive machinery with "a set of what we shall call 'correspondence principles' that connect the symbols and strings of the calculus to states of affairs in the world," thus assigning empirical content to the formal model: "such a theory would list every grammatical property that a language could exhibit and provide a correspondence principle for each. These principles would associate a term denoting some grammatical property, such as intuitive *well-formedness* with the description of some formalism in the uninterpreted calculus, such as a *complete derivation*." And this for all levels. In addition, there would have to be a system of metaprinciples to guarantee the coherent interpretation of formal grammars (e.g., what must be interpreted and what can be left as unrelated to actual behavior). This is a far-reaching extension of the small, fragmentary, and what the authors consider less than adequate pieces of interpretation found here and there in linguistics: "Three notable examples are Chomsky's (partial) explication of the notions 'grammatical sentence,' 'ambiguous construction,' and 'synonymous sentence' (1957, pp. 2-17, 88-91)."

On close inspection, grammaticalness continues to be the central notion in linguistic research; like judgments of ambiguity, synonymy, and the rest of related notions, it makes a heavy appeal to the speaker's intuition. Yet intuition remains undefined. Its overtones of mystery and profundity (or, more appropriately, depth) help keep up the connotations of unassailability associated with the "ghost in the machine," a practice which, for some reason, appears to be reassuring to some people. But what does intuition amount to? A person's behavior is intuitive when he/she is unable to specify any explicitly formulated rules accounting for it—which happens to be the case for most, if not all, of the verbal behavior of the vast majority of people (see note 4, chapter 1). In such matters as well-formedness, multiplicity or same-

~ NOTES ~

ness of meaning and form, and so on, it all probably reduces to whether given expressions "feel right" under given circumstances. And it would be difficult to prove that this is anything but the product of specific behavioral history. A direct analysis of verbal data in all their empirical dimensions raises no problems as to "what is linguistic and what is not, what belongs in the grammar and what is extragrammatical" in the above sense.

The entire proposal that empiricism can best make a comeback through an enriched version of rationalist theory must be deemed a strange contraption. Indeed, the notion of a comeback itself is bizarre, for empiricism has been here all along—except for those who have chosen to follow the rationalist path and must now live with the consequences of their flight. (For a discussion of the historical and philosophical confusion that has permeated the rationalist-empiricist distinction among "explanatory linguists," see, e.g., Aarsleff, 1970; Wells, 1969; Zimmerman, 1969.)

5. As to the point or purpose of these efforts, one might venture to mention practical concerns. Sapon (1966) puts the case admirably in his summary of an early case report, in which he demonstrates the consequences of applying operant procedures for the establishment of productive verbal behavior in a child who displayed a near-total functional inadequacy. As he points out, the implications of applying these techniques reach beyond the obvious application to cases of delayed, absent, or defective speech to the structuring and management of language instruction in such contexts as (1) the facilitation and acceleration of language learning in extremely young children, (2) the expansion and refinement of verbal behavior in socially disadvantaged children whose language is regarded as inadequate for purposes of formal schooling, (3) the effective teaching of foreign languages in the form of programmed instruction.

Sapon is not alluding to elusive theoretical possibilities; he is speaking of specific techniques immediately available for the design of effective strategy in the engineering of verbal behavior (cf., e.g., Sapon, 1964, 1967, 1970, 1972). Studies of this sort have proliferated in recent years; the various references included in the present book constitute only a representative sample of the fast growing field of behavior modification. Ethical questions are not irrelevant. Thus Sapon writes: "Mention of therapeutic applications leads me to underscore the following point. There is real danger, in the form of distressing, and perhaps tragic, consequences that 'authoritative' statements based on theoretical zeal will not only inhibit creative experimentation, but will

~ NOTES TO CHAPTER 7 ~

misdirect the efforts of those concerned with the treatment of speech disorders."

By way of counterpoint Sapon proceeds to examine a case reported by Lenneberg (1964). The S was a moderately brain-damaged boy of five who displayed "an inability to vocalize upon command" (sic). It is instructive to ponder what Lenneberg did and, more so, what he did *not* do, as discussed by Sapon (1966, fn. 11). Lenneberg nonetheless draws certain conclusions, having a theory to support. And this is precisely the point. Sapon concludes: "In the experiment just cited, the boy displayed what might be taken as a promising first step. That the promise was not pursued in the experiment, I consider lamentable. What is much more serious is the impact of such 'authoritative' reports on the researcher, the practitioner, and the patient. . . . The image of a child assigned to a custodial institution because it is 'theoretically not possible to effect training in language' is profoundly distressing." Practical considerations probably rank low among experts concerned with the construction of intellectually satisfying theories. One wonders *what* is actually peripheral.

6. Present statements are probably an inevitable outcome of distinct biases built into the methodological framework within which the formulation is framed (see, in particular, chapter 4). Notice that even Lenneberg (1969) phrases the relation between the formal apparatus proposed and the presumed biological reality in far more cautious terms:

> Linguists, particularly those developing generative grammar, aim at a formal description of the machine's behavior. They search mathematics for a calculus to describe it adequately. . . . A totally adequate calculus has not yet been discovered. Once available, it will merely describe, in formal terms, the process of relational interpretation in the realm of verbal behavior. It will describe a set of operations; however, it will not make any claims of isomorphism between the formal operations and the biological operations they describe.

Current claims about UG being a matter of *biological necessity* suggest not only that the adequate calculus has been discovered (or at least that we are well on the way to discovering it) but also that biological rather than logical constraints have guided the development of the system of principles, conditions, rules, elements, properties, and so on—which we know not to be the case. If it were, there should be no reason not to speak of isomorphism between the formal operations and

~ NOTES ~

the biological operations they describe. This latest development in Chomsky's thinking is probably the last leg of a long journey into hyperbole.

7. In a classic, variously misunderstood paper, Skinner (1950) argues against any kind of learning theory designed to explain observable facts through appeal to "events taking place somewhere else, at some other level of observation, described in different terms, and measured, if at all, in different dimensions." The issues involved are closely related to the above remarks about the flight from the laboratory. The experimental psychologist is ultimately committed to the construction of a theory of behavior, but he has little to gain from ordinary learning theory or from formulations that concentrate on more strictly empirical parameters which do not transcend a S-R conception, no matter how elaborate the mediational apparatus invoked.

Considerable confusion has arisen from the fact that many psychologists concerned with language have appealed to one or another brand of mediational theory. Mainstream psycholinguists have consistently attacked any attempt to extend S-R frameworks to language behavior (deciding, in the process, that this was necessarily the mould into which all behavioral approaches had to be fitted). Though right in their criticizing, their criticism has been vastly misdirected in its detail (for a discussion see, e.g., Staats, 1971).

The study of contingencies of reinforcement involves a great deal more than usually goes into these simplified schemes. We want to account for the appearance of behavior, but we want to do so in all its dynamic complexity; we want to account for all the variables responsible for changes in the probability of occurrence of behavior. Ordinary learning theory as an independent field becomes obsolete. Such an approach may not clarify the nature of "mind," it may have no room for competence constructs or cognitive structures, but it provides an effective treatment of the behavior of organisms. Frequent arguments for an a priori theory to "guide research" must be contrasted with the results of several decades of cumulative work in its absence.

8. Myers (1962) reports a brief epistolary exchange with Chomsky that illustrates the present point. Discussing the formulation of the passive transformation in *Syntactic Structures*, Myers observes that it would be unfair to say that the formulism introduced by Chomsky is only a complex way of saying something already well known, namely, that many active sentences can be shifted into corresponding passive ones. In favor of the mathematical statement are its greater precision

~ NOTES TO CHAPTER 7 ~

and a degree of generality that would otherwise be lost; furthermore, it has no exception whatever.

> To clarify this point I wrote him to ask what he would do about such sentences as "This room seats thirty people," "The dress becomes Mary," and "The climate suits his health." He answered: "As to rule (34), the examples that you mention, and similar ones, I think can best be regarded as showing that *becomes, seats, suits, weighs*, etc. are not transitive verbs, in line with the reasoning on pp. 83, 84."

Myers pertinently remarks:

> Here once again we must be careful of our reactions. It is natural enough to think: "That's ridiculous. In the sentence given, *becomes* is exactly parallel to *adorns*, and everybody knows that *adorn* is a transitive verb, so of course *becomes* is too." But *becomes* is not parallel to *adorns* in its reaction to this particular transformation, and Chomsky has the mathematician's right to refine his definition in order to avoid a contradiction. *He is in quite a different position from an experimental scientist, who has no right whatever to disregard a piece of physical evidence because it happens to conflict with his theory.*

The italics have been added here. In a way, Myers' observation neatly synthesizes what constitutes the *leitmotiv* of the present study. The view we take of the subject matter narrowly determines the range of permissible means developed to account for it. All conceptual issues depend on the preliminary decision to treat natural language as a formal object or as a natural phenomenon.

~ REFERENCES ~

Aaronson, D., and R. W. Rieber, eds. 1980. *Psycholinguistic Research: Implications and Applications.* Hillside, N.J.: Lawrence Erlbaum.

Akmajian, A., R. A. Demers, and R. M. Harnish. 1979. *Linguistics: An Introduction to Language and Communication.* Cambridge, Mass.: MIT Press.

Aarsleff, H. 1970. "The History of Linguistics and Professor Chomsky." *Language* 46:570-585.

Bachrach, A. J., ed. 1962. *Experimental Foundations of Clinical Psychology.* New York: Basic Books.

Bauman, R., and J. Sherzer, eds. 1974. *Explorations in the Ethnography of Speaking.* Cambridge: Cambridge University Press.

Bellugi, U., and R. Brown, eds. 1964. *The Acquisition of Language.* Monographs of the Society for Research in Child Development, serial no. 92, vol. 29, no. 1.

Bever, T. G., J. J. Katz, and D. T. Langendoen, eds. 1976. *An Integrated Theory of Linguistic Ability.* New York: T. Y. Crowell.

Biemiller, A., ed. 1970. *Problems in the Teaching of Young Children.* Toronto: Ontario Institute for Studies in Education.

Bloch, B. 1948. "A Set of Postulates for Phonemic Analysis." *Language* 24:3-48.

Block, N., ed. 1980. *Readings in the Philosophy of Psychology.* Cambridge, Mass.: Harvard University Press.

Bloom, L. 1970. *Language Development: Form and Content in Emerging Grammars.* Cambridge, Mass.: MIT Press.

Bloomfield, L. 1914. "Sentence and Word." *Transactions of the American Philological Association* 45:65-75. Reprinted in Hockett, 1970.

———. 1926. "A Set of Postulates for the Science of Language." *Language* 2:153-164.

———. 1927a. "On Recent Work in General Linguistics." *Modern Philology* 25:211-230.

———. 1927b. Review of O. Jespersen, *The Philosophy of Grammar.* In *Journal of English and Germanic Philology* 26:444-446.

———. 1933. *Language.* New York: Holt, Rinehart and Winston.

———. 1939. *Linguistic Aspects of Science.* Chicago: University of Chicago Press.

~ REFERENCES ~

———. 1943. "Meaning." *Monatshefte für Deutschen Unterricht* 35:101-106. Reprinted in Hockett, 1970.

———. 1945. "On Describing Inflection." *Monatshefte für Deutchen Unterricht* 37:8-13.

Blumenthal, A. L. 1970. *Language and Psychology: Historical Aspects of Psycholinguistics.* New York: Wiley.

Bolinger, D. L. 1964. "Around the Edge of Language: Intonation." *Harvard Educational Review* 34:282-296.

Bowers, F. 1969. "The Deep Structure of Abstract Nouns." *Foundations of Language* 5:520-523.

Brame, M. K., R. M. Smaby, E. Bach, and R. Stern. 1978. *Semantics and Grammatical Theory.* New York: Haven Publishing Corporation.

Brown, R. 1973. *A First Language: The Early Stages.* Cambridge, Mass.: Harvard University Press.

Carden, G. 1976. "Syntactic and Semantic Data: Replication Results." *Language in Society* 5:99-104.

Catania, A. C. 1972. "Chomsky's Formal Analysis of Natural Languages: A Behavioral Translation." *Behaviorism* 1:1-15.

———. 1973. "The Psychologies of Structure, Function, and Development." *American Psychologist* 28:434-443.

———, and T. A. Brigham, eds. 1979. *Handbook of Applied Behavior Analysis.* New York: Irvington Publishers.

Chao, W. R. 1962. "Models in Linguistics and Models in General." In Nagel, Suppes, and Tarski, 1962.

Chomsky, N. 1955. *The Logical Structure of Linguistic Theory.* Mimeograph. Cambridge, Mass.: MIT Library.

———. 1956. "Three Models for the Description of Language." *I.R.E. Transactions on Information Theory,* IT-2:113-124.

———. 1957. *Syntactic Structures.* The Hague: Mouton.

———. 1959. Review of B. F. Skinner, *Verbal Behavior.* In *Language* 35:26-58.

———. 1961. "Some Methodological Remarks on Generative Grammar." *Word* 17:219-239.

———. 1962a. "Explanatory Models in Linguistics." In Nagel, Suppes, and Tarski, 1962.

———. 1962b. "A Transformational Approach to Syntax." In Hill, 1962. Reprinted in Fodor and Katz, 1964.

———. 1963. "Formal Properties of Grammars." In Luce, Bush, and Galanter, 1963.

~ REFERENCES ~

Chomsky, N. 1964. "Current Issues in Linguistic Theory." In Fodor and Katz, 1964.

———. 1965. *Aspects of the Theory of Syntax*. Cambridge, Mass.: MIT Press.

———. 1966. *Cartesian Linguistics*. New York: Harper and Row.

———. 1967a. "The Formal Nature of Language." Appendix to Lenneberg, 1967. Included also in Chomsky, 1972.

———. 1967b. "Recent Contributions to the Theory of Innate Ideas." *Synthese* 17:2-11.

———. 1967c. In Jakobovits and Miron, 1967.

———. 1968. "Linguistics and Philosophy." Included in Chomsky, 1972.

———. 1972. "Form and Meaning in Natural Languages." Included in Chomsky, 1972.

———. 1972. *Language and Mind*. New York: Harcourt, Brace, Jovanovich.

———. 1975. "Knowledge of Language." In Gunderson, 1975.

———. 1976. *Reflections on Language*. London: Pantheon.

———. 1977. *Essays on Form and Interpretation*. Amsterdam: North-Holland.

———. 1980. *Rules and Representations*. New York: Columbia University Press.

———, and G. A. Miller. 1963. "Introduction to the Formal Analysis of Natural Languages." In Luce, Bush, and Galanter, 1963.

Clifton, C., Jr. 1967. "The Implications of Grammar for Word Associations." In Salzinger and Salzinger, 1967.

Cofer, C. N. 1968. "Problems, Issues, and Implications." In Dixon and Horton, 1968.

Cole, R. E., ed. 1977. *Current Issues in Linguistic Theory*. Bloomington, Ind.: Indiana University Press.

Cooper, W. E. and E.C.T. Walker, eds. 1979. *Sentence Processing*. Hillsdale, N.J.: Lawrence Erlbaum.

Danks, J. H., and S. Glucksberg. 1980. "Experimental Psycholinguistics." *Annual Review of Psychology* 31:391-417.

Davidson, D., and G. Harman, eds. 1972. *Semantics of Natural Language*. Dordrecht: Reidel.

Day, S. B., ed. 1975. *Communication of Scientific Information*. Basel: S. Karger AG.

Derwing, B. L. 1973. *Transformational Grammar as a Theory of Language Acquisition*. Cambridge: Cambridge University Press.

~ REFERENCES ~

Dixon, T. R., and D. L. Horton, eds. 1968. *Verbal Behavior and General Behavior Theory.* Englewood Cliffs, N.J.: Prentice-Hall.

Einstein, A. 1934. *Essays in Science.* New York: Philosophical Library.

Fillenbaum, S. 1971. "Psycholinguistics." *Annual Review of Psychology* 22:251-308.

Fillmore, C. J., D. Kempler, and W. S.-Y. Wang, eds. 1979. *Individual Differences in Language Ability and Language Behavior.* New York: Academic Press.

Fodor, J. A. 1968. *Psychological Explanation: An Introduction to Philosophy of Psychology.* New York: Random House.

———. 1975. *The Language of Thought.* New York: T. Y. Crowell.

———, T. G. Bever, and M. Garrett. 1974. *The Psychology of Language. An Introduction to Psycholinguistics and Generative Grammar.* New York: McGraw-Hill.

———, and M. Garrett. 1966. "Some Reflections on Competence and Performance." In Lyons and Wales, 1966.

———, and J. J. Katz, eds. 1964. *The Structure of Language: Readings in the Philosophy of Language.* Englewood Cliffs, N.J.: Prentice-Hall.

French, P. A., T. E. Uehling, and H. K. Wettstein, eds. 1977. *Studies in the Philosophy of Language.* Minneapolis: University of Minnesota Press.

Fries, C. C. 1961. "The Bloomfield 'School.'" In Mohrmann, Sommerfeld, and Whatmough, 1961.

Fromkin, V. 1968. "Speculations on Performance Models." *Journal of Linguistics* 4:47-68.

Gilbert, R. M., and J. R. Millenson, eds. 1972. *Reinforcement: Behavioral Analysis.* New York: Academic Press.

Glanzer, M. 1967. "Psycholinguistics and Verbal Learning." In Salzinger and Salzinger, 1967.

Goldiamond, I. 1966. "Perception, Language and Conceptualization Rules." In Kleinmuntz, 1966.

Goodman, N. 1967. "The Epistemological Argument." *Synthese* 17:24-28.

Gough, P. B., and J. J. Jenkins. 1963. "Verbal Learning and Psycholinguistics." In Marx, 1963.

Greenspoon, J. 1962. "Verbal Conditioning and Clinical Psychology." In Bachrach, 1962.

———, and A. J. Brownstein, 1967. "Awareness in Verbal Conditioning." *Journal of Experimental Research in Personality* 2:295-308.

REFERENCES

Gregory, R. L. 1961. "The Brain as an Engineering Problem." In Thorpe and Zangwill, 1961.

Gross, M. 1972. *Mathematical Models in Linguistics*. Englewood Cliffs, N.J.: Prentice-Hall.

———. 1979. "On the Failure of Generative Grammar." *Language* 55:859-885.

Gumperz, J. J., and D. Hymes, eds. 1964. *The Ethnography of Communication. American Anthropologist* (Special Publication). Part 2, vol. 66, no. 6.

Gumperz, J. J., and D. Tannen. 1979. "Individual and Social Differences in Language Use." In Fillmore, Kempler, and Wang, 1979.

Gunderson, K., ed. 1975. *Language, Mind and Knowledge*. Minneapolis: University of Minnesota Press.

Guttenplan, S., ed. 1975. *Mind and Language*. Oxford: Clarendon Press.

Halle, M., and K. M. Stevens. 1964. "Speech Recognition: A Model and a Program for Research." In Fodor and Katz, 1964.

———, J. Bresnan, and G. A. Miller, eds. 1978. *Linguistic Theory and Psychological Reality*. Cambridge, Mass.: MIT Press.

Harman, G. 1963. "Generative Grammars without Transformational Rules: A Defense of Phrase Structure Grammar." *Language* 39:597-616.

———, ed. 1974. *On Noam Chomsky: Critical Essays*. New York: Doubleday.

Harris, Z. S. 1942. "Morpheme Alternants in Linguistic Analysis." *Language* 18:169-180.

———. 1944. "Yokuts Structure and Newman's Grammar." *International Journal of American Linguistics* 10:196-211.

———. 1951a. Review of D. G. Mandelbaum, ed., *Selected Writings of Edward Sapir*. In *Language* 27:288-333.

———. 1951b. *Methods in Structural Linguistics*. Chicago: University of Chicago Press.

———. 1952. "Discourse Analysis." *Language* 28:1-30.

———. 1957. "Co-occurrence and Transformation in Linguistic Structure." *Language* 37:283-340.

———. 1959. "The Transformational Model of Language Structure." *Anthropological Linguistics* 1:27-29.

———. 1962. *String Analysis of Sentence Structure*. The Hague: Mouton.

———. 1965. "Transformational Theory." *Language* 41:363-401.

~ REFERENCES ~

———. 1976. "On a Theory of Language." *The Journal of Philosophy* 73:253-276.

Hill, A. A., ed. 1962. *Proceedings of the Third Texas Conference on Problems of Linguistic Analysis in English*, 1958. Austin, Tex.: The University of Texas Press.

Hintikka, J., J.M.E. Moravcsik, and P. Suppes, eds. 1973. *Approaches to Natural Language*. Dordrecht: Reidel.

Hiż, H. 1960. "The Intuition of Grammatical Categories." *Methodos* 12:1-9.

———. 1967. "Methodological Aspects of the Theory of Syntax." Review of N. Chomsky, *Aspects of the Theory of Syntax*. In *The Journal of Philosophy* 64:67-74.

———. 1968. "Computable and Uncomputable Elements of Syntax." In van Rootselaar and Staal, 1968.

———. 1975. "Specialized Languages of Biology, Medicine and Science, and Connections between Them." In Day, 1975.

———. 1976. "On Some General Principles of Semantics of Natural Language." *Philosophica* 18:129-138.

Hockett, C. E. 1947. "Problems of Morphemic Analysis." *Language* 23:321-343.

———. 1948. "A Note on Structure." *International Journal of American Linguistics* 14:269-271.

———. 1952. "A New Study of Fundamentals." Review of Z. S. Harris, *Methods in Structural Linguistics*. In *American Speech* 27:117-121.

———. 1954. "Two Models of Grammatical Description." *Word* 10:210-231.

———. 1968. *The State of the Art*. The Hague: Mouton.

———, ed. 1970. *A Leonard Bloomfield Anthology*. Bloomington, Ind.: Indiana University Press.

Hoenigswald, H. 1977. "Intentions, Assumptions and Contradictions in Historical Linguistics." In Cole, 1977.

Holz, W. C., and N. Azrin. 1966. "Conditioning Human Verbal Behavior." In Honig, 1966.

Honig, W. K., ed. 1966. *Operant Behavior: Areas of Research and Application*. New York: Appleton-Century-Crofts.

———, and J.E.R. Staddon, eds. 1977. *Handbook of Operant Behavior*. Englewood Cliffs, N.J.: Prentice-Hall.

Hook, S., ed. 1969. *Language and Philosophy*. New York: New York University Press.

Horner, V. 1968. "The Verbal World of the Lower-Class Three-Year-

REFERENCES

Old: A Pilot Study in Linguistic Ecology." Unpublished doctoral dissertation, University of Rochester.

Hymes, D. 1964. "Introduction: Toward Ethnographies of Communication." In Gumperz and Hymes, 1964.

———. 1972. Review of J. Lyons, *Noam Chomsky*. In *Language* 48:416-427.

———. 1974. *Foundations in Sociolinguistics*. Philadelphia: University of Pennsylvania Press.

Jakobovits, L. A., and M. S. Miron, eds. 1967. *Readings in the Psychology of Language*. Englewood Cliffs, N.J.: Prentice-Hall.

Jespersen, O. 1924. *The Philosophy of Grammar*. London: George Allen and Unwin.

Johnson-Laird, P. N. 1974. "Experimental Psycholinguistics." *Annual Review of Psychology* 25:135-160.

Joos, M., ed. 1957. *Readings in Linguistics*. Washington, D.C.: American Council of Learned Societies.

Julià, P. 1968a. "Some Methodological Remarks Concerning the Specification of Verbal Response Topography." Research report, Institute for Behavioral Research, Silver Spring, Md.

———. 1968b. "Some Methodological Remarks on Contemporary Models of Linguistic Performance." Paper read at the Psychology Colloquium, Department of Psychology, Dalhousie University, Halifax, Nova Scotia, Canada.

———. 1973. "La fonética experimental." In Roca-Pons, 1973.

———. 1974. "Del análisis experimental del comportamiento verbal." Invited address, Psycholinguistics Symposium, XV Interamerican Congress of Psychology, Bogotá, Colombia.

———. 1975. "Del análisis funcional de la conducta verbal." *Mexican Journal of Behavior Analysis* 1:269-284.

———. 1979. "Regularization: Formal and Functional." *Abstracts of the Sixth International Congress of Logic, Methodology and Philosophy of Science* 6:153-159. Hannover, Germany.

———. 1980a. *El formalismo en psicolingüística: Reflexiones metodológicas*. Madrid: Fundación Juan March.

———. 1980b. "Ambiguity in Linguistic Theory." Paper presented at the Second Meeting of the North-American Catalan Society, Yale University. In press.

———. "Verbal Processes" (in preparation).

Kanfer, F. H. 1968. "Verbal Conditioning: A Review of Its Current Status." In Dixon and Horton, 1968.

~ REFERENCES ~

Kantor, J. R. 1936. *The Objective Psychology of Grammar.* Bloomington, Ind.: Indiana University Press.
———. 1975. "Psychological Linguistics." *Mexican Journal of Behavior Analysis* 1:249-268.
———. 1977. *Psychological Linguistics.* Chicago: Principia Press.
Katz, J. J. 1964. "Mentalism in Linguistics." *Language* 40:124-137.
———. 1971. *The Underlying Reality of Language and Its Philosophical Import.* New York: Harper and Row.
———, and T. G. Bever. 1976. "The Fall and Rise of Empiricism." In Bever, Katz, and Langendoen, 1976.
———, and J. A. Fodor. 1963. "The Structure of a Semantic Theory." *Language* 39:170-210.
———, and P. Postal. 1964. *An Integrated Theory of Linguistic Descriptions.* Cambridge, Mass.: MIT Press.
Keller, F. S., and W. N. Schoenfeld. 1950. *Principles of Psychology.* New York: Appleton-Century-Crofts.
Kiefer, H. E., and M. K. Munitz, eds. 1970. *Language, Belief, and Metaphysics.* Albany: State University of New York Press.
Kleinmuntz, B., ed. 1966. *Problem Solving.* New York: Wiley.
Koch, S., ed. 1963. *Psychology: A Study of a Science.* Vol. 5. New York: McGraw-Hill.
Koutsoudas, A. 1963. "The Morpheme Reconsidered." *International Journal of American Linguistics* 29:160-170.
Krasner, L. 1958. "Studies of the Conditioning of Verbal Behavior." *Psychological Bulletin* 55:148-170.
Kuhn, T. S. 1962. *The Structure of Scientific Revolutions.* Chicago: University of Chicago Press.
Kuno, S. 1980. "Functional Syntax." In Moravcsik and Wirth, 1980.
Labov, W. 1972. *Sociolinguistic Patterns.* Philadelphia: University of Pennsylvania Press.
Lenneberg E. H. 1964. "The Capacity for Language Acquisition." In Fodor and Katz, 1964.
———. 1967. *Biological Foundations of Language.* New York: Wiley.
———. 1969. "On Explaining Language." *Science* 164:635-643.
Liberman, A. M. 1970. "The Grammars of Speech and Language." *Cognitive Psychology* 1:301-323.
Lounsbury, F. G. 1953. "The Method of Descriptive Morphology." *Oneida Verb Morphology.* Yale University Publications in Anthropology, no. 48.
Luce, R. D., R. R. Bush, and E. Galanter, eds. 1963. *Handbook of Mathematical Psychology.* Vol. II. New York: Wiley.

REFERENCES

Lyons, J. 1970. *Chomsky.* London: Fontana-Collins.
———, and Wales, R. J., eds. 1966. *Psycholinguistic Papers: The Proceedings of the 1966 Edinburgh Conference.* Edinburgh: Edinburgh University Press.
MacCorquodale, K. 1969. "B. F. Skinner's *Verbal Behavior*: A Retrospective Appreciation." *Journal of the Experimental Analysis of Behavior* 12:831-841.
———. 1970. "On Chomsky's Review of Skinner's *Verbal Behavior*." *Journal of the Experimental Analysis of Behavior* 13:83-99.
Mach, E. 1914. *The Analysis of Sensations.* (German original, 1897). Chicago: Open Court.
MacKay, D. G., and T. G. Bever. 1967. "In Search of Ambiguity." *Perception and Psychophysics* 2:193-200.
McLeish, J., and J. Martin. 1975. "Verbal Behavior: A Review and Experimental Analysis." *Journal of General Psychology* 93:3-65.
McNeill, D. 1970. *The Acquisition of Language: The Study of Developmental Psycholinguistics.* New York: Harper and Row.
Marx, M. H., ed. 1963. *Theories in Contemporary Psychology.* New York: Macmillan.
Matthews, P. H. 1979. *Generative Grammar and Linguistic Competence.* London: George Allen and Unwin.
Menyuk, P. 1969. *Sentences Children Use.* Cambridge, Mass.: MIT Press.
Miller, G. A. 1951. *Language and Communication.* New York: McGraw-Hill.
———. 1956. "Human Memory and the Storage of Information." *I.R.E. Transactions on Information Theory* IT-2:129-137.
———. 1962. "Some Psychological Studies of Grammar." *American Psychologist* 17:748-762.
———. 1965. "Some Preliminaries to Psycholinguistics." *American Psychologist* 20:15-20.
———, and N. Chomsky. 1963. "Finitary Models of Language Users." In Luce, Bush, and Galanter, 1963.
———, E. Galanter, and K. Pribram. 1960. *Plans and the Structure of Behavior.* New York: Holt, Rinehart and Winston.
Mohrmann, C., A. Sommerfeld, and J. Whatmough, eds. 1961. *Trends in European and American Linguistics 1930-1960.* Utrecht: Spectrum Publishers.
Moravcsik, A., and J. R. Wirth, eds. 1980. *Syntax and Semantics.* Vol. 13. New York: Academic Press.

~ REFERENCES ~

Myers, L. M. 1962. "Two Approaches to Language." *Publications of the Modern Language Association* 77:6-10.

Nagel, E., P. Suppes, and A. Tarski, eds. 1962. *Logic, Methodology and Philosophy of Science.* Stanford, Cal.: Stanford University Press.

Osgood, C. E. 1963. "On Understanding and Creating Sentences." *American Psychologist* 18:735-751.

——. 1967. In Jakobovits and Miron, 1967.

——. 1968. "Toward a Wedding of Insufficiencies." In Dixon and Horton, 1968.

——. 1971. "Where Do Sentences Come From?" In Steinberg and Jakobovits, 1971.

——, and T. A. Sebeok, eds. 1954. *Psycholinguistics: A Survey of Theory and Research Problems.* Baltimore: Waverly Press.

——, C. E., J. Suci, and P. H. Tannenbaum. 1957. *The Measurement of Meaning.* Urbana, Ill.: University of Illinois Press.

Peters, S., and R. Ritchie. 1973. "On the Generative Power of Transformational Grammars." *Information Sciences* 6:49-83.

Piattelli-Palmarini, M., ed. 1980. *Language and Learning: The Debate between Jean Piaget and Noam Chomsky.* Cambridge, Mass.: Harvard University Press.

Pimsleur, P., and T. Quinn, eds. 1971. *The Psychology of Second Language Learning.* Cambridge: Cambridge University Press.

Plath, W. 1961. "Mathematical Linguistics." In Mohrmann, Sommerfeld, and Whatmough, 1961.

Postal, P. 1964a. "Underlying and Superficial Linguistic Structure." *Harvard Educational Review* 34:246-266.

——. 1964b. *Constituent Structure: A Study of Contemporary Models of Syntactic Description.* Supplement to vol. 30 of *International Journal of American Linguistics.* Bloomington, Ind.

Premack, D. 1969. "Language: On the Difference between Training a Chimp to Press a Lever and Telling It to Press the Lever." Invited address, American Psychological Association Meetings, Washington, D.C.

——. 1971. "On the Assessment of Language Competence in the Chimpanzee." In Schrier and Stollnitz, 1971.

Putnam, H. 1967. "The 'Innateness Hypothesis' and Explanatory Models in Linguistics." *Synthese* 17:12-23.

Pylyshyn, Z. W. 1972. "Competence and Psychological Reality." *American Psychologist* 27:546-552.

~ REFERENCES ~

Pylyshyn, Z.W. 1973. "The Role of Competence Theories in Cognitive Psychology." *Journal of Psycholinguistic Research* 2:21-50.

Quine, W.V.O. 1953. *From A Logical Point of View*. Cambridge, Mass.: Harvard University Press.

———. 1960. *Word and Object*. Cambridge, Mass.: MIT Press.

———. 1970. "Philosophical Progress in Language Theory." In Kiefer and Munitz, 1970.

———. 1972. "Methodological Reflections on Current Linguistic Theory." In Davidson and Harman, 1972.

Reber, A. S. 1973. "On Psycho-Linguistic Paradigms." *Journal of Psycholinguistic Research* 2:289-319.

Richelle, M. 1973. "Analyse formelle et analyse fonctionelle du comportement verbal: Notes sur le débat entre Chomsky et Skinner." *Bulletin de Psychologies* 26:252-259.

Robinson, G. 1977. "Procedures for the Acquisition of Syntax." In Honig and Staddon, 1977.

Roca-Pons, J., ed. 1973. *El Lenguaje*. Barcelona: Teide.

Ross, J. R. 1979. "Where's English?" In Fillmore, Kempler, and Wang, 1979.

Salzinger, K. 1959. "Experimental Manipulation of Verbal Behavior: A Review." *Journal of General Psychology* 61:65-94.

———. 1967. "The Problem of Response Class in Verbal Behavior." In Salzinger and Salzinger, 1967.

———. 1973a. "Inside the Black Box, with Apologies to Pandora." A review of U. Neissner, *Cognitive Psychology*. In *Journal of the Experimental Analysis of Behavior* 19:369-378.

———. 1973b. "Some Problems of Response Measurement in Verbal Behavior: The Response Unit and Intraresponse Relations." In Salzinger and Feldman, 1973.

———. 1975. "Are Theories of Competence Necessary?" *Annals of the New York Academy of Sciences* 263:178-196.

———. 1979. "Language Behavior." In Catania and Brigham, 1979.

———. 1980. "Ecolinguistics: A Radical Behavior Theory Approach to Language Behavior." In Aaronson and Rieber, 1980.

———, and R. S. Feldman, eds. 1973. *Studies in Verbal Behavior: An Empirical Approach*. New York: Pergamon Press.

———, and S. Salzinger, eds. 1967. *Research in Verbal Behavior and Some Neurophysiological Implications*. New York: Academic Press.

Sapir, E. 1921. *Language*. New York: Harcourt, Brace and World.

Sapon, S. M. 1964. "Micro-Analysis of Second Language Learning." *International Review of Applied Linguistics* 3:131-136.

~ REFERENCES ~

———. 1965. " 'Receptive' and 'Expressive' Language." Paper presented at the American Psychological Association Meetings, Division 7.

———. 1966. "Shaping Productive Verbal Behavior in a Non-Speaking Child: A Case Report." *Georgetown University Monograph Series*, no. 19, pp. 157-175.

———. 1967. "Contingency Management in the Modification of Verbal Behavior in Disadvantaged Children." Paper presented at the American Psychological Association Meetings, Division 25.

———. 1970. "Engineering Verbal Behavior." In Biemiller, 1970.

———. 1971. "On Defining a Response: A Crucial Problem in Verbal Behavior." In Pimsleur and Quinn, 1971.

———. 1972. "Problems in the Modification of Verbal Behavior." Address to the Annual Meetings of the National Society for Autistic Children, Flint, Mich.

Saporta, S., and J. R. Bastian, eds. 1961. *Psycholinguistics: A Book of Readings*. New York: Holt, Rinehart and Winston.

———. 1965. Review of S. Koch, ed., *Psychology: A Study of a Science*, vol. 6. In *Language* 41:95-100.

Saussure, F. de. 1916. *Cours de linguistique générale*. Paris: Payot.

Schiefelbusch, R. L., and L. L. Lloyd, eds. 1974. *Language Perspectives: Acquisition, Retardation, and Intervention*. Baltimore: University Park Press.

Schlesinger, I. M. 1971. "Production of Utterances and Language Acquisition." In Slobin, 1971.

Schoenfeld, W. N. 1971. Review of P. Black, ed., *Physiological Correlates of Emotion*. In *Communications in Behavioral Biology* 5:397-398.

———, and S. H. Baron. 1965. "Ethology and Experimental Psychology." *Science* 147:634-635.

———, and W. W. Cumming. 1963. "Behavior and Perception." In Koch, 1963.

Schrier, A. M., and F. Stollnitz, eds. 1971. *Behavior of Nonhuman Primates*, vol. 4. New York: Academic Press.

Segal, E. F. 1972. "Induction and the Provenance of Operants." In Gilbert and Millenson, 1972.

———. 1975. "Psycholinguistics Discovers the Operant: A Review of Roger Brown's *A First Language: The Early Stages*." In *Journal of the Experimental Analysis of Behavior* 23:149-158.

———. 1977. "Toward a Coherent Psychology of Language." In Honig and Staddon, 1977.

~ REFERENCES ~

Skinner, B. F. 1938. *The Behavior of Organisms*. New York: Appleton-Century-Crofts.

———. 1947. "Current Trends in Experimental Psychology." Included in Skinner, 1972.

———. 1950. "Are Theories of Learning Necessary?" Included in Skinner, 1972.

———. 1953. *Science and Human Behavior*. New York: Macmillan.

———. 1957. *Verbal Behavior*. New York: Appleton-Century-Crofts.

———. 1961. "The Flight from the Laboratory." Included in Skinner, 1972.

———. 1963. "Behaviorism at Fifty." Included in Skinner, 1969.

———. 1965. "What is the Experimental Analysis of Behavior?" *Journal of the Experimental Analysis of Behavior* 9:213-218.

———. 1969. *Contingencies of Reinforcement: A Theoretical Analysis*. New York: Appleton-Century-Crofts.

———. 1972. *Cumulative Record*. New York: Appleton-Century-Crofts.

———. 1974. *About Behaviorism*. New York: Alfred Knopf.

Slobin, D. I. 1966. "Comments on McNeill's 'Developmental Psycholinguistics.'" In Smith and Miller, 1966.

———, ed. 1971. *The Ontogenesis of Grammar: Some Facts and Several Theories*. New York: Academic Press.

Smith, F., and G. A. Miller, eds. 1966. *The Genesis of Language*. Cambridge, Mass.: MIT Press.

Staats, A. W. 1968. *Learning, Language, and Cognition*. New York: Holt, Rinehart and Winston.

———. 1971. "Linguistic-Mentalistic Theory Versus an Explanatory S-R Learning Theory of Language Development." In Slobin, 1971.

———. 1974. "Behaviorism and Cognitive Theory in the Study of Language: A Neopsycholinguistics." In Schiefelbusch and Lloyd, 1974.

Steinberg, D. D., and L. A. Jakobovits, eds. 1971. *Semantics*. Cambridge: Cambridge University Press.

Stern, R. 1978. Introduction. In Brame, Smaby, Bach, and Stern, 1978.

Swadesh, M. 1935. "The Phonemic Principle." *Language* 10:117-129.

Thorpe, W. H., and O. L. Zangwill, eds. 1961. *Current Problems in Animal Behavior*. Cambridge: Cambridge University Press.

Turner, M. B. 1967. *Philosophy and the Science of Behavior*. New York: Appleton-Century-Crofts.

van Rootselaar, B., and J. F. Staal, eds. 1968. *Logic, Methodology and Philosophy of Science*. Amsterdam: North-Holland.

~ REFERENCES ~

Verhave, T. 1972. "The Language and Mind of a Polemicist: Some Reflections on *Language and Mind*, by N. Chomsky." *Journal of Psycholinguistic Research* 1:183-195.

Wales, R., and H. Toner. 1979. "Intonation and Ambiguity." In Cooper and Walker, 1979.

Wallace, A.F.C. 1961. "On Being Just Complicated Enough." *Proceedings of the National Academy of Science* 47:458-464.

Wells, R. S. 1947. "Immediate Constituents." *Language* 23:81-117.

———. 1969. "Innate Knowledge." In Hook, 1969.

Wexler, K., and P. W. Culicover. 1980. *Formal Principles of Language Acquisition*. Cambridge, Mass.: MIT Press.

Wiener, N. 1948. *Cybernetics*. New York: Wiley.

Williams, J. H. 1964. "Conditioning of Verbalization: A Review." *Psychological Bulletin* 62:383-393.

Winokur, S. 1976. *A Primer of Verbal Behavior: An Operant View*. Englewood Cliffs, N.J.: Prentice-Hall.

Yngve, V. 1960. "A Model and a Hypothesis for Language Structure." *Proceedings of the American Philosophical Society* 104:444-466.

Zimmerman, M. 1969. "Is Linguistic Rationalism a Rational Linguistics?" In Hook, 1969.

~ INDEX ~

Aaronson, D., 168n.10
Aarsleff, H., 200n.4
acceptability: *vs.* grammaticalness, 122; and pragmatics, 197n.3
Akmajian, A., 181n.3
ambiguity: Chomsky *vs.* Hiż on, 179n.1; and context, 163n.2; and formalism, 187-188n.5; and linguistic theory, 54-55; and PSG, 49-50; resolving of, 159-160n.3, 187n.5; and TGG, 50, 56, 63, 73-74, 159-160n.3; in unknown language, 59, 63
anomalies, *see* errors
aphasia, 119
artificial intelligence, 15, 174n.4
associationist paradigm, 13
Azrin, N., 147n.5

Baron, S. H., 147-148n.6
Bauman, R., 177n
behavior: deliberation as, 113; and environmental events, xiv; experimental analysis of, 13, 144-147n.4, 150-151n.8, 175-176n.17; language as, xi, 8, 13, 41, 68-69, 119, 143-144n.3, 165-166n.5; topography of, 150n.8, 151n.1; *vs.* traces of behavior, xi, 153n; variables determining, 119-120, 144-145n.4; verbal *vs.* nonverbal, xiii-xiv, 11, 120
behavioral processes, xiv, 113, 144-147n.4, 158n
behavioral repertoire, 149-150n.7, 188-189n.6
behaviorism: and Bloomfield, 23; mistaken identification with descriptive linguistics, 123, 190n.8

belief: as behavior, xiii-xiv, 116; Chomsky on study of, xiii, 117, 133
Bellugi, U., 176n
Bever, T. G., 131, 188n.5, 190-191n.8, 198n
Bloch, B., 23, 30, 33
Block, N., 143n.1
Bloom, L., 178n.17
Bloomfield, L., 19, 20-29, 30, 31, 32, 35, 38, 51, 56, 95, 152n.2
Blumenthal, A. L., 7
Boas, F., 19, 29
Bolinger, D. L., 154n.5
Bowers, F., 182n.4
brain: as black box, 85-86; and innate mental structure, 133, 135; Katz on, 174-175n.16; recursive rules represented in, 81. *See also* mind
Brown, R., 176n, 178n.17, 194-195n
Brownstein, A. J., 147n.5

Carden, G., 181n.4
Catania, A. C., 159-160n.3, 187n.5, 192n.2, 193-194n, 195n
Chao, W. R., 161-162n.1
Chomskian revolution, 131, 198n
Chomsky, N.: apriorism of, 12-13, 67-70, 192n.1 (*see also* methodology); on communication process, 79, 171n; on competence and performance, 65-70, 84, 98-99, 110-120, 126, 171-172n.12; contribution of, 42, 66, 107-108, 123-124, 135, 157n.1, 161n.1, 191n.10; *vs.* Descartes, 131-132; and environmental factors, 177-178n, 179n.1; extreme position of, xiv-xv; on

~ INDEX ~

Chomsky, N. (*cont.*)
  FSG, 45-47; and Harris, 39-40, 157n.1, 190-191n.8, 197-198n.4; and Hockett, 37, 38, 40; impact of, xiv, 6; and justification of grammars, xv, 51, 63-64, 75-76, 96-97, 100-103, 109; and "knowledge," xiii-xiv, 99, 118-119, 133; on language learning, 123-124 (*see also* language learning); on linguistic theory, 43-45, 53-54, 61, 63, 65, 66, 67, 70-78, 89-90, 101-102, 103, 124, 130-131; on meaning, 9, 39, 71; mentalism of, 100, 131-140, model formulation by, 87-88; on models, xiii, 163n.1 (*see also* explanatory models); 1957 views of, 52-62; 1962 views of, 65-84, 114; 1965 views of, 93-106; 1976 views of, 132-141; on operant conditioning, 10-12, 68-70, 83, 136-137, 150-151n.8, 188n.6, and philosophy, 131, 196-197n.3; *vs.* Plato, 131-132; on PSG, 47-48, 49-50; psychologism of, 179n.1; rationalism of, 66, 99-100, 103, 131-132; on rules, 43-44, 63, 69, 106, 115, 117, 118, 137, 167n.10, 191n.10; and de Saussure, 66-67, 100; on semantics-syntax relation, 57-62, 71, 94-97, 104-105. See also transformational-generative grammar
Clifton, C., Jr., 7
Cofer, C. N., 5, 6, 8, 185n.2
cognitive entities, 13-15, 18, 81, 83, 89-90, 116, 141, 145n, 173-174n.14, 174-175nn.15, 16
cognitive structures: Chomsky's assumption of, 132-134; origin of, 133, 136, 138
competence, 65-66, 67, 70; and behavior, 186n.3; communicative, 177n; and environment, xiii; grammatical, 122; and grammaticalness, 181n.4; and intuition, 66, 117; models of, 69-71, 75-80, 82-84, 111, 112, 114, 116, 118, 122-123; *vs.* performance, 17, 65, 81, 87-88, 98, 108, 110-123, 126, 174n.15; pragmatic, 122; questionable emphasis on, 107-108; and structuralism, xii; and study of performance, 98, 99
computing machines, Wiener on, 173n
content paradigm, 14
context, 179n.1, 187n.5
contingencies of reinforcement, 70, 145-146n, 173n, 188n, 193n, 196.2, 202n.7
conversation analysis, 96
Cooper, W. E., 175n.16
creativity, 55-56, 67-68, 100, 110-111, 113, 118-121, 125, 182-185n.5. See also infinity
Culicover, P. W., 143n.1
Cumming, W. W., 166n.7

Danks, J. H., 7, 15
Davidson, D., 197n.3
deep structures, 93, 94-96, 105, 106, 123-124; and logical analysis, 106
dependent variable, xi; behavior as, 144n.4; and meaning, 149n
depth hypothesis and performance simulators, 168-169n.11
Derwing, B. L., 192n.1
description *vs.* explanation, xii, 37, 90-91, 123, 124, 130
descriptive adequacy, xii, 52-54, 63, 100-101, 103, 111
descriptive linguistics: *vs.* explanatory, 21, 25, 90-91; and manipulation of data, xii, 119, 124, 139-140
dialect, 157n.1, 181n.4; *vs.* sublanguage, 184n
discourse analysis, 96, 180n
discriminative stimulus, 117,

~ INDEX ~

144n.4; and meaning, 173n, 196n.2
Dixon, T. R., 7, 8
dualism: Chomsky's assumption of, 57, 61; and formalism, 17, 151n.1; and form *vs.* meaning, xii, 97; and structural analysis, 155n.7; in TGG, 57, 97, 99

Einstein, A., 140
empiricism: Chomsky's shift from, 65, 66; Harris', 190-191n.8; and linguistic subjectivity, 182n.4
empiricist "counterrevolution," 198-200n.4
errors and competence *vs.* performance, 73, 74, 97-98, 121-122, 181-182n.4
ethology: and nativism, 12; significance of, 147n.6
evaluation procedure: Chomsky's black box as, 53, 70, 75-76, 91; in justification of grammars, 53-55, 101-102; limitations imposed by, 117
explanatory adequacy, xii, 54-56, 63, 100, 101-103, 111
explanatory linguistics, 37, 90-91; mistaken assumptions of, 6, 16-17, 125; TGG as, 6, 123-124
explanatory model(s), xiii, xv, 6, 85-86; formalized grammar as, 74; and perceptual devices, 111-112; scientific study through, 108; suggestion of structure in, 88; TGG as, 87 *See also* models
explanatory power: as adequacy criterion, 4; and black box, 86; of Chomsky's metatheory, 40, 54-56, 101-103; and formal sciences, 191n.10; and nativism, 84, 110; requirements for, 54-56, 65, 97, 101-102; and semantics, 57, 59

Fillenbaum, S., 7

finite-state grammars(FSG), 45-47
"Flight to the Inner Man," Skinner on, 130
"Flight to Laymanship," Skinner on, 129
"Flight to Mathematical Models," Skinner on, 129-130
"Flight to Real People," Skinner on, 129
Fodor, J. A., 7, 95, 118, 121, 143n.1, 171n, 175n.16
form: *vs.* content, 112-113; and meaning, 57-63, 71, 97, 112-113, 181n.3, 197n.3; systematic analysis of, xi
formalism: and ambiguity, 187-188n.5; and behavioral analysis, 6, 150-151n.8, 192-196n.2; dualism entailed by, 17, 151n.1; and meaning, 197n.3; self-delusion of, 63, 71-72, 80-81, 203n; Skinner on, 149n
formal sciences: and explanatory power, 191n.10; models in, 162n; treatment of infinity in, 157n.1
French, P. A., 197n.3
Fries, C. C., 22, 23-24
Fromkin, V., 169-171n.12
functional syntax, 177n

Garrett, M., 7
generative grammar, 100, 102, 104; *vs.* facts of performance, 112-114, 156n.1; incomplete work on, 119; and linguistic universals, 104, 109; recursive property of, 106, 111. *See also* transformational-generative grammar
genetic fallacy, 108, 109
ghost in the machine: exorcising of, 133, 136, 141; and intuition, 199n
Glanzer, M., 7, 9
Glucksberg, S., 7, 15
Goldiamond, I., 173n
Goodman, N., 117

~ INDEX ~

Gough, P. B., 5, 7, 9
grammar: formalized, 70, 73, 83-84; and meaning, 26, 29-30, 120, 181n.3; as "revealing," 45 (see also explanatory power); traditional categories of, 19, 75, 105, 106, 127; universal, 105, 106-107, 131, 137-138, 201-202n.6. See also evaluation procedure; transformational-generative grammar
grammaticalness: vs. acceptability, 122; and competence, 65-66, 181n.4; criteria for, 45, 46-47, 52, 55-56, 66, 74, 98, 156-157n.1, 157-159n.2, 184n, 190n.8; and intuition, 52, 74, 158-159n, 199n; and prescriptivism, 181n.4, subjectivity of, 182n.4; and test of adequacy for grammar, 45, 52
Greenspoon, J., 147n.5
Gregory, R. L., 86
Gross, M., 119, 156n
Gumperz, J. J., 181n.4
Gunderson, K., 197n.3
Guthrie, E. R., 186n.2
Guttenplan, S., 197n.3

Halle, M., 95, 170-171n, 175n.16
Hampshire, Stuart, 132
Harman, G., 48, 197n.3
Harris, Z. S., 23, 30, 31, 32, 33, 36, 38, 39, 51, 94, 155n.7, 157n, 179-180n.2, 190-191n.8, 194n, 197n.4
heuristic devices, 53, 76-77, 80, 87
Hintikka, J., 197n.3
Hiż, H., 39, 105-106, 108, 111, 162n, 178-179n.1, 183-184n
Hockett, C. E., 26, 29, 30, 31, 32, 33-39, 40, 51, 52, 75, 90, 154n.5, 182-183n.5
Hoenigswald, H., 192n.10
Holz, W. C., 147n.5
Hook, S., 196-197n.3
Horner, V., 178n.17
Horton, D. L., 7, 8

Humboldt, W. von, 100
Hymes, D., 21, 107, 177n
hypothesis: and black box vs. cybernetics, 86; circularity of input-output, 83-84; explanatory, xii, 4; innateness, 82, 104, 108, 134-135, 136, 137-138, 201n.6; on nature of mind, 126-127; vagueness of input-output, 69-71, 84, 91-92, 115-117, 123, 126-127, 135

idealization: and "degeneracy," 65-66, 121-122; as escape, 128, 170n; formal grammar as, 73, 97-98; and grammaticalness, 190n.8; of "what is learned," 73, 90. See also methodology
idealized speaker-listener, xiii, 97-98, 108
immediate constituent (IC) analysis, 32, 47-48
independent variable(s), xi, 63; in change of verbal environment, 157n.1; linguistic context as, 187n.5; and meaning, xii, 63, 149n; and rate, 144n.4; and response class, 119-120
infinity: finite representation of, 6, 45, 52, 81, 94, 100, 111, 137, 155n.7, 156-157n.1, 173n; and monolithic view of language, 118-121, 125, 156-157n.1, 182-185n.5
information measurement, Cofer on, 5
information theory, 8, 9
innateness hypothesis, 82, 104, 108, 134-135, 136, 137-138, 201n.6. See also competence
inner states, in behavioral analysis, 130, 145n
intuition: and formalized grammar, 55, 56, 83-84, 117; about form vs. meaning, 59-60; and grammaticalness, 52, 66, 74, 158-159n, 199n; in language learning, 87-88, 103,

INDEX

116, 117; nature of, 199-200n.4. See also knowledge of language

Jakobson, R., 104
Jenkins, J. J., 5, 7, 9
Jespersen, O., 27
Johnson-Laird, P. N., 7
Joos, M., 20, 21, 31, 32, 180n
Julià, P., 113, 116, 119, 124, 151n.8, 167n.8, 170n, 185n.5, 186n.3, 188n.5

Kanfer, F. H., 147n.5
Kantor, J. R., 152n.3, 182n.4, 186n.2
Katz, J. J., 95, 121, 131, 143n.1, 168n.10, 169n.11, 171n, 174n.16, 190-191n.8, 198n
Keller, F. S., 150n.7
knowledge of language: vs. "ability," 133; as behavior, xiii-xiv; competence as, 66, 98-99, 124, 128, 133; vs. experience, 118-121, 183-185n.5; and knowledge of arithmetic, 69, 80-81, 82; "range of variance" for, 117; vs. "use" of language, 57, 69, 108, 113-114, 125, 126-127, 140, 141. See also competence; performance
Koutsoudas, A., 154n.6
Kozhevnikov, V., 170n
Krasner, L., 11
Kuhn, T. S., 128
Kuno, S., 177n

Labov, W., 181n.4
language: as autonomous system, xi, 6, 8, 28-29, 30, 40-41, 152-154n.4, 155n.7, 165n.3, 175n.17; as behavior, xi, 8, 13, 41, 68-69, 119, 143-144n.3, 148-150n.7, 165-166n.5; change in, 27, 28, 29; Chomsky's view of, 43-44, 57, 68, 71, 99-100, 106-107, 185n.6 (see also competence); as formal object vs. natural phenomenon, xi, xii, xiv, 175n.17, 203n; "innate faculty" of, 134-135, 136, 137-138, 201n.6 (see also competence); as mirror of mind, xiii, 132; as recursively enumerable set, xii, 106, 111, 125; de Saussure's view of, 20-21, 66-67, 151n.1; as well-defined system, 98, 157n.1, 182-185n.5, 190n.8
language learning: Chomsky on, 69-70, 73, 75-77, 80, 87, 92, 117-119, 134-135, 141, 167n.10, 175-176n.17; and "degenerate" performance, 73, 74, 121-122, 125, 189-190n.7; and evaluation procedure, 70, 75-76, 91, 102, 117-119; vs. performance, 80, 92; rate of, 165n.4; semantics in, 71, 92; variability in, 165n.4; and verbal environment, xiv, 91, 92, 111-112, 134, 168n, 175-178n.17
learning theory: vs. biological concerns, 134-137; in early psycholinguistics, 5; status of, 202n.7
Lenneberg, E. H., 148n.6, 201n.5, 201n.6
lexicon, 29, 30; in standard TGG, 93-94
Liberman, A. M., 170n
linguistic theory: current trends in, 90, 96, 106, 155n.7, 177n, 184-185n.5; goals of, 42, 53-56, 130, 185n.5; and theoretical science, 128, 139-140. See also Chomsky
Lounsbury, F. G., 34, 58
Luce, R. D., 65
Łukasiewicz, J., 168n.11
Lyons, J., 131

McCarthy, D., 165n.4
MacCorquodale, K., 10, 150n.7, 159n.2, 185n.2, 186n.3
Mach, E., 3-5, 16
MacKay, D. G., 188n.5

223

~ INDEX ~

McLeish, J., 91
McNeill, D., 168n.10
Martin, J., 91
Matthews, P. H., 102
meaning: Bloomfield on, 25-28; and discriminative behavior, 173n, 181n.3, 196n.2; elusiveness of, xi-xii, 62; and form, 57-63, 71, 97, 112-113, 181n.3, 197n.3; operant interpretation of, 149n; Osgood's theory of, 5. *See also* semantics
mediation: appeal to, 202n.7; by black box, 86
mentalism: and "biological necessity," 131-138; experimental, 118, 140; explanatory vs. descriptivism, 25, 100; and form vs. meaning, xii
Menyuk, P., 176n
metatheory: as black box, 70-71, 73-78, 84, 86-87; as input-output machine, 53-54, 56, 63, 66, 91; linguistic theory as, 4, 6, 16, 44, 63. *See also* competence; evaluation procedure
methodology: interdisciplinary, 3-5, 16-17; in natural science, 12, 128-130, 134, 138-140, 203n; over-reliance on thought experimentation, 192n.1; theoretical apriorism, xii, 29, 67-68, 109, 117, 132-134, 142, 172n.3, 192n.1; theory testing as, 12-13, 83, 117, 125. *See also* description vs. explanation; metatheory; models
Miller, G. A., 7, 9, 65, 67, 69, 78, 114, 169n.11, 171n, 172n.13, 175n.15
mind: as behavior, 127; Chomsky on, 126-128, 131-140; as equivalent to nervous system, 89
model(s): algebraic, 78, 82; black box, 85-89, 123; competence, 69-71, 75-80, 82-84, 111, 112, 114, 116, 118, 122-123, 169-172n.12; cybernetic, 85-86, 88-89, 167n.9; formal vs. structural, 84-85; FSG, 45-47; function of, 84, 162n, 172n.13; Hockett on, 33-36; IA, 31-32, 33, 38; input-output, 53-54, 63, 66, 70-71, 79, 84; IP, 33, 38, 154n.6; of learning vs. performance, 92, 129; mathematical, 129-130, 163-165n.3; mathematical vs. physical, 161-162n; as metaphor, 84; perceptual, 80, 83, 92, 115, 116; performance, 79-80, 83, 111, 112, 115-116, 118, 123, 169-171n.12; PSG, 45-46, 47-48, 49-50; senses of, 162-163n.1; significance of, 91; statistical, 164-165n.3; stochastic, 82; structural, 85, 86, 164-165n.3; TG, 45-46, 48-50, 73-77, 87, 101-103; word-by-word, 47; WP, 33
morphology: and phonology, 30-31; and syntax, 30-31, 60, 154n.6
Myers, L. M., 202-203n.8

Nagel, E., 161n.1
nativism: and ethology, 12; and explanatory power claims, 84, 124; and language as object, 175n.17. *See also* innateness hypothesis
nature-nurture controversy, 139
neurolinguistics, 90, 174-175n.16

operant, characterization of, 149n
operant conditioning: and language, 11, 145-147n.4, 147n.5, 200-201n.5 (*see also* verbal behavior); modification of verbal behavior through, 147n.5, 200-201n.5; and Reber's survey, 14; summary statement of, 144-147n.4
Osgood, C. E., 5, 9, 13

perceptual models, 80, 83, 92, 115, 116. *See also* speaker-listener relation

224

INDEX

performance: in Chomsky's view, 65-66, 67-68, 99, 112, 126; *vs.* competence, 17, 65-66, 81, 87-88, 98, 108, 110-123, 126; "degeneracy of," 97-98, 121-122, 125, 189-190n.7, 191n.9; *vs.* "generating" sentences, 113, 185-186n.2; *vs.* learning, 92, 129; mechanisms of, 71, 108, 109, 123, 126-127; models of, 79-80, 83, 111, 112, 115-116, 118, 123, 169-171n.12; proper study of, 108, 118-123, 128-130, 136, 138-140; variables determining, 80, 113, 118-121, 186n.3, 187n.4. *See also* behavior
Peters, S., 104
philology, legacy of, xi, 152n.3
phonetic laws, Bloomfield on, 24
phonetics: descriptive, 153n, 154n.5; experimental, 170-171n
phonology: and grammar, 30-31, 154n.5; and morphology, 30, 31, 154n.5; universals in, 104-105. *See also* transformational-generative grammar
phrase-structure grammars (PSG): Chomsky on, 9, 45-46, 47-50; Harman on, 48. *See also* transformational-generative grammar
physiological psychology, status of, 147-148n.6
Piatelli-Palmarini, M., 138
Pike, K., 38
Plath, W., 163-164n.3
Postal, P., 10, 14, 34, 95
pragmatic competence, 122
pragmatics, status of, 197n.3
Premack, D., 14, 147n.6
processes: behavioral, 113, 145-146n; cognitive, 90, 117, 145n (*see also* cognitive entities); finite-state Markov, 46-47; of synthesis and analysis, 56, 114
process paradigm, 13-14
psycholinguistics: Chomsky's impact on, xiv, 15; current trends in, 13-15; as field, 4-8, 90; role of linguistics in, 4-7, 8, 14-17
psychology: Bloomfield on, 24-25; laboratory role in, 12, 145-146n; and psycholinguistics, 4-8, 9-13, 15-18. *See also* behavior; stimulus-response psychology
Putnam, H., 138
Pylyshyn, Z. W., 174n.15

Quine, W.V.O., 52, 106, 168n.10, 177n, 197n.3

rationalism: Chomsky's commitment to, xiii, 99-100, 123, 131-132; enriched version of, 200n.4; and experience, xiii, 91, 103, 117, 123-124; and "language faculty," 134
rationalist revolution, 197-198n.4
Reber, A. S., 13, 14, 15
reinforcement: as behavioral variable, 70, 117, 145n, 167n.9; and meaning, 196n.2. *See also* contingencies of reinforcement
response, in analysis of verbal behavior, 119-120, 149n, 150-151n.8
response class, 119-120, 150-151n.8
Richelle, M., 186n.3
Rieber, R. W., 168n.10
Ritchie, R., 104
Robinson, G., 192n.2, 196n.12
Ross, J. R., 181n.4
rules: bases for, 137; and grammatical process, 32; and innateness view, 71, 100, 117, 148n.6, 176n; internalization of, 87, 92, 117, 167n.10; as "laws," 43, 63, 87; nature of, 146-147n.4, 191-192n.10; relevance of, 44, 69, 113, 115, 118-119, 125, 183-184n.4, 191-192n.10

~ INDEX ~

Salzinger, K., 15, 91, 147n.5, 186n.3, 187n.4, 196n.2
Sapir, E., 20, 21, 27, 28, 30, 31, 32, 200n.5
Sapon, S. M., 160-161n.4, 165nn.4, 5, 166n.6, 196n.2, 200-201n.5
Saporta, S., 5, 167n.8
Saussure, F. de, 19, 20, 25, 27, 28, 66-67, 100, 151n.1
Schlesinger, I. M., 168
Schoenfeld, W. N., 147-148n.6, 150n.7, 166n.7
Sebeok, T. A., 5
Segal, E. F., 187n.4, 192-193n.2, 194-195n.5
semantics: generative, 198n; and grammar, 26, 30, 39-40, 62, 120, 181n.3; interpretive, 198-199n; and language learning, 71, 92; proliferation of theories of, 197n.3; in TGG, 49-50, 57-62, 94-97
sentence atomism, 40, 45, 74, 95, 96, 163n.2, 178-179n.1
Sherzer, J., 177n
simplicity, as criterion, 36, 52, 54, 102
Skinner: autoclitic formula of, 195n; basic outlook of, 13, 143-144nn.3, 4, 144-147n.4, 148-150n.7; and function of laboratory, 12; in Gough-Jenkins characterization of psycholinguistics, 5; and introspection, 99; on knowledge and usability, 119; "language" defined by, 143n.3; on language learning, 167-168n 10, 176n; on learning theory, 202n.7; and mental processes, 173n; on physiological psychology, 147-148n.6; on psychologists' "Flights," 128-130; on research, 172n.13
Slobin, D. I., 14

sociolinguistics, 157n.1, 177n, 181n.4
speaker-listener relation, 56, 62, 80, 82-83, 92, 99, 116, 125, 150n.7, 160-161n.4, 165n.5-166n.6, 187n
Staats, A. W., 13, 193n
Stern, R., 104.
Stevens, K. M., 171n
stimulus-response (S-R) psychology, 7-8, 144n.4, 202n.7; operant conditioning confused with, 10-11, 175-176n, 202n.7
stratificational grammar, 38
string analysis, 179n.2
structural linguistics: Bloomfield's principles for, 22-23; and Chomsky's achievements, xiv, 51-52, 107-108, 123-124; conception of language in, 28-29, 40-41, 152-154n.4; early history of, 19-28; models in, 32-36, 41; post-Bloomfieldian, 29-40, 51, 57; scientific status for, 37, 40; and spoken *vs.* written language, xi, 153n, 154n.5
structure, psychology of, 193n
sublanguages, 118-119, 168n.10, 183-185n.5
suprasegmental features, 30-31, 154n.5
surface structures, 93, 94-96, 103, 105, 106, 123-124; and semantic interpretation, 94
Swadesh, M., 28
syntax: and Chomsky's structuralism, 107-108; and morphology, 30-31, 154n.6; and semantics, 26, 39-40, 45, 57-62, 93-97; universals of, 105-106. *See also* transformational-generative grammar

tagmemics, 38
Tannen, D., 181n.4
text analysis, 96
Tolman, E. C., 186n.2
Toner, H., 188n.5

~ INDEX ~

Trager, G., 30
transformational-generative grammar (TGG), 46, 48-50; assumptions underlying, 42-45, 47, 63, 124, 130-131; "empirical" status of, 108, 127-128, 140, 192n.1; as explanatory model, 6, 73-78, 103 (see also explanatory models); as idealization, 73, 97-98; and infinity of sentences, 52, 94, 100, 137, 156-157n; levels in, 51, 55, 58, 63; phonological rules in, 94; semantic rules in, 94; semantics in, 49-50, 57-62, 94-97; standard theory of, 93-97; syntactic rules in, 93-94. See also explanatory power
Turner, M. B., 84-86

understanding, undue emphasis on, 55, 61-62, 111. See also ambiguity; speaker-listener relation
unit of verbal behavior: and formalism, 5, 15, 44, 75, 78, 119-120, 125, 127, 149n, 156-157n.1, 158-159n.2, 176n, 179-180n.2, 196n.2; plasticity and variability of, 125; Skinner's definition of, 149n, 150-151n.8. See also sentence atomism; word
universal grammar, "biological necessity" of, 137-138, 201n.6
universals: formal, 104, 105-106, 109; substantive, 104-105, 109; perception of, 172-173n.14, 189-190n.7

verbal associations, study of, 5, 7
verbal behavior: vs. competence model, 123; Skinner's analysis of, 13, 148-150n.7; unit of, 149n, 150-151n.8. See also behavior; performance
verbal community, see verbal environment
verbal environment: change of, 118-119, 168n.10; and definition of verbal behavior, 143-144n.3; and language learning, xiv, 91, 92, 111-112, 134, 168n.10, 177n; mistaken notion of, 69-70, 84, 91, 92, 175-176n.17; new studies on, 178n.17
verbal learning, 7, 8
verbal repertoire, 149n
Verhave, T., 9

Wales, R., 188n.5
Walker, E.C.T., 175n.16
Wallace, A.F.C., 9
Weiss, A. P., 152n.2
well-definition, as an assumption, 98, 182-183n.5
well-formedness and meaningfulness, 47. See also grammaticalness
Wells, R. S., 32, 200n.4
Wexler, K., 143n.1
Whorf, B. L., 21
Wiener, N., 88, 89, 172-173n.14, 189n.7
Williams, J. H., 147n.5
Winokur, S., 150n.7
Woodworth, R. S., 85
word, 30-31, 60, 61, 157n.1, 158n, 180n; Skinner on, 149n. See also unit of verbal behavior

Yngve, V., 168-169n.11

Zimmerman, M., 200n.4

Library of Congress Cataloging in Publication Data

Julià, Pere.
Explanatory models in linguistics.

Bibliography: p.   Includes index.
1. Linguistic models.   2. Psycholinguistics.
3. Generative grammar.   I. Title.
P128.M6J84   1983   410   82-47602
ISBN 0-691-06524-1

GPSR Authorized Representative: Easy Access System Europe - Mustamäe tee 50, 10621 Tallinn, Estonia, gpsr.requests@easproject.com

www.ingramcontent.com/pod-product-compliance
Lightning Source LLC
Chambersburg PA
CBHW080732300426
44114CB00019B/2560